International
Library of the
Philosophy of
Education

Children's
rights

International
Library of the
Philosophy of
Education

General Editor

R. S. PETERS

Professor of Philosophy of Education
Institute of Education
University of London

Children's rights

A philosophical study

C.A.Wringe

Department of Education
University of Keele

ROUTLEDGE & KEGAN PAUL
London, Boston and Henley

First published in 1981
by Routledge & Kegan Paul Ltd
39 Store Street, London WC1E 7DD,
9 Park Street, Boston, Mass. 02108, USA and
Broadway House, Newtown Road,
Henley-on-Thames, Oxon RG9 1EN
Printed in Great Britain by
Billing & Sons Ltd
Guildford, London, Oxford and Worcester

British Library Cataloguing in Publication Data

Wringe, C.A.
Children's rights. - (International library of the
philosophy of education)
1.   Children's rights
I.   Title   II.   Series
323.4   HQ789.A5

ISBN   0-7100-0852-X

TO SALLY

Contents

General editor's note

There is a growing interest in philosophy of education amongst
students of philosophy as well as amongst those who are more
specifically and practically concerned with educational problems.
Philosophers, of course, from the time of Plato onwards, have
taken an interest in education and have dealt with education in
the context of wider concerns about knowledge and the good of
life. But it is only quite recently in this country that philosophy
of education has come to be conceived of as a specific branch of
philosophy like the philosophy of science or political philosophy.

To call philosophy of education a specific branch of philosophy
is not, however, to suggest that it is a distinct branch in the
sense that it could exist apart from established branches of
philosophy such as epistemology, ethics and philosophy of mind.
It would be more appropriate to conceive of it as drawing on
established branches of philosophy and bringing them together
in ways which are relevant to educational issues. In this respect
the analogy with political philosophy would be a good one. Thus
use can often be made of work that already exists in philosophy.
In tackling, for instance, issues such as the rights of parents
and children, punishment in schools, and the authority of the
teacher, it is possible to draw on and develop work already done
by philosophers on 'rights', 'punishment', and 'authority'. In
other cases, however, no systematic work exists in the relevant
branches of philosophy - e.g. on concepts such as 'education',
'teaching', 'learning', 'indoctrination'. So philosophers of education have had to break new ground - in these cases the philosophy
of mind. Work on educational issues can also bring to life and
throw new light on long-standing problems in philosophy. Con-
centration, for instance, on the particular predicament of children
can throw new light on problems of punishment and responsibility.
G.E. Moore's old worries about what sorts of things are good in
themselves can be brought to life by urgent questions about the
justification of the curriculum in schools.

There is a danger in philosophy of education, as in any other
applied field, of polarization to one of two extremes. The work
could be practically relevant but philosophically feeble; or it
could be philosophically sophisticated but remote from practical
problems. The aim of the new International Library of Philosophy
of Education is to build up a body of fundamental work in this
area which is both practically relevant and philosophically competent. For unless it achieves both types of objective it will fail to
satisfy those for whom it is intended and fall short of the conception

of philosophy of education which the International Library is meant to embody.

Twelve years ago the children's rights movement, as represented by the Little Red School Book, was an unknown phenomenon. In the first chapter of his book Dr Wringe gives an interesting and well-documented account of how the movement developed. At the end of the book he assesses the claims made for and by children during the course of the movement - e.g. the right to refuse to wear uniforms, to participate in school government, to enjoy social relations, etc. This brings the philosophical discussion of rights in the middle of the book down to earth and gives Dr Wringe's book a sense of reality. So also does his admission at the start that his interest in the topic of rights arose from his experience as a young teacher, when he was confronted with the conflict of preserving order in class and the claims of independence for his pupils.

The philosophical section of Dr Wringe's book discusses traditional theories of rights and their justification. Rights as freedoms are distinguished from welfare rights and the question is raised whether the latter are properly called rights. His analysis is applied to the various rights claimed for the children. He is very judicious, when dealing with claims for participation by pupils in school government, in de-limiting the spheres in which such claims are reasonable. He also makes the important point that the claims for children's rights go far beyond the more moderate appeals of the child-centred movement.

There are many teachers who are hostile to claims for children's rights - often because of ignorance of the type of philosophical case that can, with reservations, be made for them. Dr Wringe has written a clear and interesting book that throws light on a controversial issue of considerable importance. It should be read by teachers, parents and administrators and anyone else interested in the welfare of children.

R.S. Peters

Preface

At a personal level my interest in the question of children's rights dates back to my experience as a newly qualified schoolmaster, for whom the relations of authority and obedience between teachers and pupils were not yet something to be taken for granted. As such I frequently found myself 'caught' between the seemingly proper requirements of the school for the prompt establishment of good order and endeavour, and the intuition   thoroughly justified as it now seems – that young people were entitled to a greater degree of independence, consideration and respect than they sometimes received.

Since then I have found this apparent conflict an increasingly absorbing topic of academic enquiry, ultimately leading on to a consideration of some of the central questions of political philosophy. These include not only the nature of rights and their relation to other moral and political concepts, but also the relationship in which the individual stands to the community as a whole and in which the generations, young and old, parents and children, teachers and pupils stand to each other.

These are some of the fundamental issues with which I am concerned in the following pages. At this point it is appropriate to acknowledge my debts to my own philosophical elders and betters, notably Professor R. S. Peters and Mrs Pat White. Apart from my general philosophical indebtedness, I have to thank Professor Peters for his encouragement to work my material into publishable form. My sincere gratitude is due to Mrs White for her patient and constructive discussion of all the main arguments I advance.

Introduction

The notion that children should be treated less harshly and dealt with in a less authoritarian manner has long been an important theme in educational writing, and dates back to Rousseau and beyond. It is true that in advocating a more child-centred pedagogy some writers have not failed to appeal to the humane sentiments of their readers on children's behalf. The main burden of such writing, however, has been that to follow the natural development and interests of the child, to provide agreeable conditions in which to learn, to encourage rather than to coerce, is the most effective way of achieving certain educational aims.

More recently, however, a new note has entered the argument. The view has been maintained, forcefully in some cases, that children should be allowed a certain independence and equality of consideration, not only because that is more effective educationally, or more worthy of humane and rational parents and teachers, but because children are entitled to be so treated, as of right.

Not only are children held to have rights, but certain established practices are held to infringe those rights and to justify protest and demands for implementation as unabashed, peremptory and insistent as those which are appropriate when the rights of adults are ignored. A particular feature of the situation is that when such claims are made, opposition is seldom addressed to the actual claims in question but to the more general issue of whether children may be said to have rights at all and more especially whether it is permissible for them to actively seek their recognition.

The term 'rights' has become an indispensable term in the vocabulary of those campaigning on behalf of various groups in society. The claim to rights may be as precise as the letter of the law, or as broad as the ideals of international bodies. It may carry overtones of the day-to-day morality of doing as one would be done by as well as of the fundamental assumptions shared by all who support a democratic way of life. To use the term, therefore, may be at once to cast a doubt on the legal and moral rectitude of one's opponent's position and to brand him as a reactionary, not to say as a tyrant and an aggressor. No consensus exists as to what it is to have a right or even under what general conditions the claim to have a right may be justified.

A major part of the present study is therefore concerned with the elucidation of these broad questions before considering the application of conclusions reached to the case of children and pupils. Although our main purpose is a philosophical one, however, it will be helpful in establishing the practical context of our enquiry to

begin with a brief historical review of the children's rights movement, particularly during the years 1969-72 when the controversy
was at its height. Such a review, it is hoped, will indicate the
considerable range of sources from which such claims have eman-
ated and show that the movement has at least been sufficiently
concerted to pose for school authorities and adult bodies both
problems of administration and questions of general attitude and
policy.

The claim that
children have rights

1　The children's rights movements

PUPIL MILITANCY AND ADULT POLEMICS (1)

Following the events of May 1968 at various European and British universities the spread of militancy into secondary schools was widely anticipated. In France *Lycéens* were already involved in the student unrest of 1968 and by 1969 pupils' joint management committees (*Schülermitverwaltungen*) were established in *Gymnasien* in certain German *Länder*, only to be stigmatised by many of the pupils whom they were meant to placate as *'eine Farce'*.

It is perhaps small wonder that as student militancy became old hat, the exploits and utterances of members of the Schools' Action Union should rapidly be seized upon as 'news'. When on the last day of Christmas Term 1969 this organisation mounted a strike and marched on County Hall, five pupils of an East London comprehensive school were suspended. Significantly, the issue which divided the governors and others who discussed the case was not the validity of the pupils' demands contained in a letter handed in at County Hall, but whether those suspended were properly to be described as 'truants' and 'recalcitrants', who might easily be dealt with inside the traditional framework of school discipline, or whether they were 'strikers', to be treated according to different canons.(2) It is perhaps an indication of the tense atmosphere surrounding pupil militancy that the five pupils in question were eventually expelled and the then Minister of State for Education asked the Inner London Education Authority for a full report.(3) The SAU were again in the news in February 1970 when it was revealed that the headmaster of one of their members had written about his political activities to a university which had subsequently rejected his application for entrance.(4) In July of that year the speech day at a well-known London public school was interrupted by SAU activities,(5) and in November a boy was suspended at a school in Suffolk after 'openly defying school rules' by publishing an article in 'Vanguard', the organ of the SAU.(6) In the same month some of the specific demands of the SAU were widely reported following the organisation's conference in Manchester.(7) In December a 'good natured strike' over the dismissal of a teacher at Holland Park Comprehensive School also threw up demands for increased pupil representation.(8) Apart from eight boys being transferred from one secondary modern school to another for 'trying to start a union',(9) 1971 appears to have been rather quiet from the point of view of actual pupil militancy, though as will be seen, the

5

children's rights movement continued to proceed on other fronts.
The two most significant events in this field in 1972 were the so-
called 'Schools' Demo' on the 17 May (10) and the inauguration of
the National Union of School Students a few days later.(11)

Though estimates of numbers vary to some extent, it appears
that 2,500 pupils absented themselves from school to attend the
SAU 'Schools' Demo'. After the pupils had rallied in Trafalgar
Square an attempt was made to 'storm' County Hall. Fourteen
juveniles and, perhaps rather surprisingly, ten adults were
arrested and the 'demo' was widely reported as being badly organised and lacking in leadership.(12)

Although the 'demo' achieved no obvious practical results, it
does at least appear to have provoked some thought regarding
the powers and responsibilities of heads. Shortly before the
demonstration, the Chief Officer of the Inner London Education
Authority is reported to have written to head teachers to the
effect that it was neither wise nor proper for them to give pupils
permission to be absent from school in order to attend the demonstration. Absence from school to attend the demonstration was
described unambiguously as truancy and heads were advised
(though not all of them agreed) that the responsibility for seeing
that pupils attended school lay with parents.(13)

The inaugural conference of the National Union of School Students also took place in May 1972 following a motion at the previous conference of the National Union of Students, which already
claimed to have some 12,000 members in secondary schools. Area
conferences of school students were organised in London and ten
provincial centres and a steering committee was elected. In her
inaugural speech, the first President of the NUSS declared that
the main aim in the union's twenty-five-point policy statement was
the achievement of a greater degree of democracy in schools and
ultimately a say at national level in decision-making. She was,
however, at pains to distinguish the 'moderate' and 'non-political'
programme of the NUSS from that of the SAU. School strikes were
not regarded as part of the NUSS programme. It was hoped to
gain the co-operation of adult bodies such as the National Union
of Teachers, or at least of its younger members. Another member
of the NUSS executive is reported to have said that joint campaigning with the National Council for Civil Liberties was unlikely,
even though the two organisations had certain aims in common.(14)

The spread of militancy among school pupils was followed by the
development of a supporting underground literature. 'The Little
Red School Book' appeared in the spring of 1971, translated and
adapted for use by English pupils.(15) The first edition of the
magazine 'Children's Rights'(16) appeared in November of that
year and continued to appear more or less monthly until the following September. The seven editions of the magazine featured
such topics as alternative education, exam resistance, children in
care, and children's rights in the matter of arrest (the controversial 'Children's Bust Book'). Contributors included such well-
known names as John Holt, Leila Berg and Chris Searle. The

editorial board was listed as Paul Adams, Leila Berg, Nan Berger, Michael Duane, John Holt, A. S. Neill, Robert Ollendorff and Viv Berger, though after the controversy over the 'Children's Bust Book' it was revealed that this board was not intended to edit or even see copy, membership being something of an 'empty title' intended to 'pull in the customers'. After the appearance of the 'Children's Bust Book' the editor (Julian Hall) was 'sacked' and the seventh and final edition appeared under the name of 'Kids'. The organisation then decided to continue its work in the form of a 'Children's Rights Workshop' which later published occasional pamphlets and held discussion meetings.(17) 'Children's Rights' was by far the most substantial magazine of its kind. Others, often locally based, included 'Mother Grumble' (North East), 'Brain Damage' (Oxford), 'Carfax Comic' (Oxford), 'Pigeon' (Slough), 'Hackney Miscarriage' (East London).(18)

To see the push for children's rights merely as a downward seepage of university unrest would be mistaken for a number of causes appear to have contributed to the intensity with which this topic was debated during the period 1969 to 1972, when the controversy was at its height. To begin with, much of the impetus came not from pupils and their organisations, but from adults and, in particular, from adult writers. The idea of the school as a democracy, or at least as a kind of constitutional monarchy, has an honourable history in the tradition of progressive education at least as old as Homer Lane's Little Commonwealth and the teaching and writings of A. S. Neill. In January 1971, however, the theme received special prominence in a work in which three progressive educationalists, two Reichian psychologists and a prominent member of the National Council for Civil Liberties discussed various aspects of the struggle for 'children's rights and their contemporary denial'.(19) The year 1971 also saw the beginnings of the 'deschooling' debate in Britain and although the preoccupations of Illich and his followers are in important respects different from those of the children's rights movement, the emphasis of the deschoolers on the supposedly stultifying and custodial nature of schooling and the promise of less institutionalised alternatives became an important element in children's rights literature.

Professional writers on education were not the only adults to involve themselves in the issue of children's rights. Though major personalities in the two main political parties refrained from taking up an identifiable position, one Labour MP is reported as advocating that not only teachers, but also pupils should have a larger say in the determination of the school curriculum.(20) At the other extreme, a Monday Club pamphlet published in August 1970 under the title 'Who's getting at our Kids?' alleges the existence of an actual conspiracy to 'suborn the hearts and minds of a section of the British youth'. The subversive nature of the movement lay, so the pamphlet claimed, in the portrayal of authority as 'an instrument of bourgeois capitalism' and the movement for democracy in schools is condemned as 'a logical preparation for worker control and industrial soviets'.(21)

On what some may consider a more serious level, the National
Council for Civil Liberties in January 1971 began publication of a
series of Discussion Papers under the general title of 'Children
Have Rights'. The first of these relates specifically to children
in school and points to aspect of the pupils' legal position vis-à-
vis school authorities which were considered unsatisfactory.(22)
In April of the following year the NCCL in conjunction with the
London Co-operative Society's Education Department organised a
London 'Conference on Children's Rights' which was attended by
such figures as Brigid Brophy, Joan Lestor, Francis Deutsch,
Peter Newell and Anna Shearer, each with an axe to grind. The
SAU and YAK (Youth Action Kommittee) were represented. So
also was the NUT, whose representative was sharply critical of
some of the NCCL's recommendations.(23) Shortly after the 'Conference on Children's Rights' the annual general meeting of the
NCCL passed 'more or less unanimously' an executive resolution
calling for a vigorous campaign on three particular children's
rights in schools, namely, the abolition of corporal punishment,
the right of children to determine their personal appearance in
school and the need for effective channels for participation by
pupils in the running of schools.(24) Later in the year an NCCL
group in south-east London urged that the power of heads should
be curbed and suggested, prophetically, that the shifting of head
teachers' powers and responsibilities to a more representative
body might be facilitated by introducing changes into the Model
Articles of Government and Management of Schools.(25)

Like the NCCL, the Advisory Centre for Education also chose
to promote discussion of certain educational issues in terms of
pupils' rights by publishing in the April 1971 issue of 'Where?'
its so called Draft Charter of Children's Rights, posters and free
off-prints of which were offered to interested readers.(26)

Official reaction to the children's rights movement from teachers' professional organisations does not appear to have been
forthcoming until spring 1972. When it came, it could, for the
most part, only be described as truculent. One representative of
the NUT expressed his union's opposition to any weakening of the
teachers' position 'in loco parentis' or the legal obligation on
children to attend school up to the age of sixteen. Another felt
that in taking up the case of children who were 'upset by being
told to do things they don't want to', such as wearing uniform,
the NCCL was concerning itself with trifles compared with 'the
infringements of liberty that result from poverty, over-crowding,
ill-equipped schools and selective higher education'.(27) Comment-
ing on the proposed formation of the NUSS, the Assistant General
Secretary of the union said that his organisation did not 'see the
necessity for a national organisation of pupils' and doubted
whether 'interference' by such an 'outside body' would be helpful
in settling the 'serious educational question' of the development
of pupil participation. In a somewhat similar vein, the Assistant
General Secretary of the National Association of Schoolmasters
expressed the view that agitation for children's rights was based

on the false premise that 'children are from an early age capable of determining what is good for them'. The same official also defended the retention of corporal punishment (for the good pupil(!) though not for the habitual delinquent) and pointed out that the legal right of the head to determine what children wore in school had already been established by 'case law in the courts'. (28)

Of all the bodies representing teachers only the NUT left-wing splinter group Rank and File appears to have expressed itself in favour of the pupils' rights movement. This group voted 'full support for students struggling by direct action to democratise the schools' and criticised the union for condemning school strikes, particularly in view of the NUT's own successful strike in 1970.(29)

Though most educational authorities were naturally extremely reticent on the whole topic of children's rights, mention must be made of an article by Sir Alex Clegg in his authority's schools' bulletin, supposedly based on a 'Bill of Rights' for school children from an American high school. The article mentions 'as a gruesome warning to head teachers' such provisions as the right of free speech, the right to publish magazines and newspapers without censorship and the right of pupils to see their own school records. The article was later said by its author to have been 'a joke'.(30)

One final factor colouring the discussion of relations between the young and adults was the passage of the 1969 Children and Young Persons Act following the 1968 White Paper 'Children in Trouble'. Neither of these, of course, related to the normal run of school pupils. The rights of young delinquents and the rights of school pupils do, however, raise the common issue of a young person's position with regard to civil rights. Discussion of both provides stuff for the charge that 'society' allows supposed rights of children to be ignored. Both issues are often raised by the same groups. The authoritarian regime in schools comes to be seen as part of a more general abuse of childhood. Some members of the SAU appear to have seen themselves pitted not only against reactionary pedagogues, but also against the machinery of the state. The magazine 'Children's Rights' encourages revolt against both school and the forces of law and order.(31) Nan Berger discusses the Children and Young Persons Act and the position of the school pupil in the same article (32) and the same series of NCCL Discussion Papers discusses the rights of children in school and the rights of young offenders before the juvenile courts.(33) It would not, perhaps, be surprising if the litigious approach, which may be suitable when considering the law and its application by the courts, were to affect a writer's perception of the school situation, if these two questions are discussed together.

RIGHTS CLAIMED FOR CHILDREN

It might be expected that the kinds of rights claimed for children in and out of school would vary widely according to the interests and preoccupations of those by whom the claims were made. Certainly such quasi-political pupils' organisations as the SAU and the NUSS (34) were more concerned with the machinery of educational democracy and its necessary conditions of freedom of speech and association. Predictably, also, the NCCL was particularly keen to safeguard freedoms already provided for by the law, and to bring about changes in the law which permits anomalies between the treatment of children and that of adults,(35) while the ACE drew attention both to the special restrictions to which children are subjected, and also the many deprivations which some of them suffer.(36) In spite of these differences of emphasis, however, there remains a very marked core of unanimity between the various groups and individuals advocating children's rights. To some extent this may result from an actual overlap of affiliation between the various organisations making the rights claims, for some of the personalities connected with the children's rights movement were active in more places than one. Nan Berger, one of the six authors of the book 'Children's Rights', was at that time a prominent member of the NCCL, while all six of the authors of this book were members of the editorial board of the magazine of the same name. Both the book and the magazine were edited by Julian Hall. It is difficult to establish a link between the magazine and the leadership of the SAU. The idiom and ethos of the two, however, exhibit marked similarities and it seems that the 'Children's Bust Book' was planned to appear shortly before the 'Schools Demo' of May 1972.(37) The ACE acknowledged the help of Leila Berg (one of the authors of 'Children's Rights') and Edwin Musim, as well as of the NCCL in the preparation of their draft charter.(38)

As we saw, however, the executive of the NUSS was careful to distinguish its aims from the more radical and political orientation of the SAU and doubted the likelihood of a joint campaign with the NCCL, given the wish of the NUSS to enlist the support of the younger members of the teaching profession.(39) Far from seeing the relative unanimity of children's rights advocates as arising from a red plot by a 'tight knit politically motivated group' to 'suborn the hearts and minds of a section of the British youth' (40) it seems more reasonable to attribute this unanimity to the fact that criticism of certain deficiencies, real or supposed, in the way children are treated by the adult world have for some time been common currency among idealistic adolescents and liberal-minded adults, though fashion and imitation may account for their simultaneous expression in terms of rights. Furthermore, as will be seen from the rights demands listed below, many of these belong recognisably to a liberal tradition of long standing, the only new feature in the situation being their application to children.

1 The demand that children should be seen as persons in their own right
If one assertion seems particularly fundamental to the children's rights movement it is that children should be seen as persons in their own right. Berger, discussing the legal position of the child, points to the common law assumption that children were the possessions of their parents, and claims that various Factory Acts, Education Acts and Children's Acts, while providing protection for children against exploitation, have done nothing to enhance their status as persons, legal or otherwise, in their own right, rather than appendages of adults.(41) The NCCL Discussion Paper, 'Children in Schools', likewise, protests against the classic assumption 'that children are the property of someone - if not of parents then the State'.(42)

   As is often the case in debates about rights of whatever section of the community, a contrast is continually drawn between the absence of children's rights in law and their evident existence in morality. In spite of their lack of legal status, it is suggested, pupils in school have a moral right to the same consideration as any one else and the same amount of respect from their teachers as the clients of any other professional body.(43) Berger points out that compulsion (in this case to attend school) would be totally unacceptable for adults in the so called free world and asks 'can there be one code of civil liberty for adults and another for children?'(44) The ACE suggests that we should be shocked by the contrast between the treatment of adults and that of children and holds that children are in fact denied certain basic rights under the 'United Nations International (sic) Declaration of Human Rights'.(45) Apart from their additional rights to special protection during their vulnerable years, the ACE draft charter states, the rights of children 'are no greater than the right of others and no less'.(46)

2 The right not to attend school
Both the NCCL and speakers at the joint national conference on children's rights draw particular attention to the way in which compulsory schooling supposedly infringes the child's right of self-determination.(47) Campaigners for children's rights frequently refer rhetorically to schooling as imprisonment and the supposedly custodial nature of educational establishments is brought out by the language of the SAU's demand that pupils should not need passes to leave school premises during the lunch-hour.(48)

3 The right to educational democracy
This demand takes a variety of forms. Berger appears to claim the right of consultation only, for she says 'children have a right which should be written into the basic Education Act, to form school councils . . . which can provide opportunities for pupils to express their views on how schools should be run'.(49) The NCCL, likewise, demands 'The provision of effective channels of

participation' and 'the official creation of school councils consist-
ing of staff, pupils, parents and possibly also governors, though
it appears to make no specific recommendations as to how the
members of such councils should be chosen or the extent of their
powers'.(50) Predictably, the SAU is more radical and more specific. Official spokesmen of the organisation are quoted as saying
that it sought 'community control of schools' and demanded 'democratically elected school councils which would refuse to allow the
head ever to be the chairman'. At the time of the Schools Demo
in May 1972 the SAU demanded 'rules to be decided and enforced
by the whole school'.(51) The NUSS also announced that it
was seeking 'more school democracy', leading eventually to the
'abolition of the head and to schools controlled by committees of
teachers, students, parents and non-teaching staff' and 'all forms
of discipline to be under the control of school committees'. To
judge from an off-the-cuff remark attributed to the first President of the NUSS, this organisation aimed to seek a voice, not
only in the management and discipline of educational institutions,
but also in matters of curriculum.(52)

A particular area in which more educational democracy was
sought was in the nature and role of governing bodies. The NCCL
recommended that these should be reconstituted and the NUSS
policy document stated this as one of the organisation's aims. Following trends in higher education, early moves were made in some
places to secure pupil representation on governing bodies. In
spite of DES advice that school governors must be over eighteen,
Wolverhampton Borough Council expressed the wish to see one,
preferably elected, governor aged eleven to fifteen for each of
the town's thirty secondary schools, possibly in an ad hoc capacity. Shortly afterwards, the Brighton Borough Council accepted
a plan to allow two pupils on the governing bodies of each of their
fourteen secondary schools, while in Warley, Worcestershire, the
Council instructed lawyers to find ways in which senior pupils
could have more say in the running of their schools.(53)

4 The right to organise democratically
A corollary of the demand for educational democracy is a demand
for the right of pupils 'to organise themselves democratically
without interference from other organisations' to implement the
rights attributed to adolescents.(54) The NUSS aimed to become
'the national voice of pupils which in future would not be ignored
in decision making and to obtain the right of joining the NUSS
without victimisation'.(55) In a letter handed in at the London
County Hall, the SAU demanded the right to organise student
meetings at break and after school on the school premises, to join
student unions and to engage in political activity including strikes.
(56) The ACE also expressed concern at the exclusion from schools
of pupils, 'who join unions or express political opinions', and says
that such actions seem contrary to Article 17 and 18 of the Universal Declaration of Human Rights concerning freedom of speech
and assembly.(57)

5 Rights of appeal, representation and redress
Many specific abuses of children's supposed civil rights are held
to result from the authority relationship existing in schools and
in particular from the power of the head teacher. It is widely
recognised that this problem largely results from the present
legal position which places on the head teacher responsibility for
everything that happens in the school. The NCCL suggests that
this problem could be partly met by changes in the model articles
of government and management of schools (58) and the ACE claims
that the child 'lives under a system from which there is no appeal
and no escape'.(59) Berger, likewise, argues 'that compulsory
education added to the legal concept of *in loco parentis* puts
teachers in an authoritarian position from which it is impossible
to escape'.(60) In school, the teacher is vested with the same
powers and responsibilities as the prudent parent, though he is
under no obligation to interpret these in accordance with the
beliefs of the child's actual parents. Except in cases of physical
punishment which can be shown to have been excessive, there is
in the matter of discipline no form of redress against the teacher,
and particularly against the head teacher. Children have a right
to expect, Berger claims, 'that parents will have access to schools
and be involved in disciplinary decisions about them'.(61) Such
provision, it is suggested, might be written into the law. 'The
legal concept of *in loco parentis* should be abolished', the NCCL
recommends, and replaced by a 'wide ranging but less exclusive
cum parente concept'. The NCCL is also concerned that pupils
should have the right 'to some means of appeal from decisions
affecting them, whether these are made by teachers or parents'.
(62) The ACE draft charter states: 'children shall have freedom of
access to suitably trained and appointed people to whom they can
take complaints and grievances. They shall have the freedom
to make complaints about teachers, parents and others, without
fear of reprisal'.(63)

6 The right of freedom in personal appearance
Specific areas in which excessive power is held to be exercised
by schools include the regulation of dress and appearance, the
limitation of free speech and expression, and the institution of
corporal punishment. 'Children, particularly adolescents', claims
the NCCL, 'should have the right to self-expression through personal appearance'. The more or less arbitrary power of head
teachers and local authorities in the matter of school uniform and
personal appearance is condemned as an infringement of these
rights. The practice of requiring parents to sign an undertaking
that their children will wear school uniform is described as 'a
mild form of blackmail on parents' and in any case morally invalid
because the pupils themselves 'have not signed nor necessarily
been consulted about signing the undertakings in question'.(64)
Berger suggests that the law should intervene to prevent head
teachers from compelling pupils to wear uniform.(65) The ACE
points out that adults who wear uniform choose their jobs and

Article 9 of the draft charter reads ' a child's personal appearance
is his own and his family's concern. No children shall be deprived
of any right or benefit as a consequence of his mode of dress,
style of hair, make-up or any other aspect of dress or appearance'.(66) The abolition of compulsory school uniform was declared
to be a policy aim of the NUSS.(67)

7 The right to freedom of expression

The right to publish without censorship by the school authorities
was demanded by the SAU in their letter handed in at County
Hall in July 1970.(68) Freedom of speech and the abolition of
censorship of school magazines, clubs and societies are one of the
policy aims of the NUSS (69) and the NCCL claims for pupils
the right to express opinion freely in school magazines 'without
any more restriction than is suffered by other publications in
society'. Head teachers, it is held, 'should not take on themselves
greater powers of censorship than those already sanctioned by the
law'.(70) According to the ACE draft charter, 'children have a
right to freedom of expression both written and verbal. They
have the right to publish their opinions on any matter whatsoever'.(71) The ACE was also concerned at the censorship of
pupils' private letters at some boarding schools.(72)

8 The abolition of corporal punishment

Corporal punishment, which has long been criticised on educational and psychological grounds, was also unanimously regarded
by all campaigners as an infringement of children's rights. Its
abolition was demanded by the SAU and sought by the NUSS,
whose first President described the head's power to cane any
pupil 'at will' as the degradation of pupils as individuals.(73) The
ACE draft charter urges that children should 'have freedom from
assault whether under guise of punishment or any other form',
and is anxious to abolish all 'such punishment as is intended to
mentally or physically humiliate the child, or cause him to lose his
self-respect'.(74) The NCCL points out that 'corporal punishment has been abolished in prisons and in Her Majesty's Forces
and consequently children are the only citizens who may legally
be beaten'. 'Pupils have the right', the NCCL claims, 'to be protected from assault of this kind in the same way as anyone else'.
(75)

9 The right to freedom of worship

The traditional right to freedom of worship should not, it is held,
be confined to adults. 'The adolescent, the young adult', claims
Ollendorff, 'has a right ... to determine on his own ... in which
way if any he wants to worship'.(76) The right to withdraw from
religious education and assembly on conscientious grounds is not
sufficiently publicised or protected. Any parents who wish to
withdraw their children from religious instruction lessons or
assemblies 'are nevertheless subjected to moral pressure' by
schools. In any case, Berger argues, 'children of secondary age

may have strong feelings on religion not shared by their parents'
and should have the right to opt out of religious instruction on
their own account rather than be dependent on the wish of their
parents.(77) Both the ACE and the NCCL see here a further
issue and stress the child's 'right to freedom from religious or
political indoctrination' 'at an age when they have no intellectual
equipment to understand its implications'.(78) The NUSS seeks
the abolition of both compulsory religious education and religious
assembly.(79)

10 The right of free access to knowledge
Further freedoms claimed for children and adolescents include the
'right of freedom of association ... within the school and outside'
(80) unrestrained by 'taboo of social, religious, racial or national
issues and snob or class values'.(81) Adams claims for the 'child
of school age (six to twelve years)' the right to free and unres
tricted access to knowlege, to enjoy 'the right to learn all secrets,
with no holds barred. This includes a right to sexual knowledge
and also, in our day and age, a right to knowledge of violence
and of the highly important role it plays in human affairs'.(82)
More guardedly, the ACE draft charter claims that 'children have
the right, at the appropriate age, to such knowledge as is necessary to understand the society in which they live. This shall
include knowledge of sex, contraception, religion, drugs including alcohol and tobacco, and other problems which openly confront
every growing child'.(83)

11 The right of sexual freedom
Perhaps most startlingly in the eyes of many adults, some writers
have claimed for the child rights of sexual freedom. Ollendorff,
for example, claims that the sexual activity which in fact takes
place among fourteen- and fifteen-year-olds should be recognised
as right.(84) Adams, likewise, claims for the child 'the right to a
life, with fullness with both sex and anger, love and hate', and
to loving relations 'with someone highly similar to himself, but not
within the family'.(85) The NUSS claims no right of sexual freedom. It does, however, seek 'better sex education' - and the issue
of free contraceptives to all pupils above the age of consent.(86)

12 Further rights claimed on behalf of children
The rights mentioned above are far from exhausting the list of
rights claimed for children. The ACE draft charter, for example,
mentions children's rights to such things as food, space, toys and
books.(87) Carl Bereiter speaks less of the child's right to make his
own mistakes (88) and John Holt's 'Escape from Childhood' argues
the case for an extensive list of rights on behalf of children.
These include the right to vote, to work, to own property, to
travel, to choose one's guardian, the right to receive a guaran-
teed income, and assume legal and financial responsibilities, the
right to control one's learning, to use drugs and to drive.(89)
Needless to say, the widely discussed right to education is also

implicit in many of the more specific claims by some of the writers
we have mentioned.

RECENT DEVELOPMENTS IN THE FIELD OF CHILDREN'S RIGHTS

The International Year of the Child (1979) was certainly effective
in once again bringing the question of children's rights to the
attention of the public and the media and may have been instrumental in stimulating a number of studies and publications.(90)
In recent years, debate on this subject has taken on a less stri-
dent and possibly more constructive tone. The SAU, NUSS and
Children's Rights Workshop have of late only rarely attracted
public notice. For the most part, the tide of educational radical-
ism has moved in other directions such as concern with deschooling, the practice of alternative education, the sociology of
knowledge, the attack on the cultural hegemony of middle-class
value judgments, and so on. Those concerned more generally
with the rights of the oppressed have switched their attention
from children to such other oppressed groups as women, consumers, social security claimants, immigrants and others.
Discussion of the rights of children has, however, continued in
serious academic contexts, showing that although the topic has
not been of constant up-to-the minute journalistic interest, many
underlying problems remain unsolved. It has, for instance, been
argued that children have a right of privacy which may be violated by the publication of examination results, especially if the
examinations in question have been compulsorily undertaken,(91)
or by certain school-home communications containing information
not available to the pupil himself, or which the pupil may not wish
his parents to receive.(92) The concept of children's rights has
received attention from both mainstream and educational philosophers. Notably, the grounds on which we distinguish those who
may claim full adult rights from those who may not have been seen
to pose problems of principle.(93) It has also been suggested
that compulsory education shares with punishment the character-
istic of raising questions about justifiable coercion,(94) and that
the concept of children's rights enables us to reject one widely
held account of rights in favour of another.(95)
As the children's rights movement has matured on all fronts,
the concern of activists in the field has been less with asserting
the grand old political rights of liberty and equality on behalf of
the young and more with ensuring that such legal protection as
exists or may be argued to exist for the rights of the young is
fully implemented and applied to the advantage of children, particularly those who are underprivileged. Articles in a two-part
special issue of the 'Harvard Educational Review' describe how,
in America, successful attempts have been made to argue in the
courts that school exclusion used as a disciplinary measure, and
certain widely employed assessment procedures, violate the constitutional, that is, legal, rights of children.(96) Citizen advocacy

groups have been active in securing these rights for pupils, and experiments have also been carried out in the development of a child advocacy function within the structure of educational and other institutions in which children are to be found.(97)

In this country, since the passing of the 1975 Children's Act it has increasingly become the practice in certain custody suits for courts to consider not only the child's best interests in the court's own interpretation of that expression, but also to take account of the child's actual expressed preferences. Some legal writers have also strongly expressed the view that the child should be an indispensable party to any such dispute, having his own legal representative, since his interest may be in conflict with those of his parents, foster parents or the local authorities.(98)

Returning to a more specifically educational context, there has been detailed treatment of the legal rights of parents, vis-à-vis schools, local authorities and the DES, by writers whose works have been deliberately pitched at the level of parent readers.(99) The Taylor Committee also took up part of the 1971 NCCL executive resolution that the articles of government and management of schools should be re-written to allow a considerably more democratic participation in the running of schools. Among other things the Committee's Report recommends that:

1 The membership of governing bodies should consist of equal numbers of local education representatives, school staff, parents (with, where appropriate, pupils) and representatives of the local community.

2 The Secretaries of State should take definitive advice on whether it is possible to change the law to enable pupils to serve as governors at sixteen without opening the whole question of the age of majority and the holding of public office.

3 Senior secondary school pupils should participate in school government to the fullest extent allowed by the law until they are eligible for membership.(100)

ALTERNATIVE STRATEGIES FOR THE DISCUSSION OF CHILDREN'S RIGHTS CLAIMS

It would be an understatement to say that not all of the 'rights' mentioned above are universally recognised. Furthermore, when the question of their possible implementation is raised, there is often much doubt as to the principles upon which such questions should be decided. Considerations advanced appear to be of three kinds.

First, reference is frequently made to the educational effects, good or bad, likely to follow from the implementation of 'pupils' rights' demands. Of the writings already mentioned, the NCCL Discussion Paper 'Children in Schools' is particularly prone to argue in this way. As regards school councils it states, 'the educational value of these would be enormous', 'it is between the ages of eleven and fifteen that it is appropriate to ensure that the

transition from infancy to adulthood is really in progress'. 'The
secondary school', the argument continues, 'is also the obvious
level at which to ensure that fundamental democratic processes
are instilled into future citizens.'(101) Those favouring the child's
right to be free of compulsory schooling likewise often support
their view with arguments of an educational nature, claiming that
compulsion destroys the child's natural spirit of enquiry, and
even that its effect is 'nothing less than the total deterrence of
almost all children from the whole idea of becoming educated'.(102)
On the question of dress and personal appearance, it may be
argued that taste in such matters is best learnt through freedom
in a situation where standards are recognised. Equally, of course,
educational arguments may certainly be advanced for the contrary
views. Insistence upon ready obedience, regular attendance and
sobriety in dress may well be defended as necessary to the good
order and sound endeavour necessary to disciplined and efficient
learning. Opposition to pupil participation in the management of
schools may well result from a sincere belief that the young,
because of their inexperience, will press for measures which are
unsound in educational terms.

A second approach to the question of pupils' rights claims is to
consider the implementation of these in terms of moral issues of a
more general kind. Compulsory schooling may be attacked on
grounds of the undesirability of compulsion as such, and defended
in terms of the value of what is learnt - either its intrinsic value
or its utilitarian value to both the child and society. Corporal
punishment and the right to be protected from it may be evaluated
by some by weighing the infliction of pain against the supposed
evils avoided in the long run. The censorship of school magazines
may be justified in terms of the triviality and offensiveness of
articles which might otherwise appear, or attacked because it prevents discontent from being aired and dealt with. Advocacy of
sexual freedom for the young has been based on the release of
energy and creativity which is supposed to result from it, while
more traditional views on this subject might be defended by pointing to the psychological and social harm to which such early
licence might be expected to lead.(103)

Third, the claims made may be discussed in terms of the rights
of the persons involved. It may, for instance, be denied that
children have rights while under the age of eighteen, while still
at school, or while entirely dependent on adult support. Certainly,
it is sometimes argued that the pupil has rarely done anything
to 'give' him the right to say how school should be run, or how
qualified teachers should conduct themselves. Alternatively,
teachers and heads may reply to militant pupils and their adult
supporters by asserting rights of their own. The head teacher
may claim his traditional, and even his legal right to control all
matters concerning organisation, management and discipline within the school. In support of his moral right to do this, he may
point to his responsibility for the educational progress, safety
and moral welfare of his pupils. In the matter of sanctions, he may

claim, on grounds of professional discretion, the right not to enter recalcitrant or disruptive pupils for examinations, or provide them with university references.

Of these three approaches it would seem that the third is the least likely to lead to progress or understanding. Talk of rights typically arises in situations of contention and it might be thought that discussion of this topic, far from clarifying an issue, often gives rise to further disagreement and to acrimony far beyond that which might have been expected from the original issues. To give but one example, no great harm seems to be entailed in a child's wearing prescribed dress during school hours, or shortish hair up to the age of leaving. Many do this with no ill effects. Equally, pupils in some schools do have liberty in these matters without disastrous results either to themselves or to their institutions. In themselves, the wearing of certain clothes or hair styles would seem small reason for excluding an adolescent from school or attempting to block his entry to institutions of higher education. In such cases it is often not what the pupil does which is considered offensive, but the assertion of his right to do it.

A further feature of rights talk is that there appears to be no way of reconciling disputes where one rights claim conflicts with another. The problem seems to stem from the fact that two rights claims, which, as a matter of contingency, seem to conflict, may often have justifications which are mutually independent. A pupil's supposed right to express without censorship any views which are not libellous (say on religious, political or sexual matters) may, for example, conflict with teachers' supposed traditional rights, rooted perhaps in the nature of their task, to require respectful and publicly unobtrusive demeanour on the part of their pupils. Nor is it immediately clear how discussion might proceed to a rational conclusion when a rights claim seems to run counter to considerations based on the general good or widely accepted practical objectives, be these educational or otherwise. Under the circumstances, one might be forgiven for wondering whether talk of rights is valuable at all in attempting to resolve conflicts in practical situations. Would it not be better, one might ask, to settle issues solely by reference to more impersonal considerations, such as what is most desirable in educational terms or most conducive to the general or social good.

It is proposed to argue, however, that such an approach would be inadequate and that though questions of what is socially or educationally desirable can certainly not be ignored, they do not exhaust the moral issues which have to be taken into account in dealing with children. I hope to show that the notion of rights has an essential part to play in our moral understanding and that this notion is applicable to the young as well as to adults. The attempt to examine particular rights claims on behalf of children, however, plunges us into complex and fundamental issues. In the immediately following chapters, therefore, the following questions will be considered:

1 What is meant by saying that someone has a right to something? (chapter 2).
2 What is the relationship between talk of rights and other kinds of moral language? (chapter 3).
3 What kinds of justification may in general be sought for various kinds of rights claim? (chapters 4-9).

Only when these questions have been exhausted would it seem profitable to turn to the further question of how the usual justification of particular rights claims is affected by the fact that the person on whose behalf the claim is made is a child.

What is a right?

Part II

2   Three traditional theories of rights

With a word as variously, and often emotively, used as 'right',
questions of justification presuppose some preliminary clarification
of meaning. Discussion of rights, furthermore, has a long and
chequered history and account has to be taken of earlier conceptions of the term if we are to understand the many, often conflicting reactions to its use in the present day. It may therefore
be useful to refer briefly to three traditional attempts to account
for the concept of rights which, if valid, would importantly affect
the way we approach the justification of rights claims in general,
and those made on behalf of children in particular.

1   RIGHTS AND POWER

The connection between rights and power or powers would seem
particularly relevant to any discussion of children's rights.
Though fathers no longer have the power of life and death over
their families, the power of adults over children is extensive in
respect of both their day-to-day existence and their long-term
interests.

The tendency to identify rights with powers may be traced back
to Hobbes and Spinoza,(1) if not beyond. Surprisingly, in view
of the apparent position of rights and power on opposite sides of
the is/ought distinction, Hume is of the opinion that:(2)

> Were there a species of creatures intermingled with men,
> which, though rational, were possessed of such inferior
> strength, both of body and mind, that they were incapable
> of all resistance, and could never, upon the highest prov-
> ocation, make us feel the effects of their resentment; the
> necessary consequence, I think, is that we should be bound
> by the laws of humanity to give gentle usage to these
> creatures, but should not, properly speaking, lie under
> any restraint of justice with regard to them, nor could they
> possess any right or property exclusive of such arbitrary
> lords.

For Hume, it would seem, possession of some degree of power is
at least a necessary condition of having a right, while the possession of unassailable powers by the stronger species appears to
entail the possession of rights which are correspondingly absolute.

The question of the relationship between rights and powers,
however, raises two issues which are sometimes confusingly conflated. On the one hand, there is the question of whether the

possession of the power to compel acquiescence or compliance is part of the meaning of having a right. On the other, there is the question of whether the possession of such power can in any way justify the claims we make on others. Both of these questions are obviously relevant to the issue of whether children have, or can have, rights.

There is certainly a technical use in jurisprudence in which some rights are called powers,(3) and in which power sometimes has the sense of authority. These uses, however, may be left out of account for the purposes of the present discussion. The possession of power in the more usual sense may also constitute a reason for granting or withholding certain rights, as when the leaders of a successful revolution in a foreign country are accorded the diplomatic rights and privileges of that country's lawful government, or when parliament declines to make a law which, however desirable, cannot be enforced. But to accept that, as a matter of expediency, what cannot be cured had better be endured, is not the same as recognising that there exists a moral right. Despite certain well-known older definitions of rights in terms of powers,(4) it would, indeed, seem hard to understand how it can seriously be maintained that the possession of power is necessary either to the definition of a right, or to its justification.

That powers are not synonymous with either legal or moral rights has been shown by reference to a host of counter-examples. A paralysed man may be powerless to intervene as a thief takes possession of his gold watch.(5) One may have the right (holding the necessary licence) to drive a car, but not have the power or capacity because of ill health or lack of a car.(6) One may have no possibility of having one's property or safety protected because the courts are corrupt.(7) If elections are poorly supervised one may have the right to vote but be powerless to exercise that right because one is obstructed, while others may well have the power to vote without having the right to do so.(8)

Nor can power be any part of the necessary justification of a claim to rights. In a tyrannical regime, the claim to rights may be the last resort of precisely those who lack the power to resist their oppressors. It is true that rights have this in common with powers, that they are connected with an agent's doing, having or receiving something or being in a position to do, have, or receive it if he so chooses. To have the power, however, is actually to be able to do, have or receive the thing in question, whereas to have the right is to have a particular kind of justification for so doing.

This being so, some mystery may seem to remain as to how such distinguished philosophers as Spinoza, Hobbes and Hume can have supposed rights and powers to be connected. Closer scrutiny of the context of their remarks, however, reveals that none of these writers was attempting to propound the perverse doctrine that power justifies a moral right in the sense in which we understand the term today. Spinoza and Hume, in particular, appear to have been concerned to explain why it is that we have the particular

legal and customary rights we have. Each acknowledges that, as
a matter of fact, those prerogatives will be recognised as rights
which correspond to the realities of power. Hobbes, for his
part, is concerned to maintain that prior to the undertakings by
which established society is created, Man's freedom is subject to
no moral constraints. In this sense the rights of an individual in
the state of nature are simply coextensive with his power, rather
than being justified or constituted by it.(9) In such a situation,
those without power, such as the newly born and the defeated
in war, may be deemed to give binding undertakings to obey
those who have them in their power. Unlike Hobbes, however,
we may not think such undertakings would be binding, or that
real or supposed undertakings constitute the only reasons why
someone should be obliged to limit his own freedom of action. In
that case we no longer have reason to think that people's rights
correspond to their powers, or are in any way dependent on
them.

2 RIGHTS AS CORRELATIVES OF DUTIES

If, as has been widely held, rights are to be defined as the correlatives of duties, the appropriate manner of deciding whether
children or any other category of individuals have certain rights
would be simply to examine the duties of others towards them in
the light of whatever ethical doctrine one felt prepared to defend.
In cases where one's ethical assumptions did not lead to the conclusion that someone has a duty which is specifically owed to
those whose rights are in question, any rights claim made on his
behalf would appear to be invalid. On such a view, once we have
a satisfactory theory of obligation we know all we need to know
about what we ought to do and any investigation of the topic of
rights is redundant duplication.(10)
  It appears that Bentham's purpose in formulating the doctrine
that to have a right is to stand to 'benefit from the performance
of a duty', was to dispel the notion that rights (along with
duties and obligations) were external entities, and to account for
the concept of a right in utilitarian terms.(11) If obligations and
duties are 'logical fictions', in the sense that they do not correspond to entities, rights are 'a kind of secondary fictitious
entity resulting out of a duty'.(12) For Bentham, therefore,
duties and obligations are primary and rights unequivocally derivative. Though a number of jurists and philosophers (13) have
followed Bentham in regarding duties or obligations as primary
and rights as secondary, others have simply held that right and
duty are merely 'different names for the same normative relation,
according to the point of view from which it is regarded,'(14)
without suggesting that either logically precedes the other.
  An established line of attack on the 'correlativist' view has
been to seek counter-examples of duties which do not confer
rights. Duties of imperfect obligation, duties to non-rational

creatures such as young children or animals, corporate duties
such as tax-paying and military service and duties to 'third party
beneficiaries' (as when A promises B to perform a service for C)
have all been suggested as possible stumbling blocks for the correlativity theory.(15) Supposed duties of imperfect obligation,
and the rights of non-rational or incompletely rational beings will
certainly be of interest to us later, but the not inconsiderable
efforts of philosophers to accommodate these and other duties to
the correlativity theory need not detain us. Our present concern
is not to discover whether there are duties which do not create
rights, but, on the contrary, whether there are rights which are
not adequately explained in terms of the duties to which they are
supposedly correlated.

Fairly clearly, this latter question can be answered in the
affirmative. Raphael identifies a category of rights which he calls
rights of action,(16) namely, those things which one has a right
to do in the sense that they are not wrong and do not infringe
the rights of others. To describe these as rights is not, as is
sometimes suggested, to be misled by an ambiguous idiom. The
notion of a right of action, sometimes described as a liberty, or
in the terminology of jurisprudence as a privilege (17) is well
established in both law and philosophy and is valuable in asserting that the logically prior condition of Man is not bondage but
independence.

In claiming that rights are no more than the correlatives of
duties, therefore, we must at least insert the proviso 'except
rights of action'. If we exclude rights of action, however, we are
by definition simply left with what Raphael calls 'rights of recipience'. These are not, as the name might seem to suggest, rights
to be given something (that is, welfare rights), but all rights
which impose duties on others whether they are rights to be given
something, or rights which are vouchsafed to individuals by imposing restraints upon others.(18) To say, however, that all
rights other than rights of action (that is, all rights of recipience)
impose duties on others is both perfectly true and perfectly vac-
uous.

Though rights and duties are certainly related, they are not
related in the straightforward and relatively uninteresting way
suggested by the correlativity theory or indeed by the view to
be considered in the following section that rights are some form
of claim. For the present it may perhaps be said that if someone
has a right (other than a right of action) there is at least a prima
facie obligation to respect that right. Arguably, a right provides
a particularly strong ground of obligation, to override which
always involves a wrong of some kind.(19)

This, however, is not by any means to say either that rights
and duties are opposite aspects of the same relationship, or that
they are most profitably explained in terms of duties. Far less is
it to say that in investigating the rights of individuals we had
best begin by seeking general grounds of obligation.

Cases are indeed frequently found where the statement 'I have

an obligation because you have a right' does not constitute a mere
restatement (as would be the case in 'A killed B because B was
killed by A'), but a genuine explanation. A man may, for example,
think that he has the right not to be rung up about a business
problem on a Sunday afternoon. The correlativity theory - particularly the version which simply holds that rights and duties
are the opposite ends of the same relationship without attempting
to specify which is primary and which is secondary - tells us no
more than that if the subordinate has the right not to be disturbed, the superior has the duty not to disturb him and vice
versa.

On this view, the subordinate's rights claim may be explicated
in two quite different ways. On the one hand, it might be held
that the superior has a duty to refrain from disturbing his subordinate because of the wrongness of desecrating the Sabbath,
or because it is socially desirable that one day a week should
be left free from business chores. Here the duty is seen as being
owed not to the subordinate, but to the community as a whole, or
to the superior's competitors and rivals who, for the sake of the
general good, have themselves accepted the penalty of refraining from badgering their employees on Sundays and may reasonably expect him to do the same.

On the other hand, it might be argued that since the subordinate is not simply an employee existing solely for the purposes of
his employer, he has a right to privacy and a degree of rest and
leisure on at least one day of the week. In this case the superior's duty would follow from the subordinate's right and not vice
versa. The justification would in some way be located in the subordinate, whose right would be primary while the duty of the
superior would be secondary. Above all, the duty of the superior
is inferred from the subordinate's right, and is not simply a
restatement of it.

Just conceivably there may be some who wish to speak of the
subordinate's having rights in both of these cases. At very least,
however, it will be conceded that the kind of right involved, the
ground for saying that the subordinate has a right and, perhaps,
most importantly of all, the grounds on which it would be legitimate to deprive him of this right will differ widely. These differences are obscured by the version of the correlativity theory
which simply states that rights are the correlatives of duties and
vice versa.

The version of the theory which makes duties primary and
rights secondary has the additional disadvantage that though it
is thoroughly consonant with the first account of the subordinate's right (which arises from the superior's duty to refrain), it
fails to explain the second. Yet it would seem to be a requirement
of our common understanding of the concept of a right that a
satisfactory account of this concept should treat the second case
as central, and perhaps even leave us in doubt as to whether it
was appropriate to speak of the subordinate's having a right in
the first case at all.

3 RIGHTS AS CLAIMS

It is not uncommon for writers simply to assume that rights are
some form of claim and then to pass on without further justification or elucidation.(20) An important distinction is, however,
to be drawn between the sense of 'claim' found 'in making a
claim' or 'claiming' and that being used when someone is said to
'have a claim'.

Much argument purporting to show that rights are claims
appears to be concerned with the first of these senses – with
making a claim or claiming. Sometimes it is suggested, quite mis-
takenly it seems to me, that one cannot conceive of having a
right without at some time claiming what one has a right to, or at
least having a tendency to do so.(21) Other writers focus on the
activity of claiming a good or freedom under a rule, and present-
ing one's credentials to show that one belongs to the category of
individuals which the rule in question specifies.(22) The view
that rights are claims in this sense is unsatisfactory on three
counts:
1 A claim that one makes is an action. It may be, for example,
encouraged, withdrawn, repulsed or entertained, and like many
other actions, may be described by such adjectives as ill-timed,
half-hearted, and impertinent – not to say justified or unjustified.
Whatever a right is, it is certainly not an action, and cannot be
characterised in any of these ways.
2 When one makes a claim to something, the essential feature in
the situation is not that one speaks 'urgently, peremptorily, or
insistently',(23) but that one's request to be given the object in
question is coupled with the actual or implied assertion that one
has the right to it. In this sense the notion of a right is logically
prior to that of a claim.
3 The picture given by the activity of claim-making suggested
above is one of legislation or the demand for legislation from
above, or of behaviour to be governed by rules thought conducive to a particular human end. Now it is true that some,
though certainly not all,(24) legal rights are created in this way,
particularly when they arise out of deliberately enacted laws and
regulations. By and large, however, such an understanding of
the concept of rights is in disaccord with the complexity of the
social world of individuals with widely different basic moral
assumptions and aspirations in which the discussion of rights
typically arises.

Turning now to claims in the sense of 'having a claim', it would
certainly seem more plausible to suggest that rights are claims in
this sense. One may have claims without pressing them or even
without knowing of them, much as one may have rights without
asserting them or being aware of them. To ignore someone's
claims merits moral censure, just as it does to ignore his rights.
Claims, like rights, may be overruled, but here, however, a difference of capital importance emerges.

The way in which claims may conflict, and in which some may

necessarily have to be overruled, is well illustrated by the situation in which a number of candidates have applied for a post.
Supposing no specific criteria to have been laid down, the person
making the appointment might consider the claims of various
applicants in terms of their seniority, qualifications, previous
loyalty to the firm, energy and talent, or even their need for
employment. All of these claims are 'valid' or 'justified' provided
the facts on which they are based are true and the qualities to
which they relate are appropriate reasons for appointing this
person rather than that. Eventually, the person making the
appointment will have to weigh the claims of the various conten-
ders, and choose one of them. Provided this is done fairly no
injustice will have been inflicted on those whose claims are over-
ridden, even though not all may accept the decision with good
grace.

If, however, one of the candidates has a right to the post, for
instance, he has been given an undertaking on which he has come
to rely, or perhaps, the office is an hereditary one, the question
of weighing claims does not arise. Though it will be argued in a
following chapter that in certain circumstances it may be legitimate or even obligatory to set aside or overrule a right, the
person on the receiving end of such an action remains the victim
of a wrong. Unlike someone whose claims are overruled, someone
whose right is set aside is entitled not only to complain, but also
to receive apology and compensation.

This implication of having a right, that even its legitimate setting aside constitutes an injustice, is lost if rights are equated
with claims, even justified or valid claims, in the sense of 'claims
that one has'. To turn down a justified claim, in the sense of
'claims that one makes', necessarily involves an injustice, for to
make a justified claim is to truly assert or imply that one has the
right to what one is claiming. As we saw, however, there are good
reasons for saying that rights cannot be claims in the sense of
'claims that one makes'.

Rights, then, are not powers, nor can they adequately be
accounted for as the correlatives of duties, nor as claims. In
attempting to tackle the question of what are someone's rights,
therefore, it is not relevant to ask whether he has the power to
coerce others, or to resist their efforts to coerce him. Nor will it
necessarily be most profitable to begin by trying to construct a
general theory of duty or by examining high-level moral principles
which may be appealed to in pressing one's claims on others.

In the following chapter an attempt will be made to provide a
positive account of what it is to have a right. This, it is hoped,
will go some way towards explaining certain troubling features of
rights talk, particularly the fact that rights sometimes appear to
conflict with each other, or with different kinds of moral consideration.

3   Rights and other forms of moral language (1)

RIGHTS AND THE GOOD

The view that rights are simply the correlatives of duties, or are some kind of claims to the implementation of a rule, would appear to imply a particular relationship between talk of rights and other kinds of moral language. The model is one in which a right is a kind of secondary or derivative concept within a framework of prior moral rules. Individual rights, like individual duties it would seem, are to be justified by rules subordinate in turn, perhaps, to an echelon of higher order principles, or directly to some further or higher good. Ultimately, rights are seen to be justified because the action they license 'is itself good or else a means to what is good'.(2) The moral pyramid is seen to be of a piece though its contours and structure may be sketched with more or less precision. Older writers provide numerous statements of this view which are often unqualified and emphatic.(3)

To accept such an understanding of the concept of rights, however, would be to commit oneself almost irresistibly to the view that to answer questions about rights it is necessary to begin by plunging oneself into a full-scale discussion of theories of ethics. (4) This, however, seems mistaken. One cannot, of course, properly claim the right to inflict injustice or wrongful harm on others. But numerous examples suggest that the validity or otherwise of a right is often independent of the character of the action it licenses and, indeed, involves 'a quite different type of moral evaluation from that used in describing an action as good or bad, right or wrong'.(5) Having the right to do something implies no positive moral value in the action itself, and certainly no tendency to increase any collective or ultimate good. A customer at a car show-room, for example, may have the right to choose a red car rather than a green one, even though the benefits of so doing may be non-existent.

Far from being calculated to increase the common weal, rights may, indeed, be seen as areas of individual autonomy, of limited sovereignty over one's own actions or those of others, which one may normally choose to exercise or not as one wills.(6) Alternatively, they may be pictured as a kind of boundary of inviolability which may not be crossed in pursuit of overall social goods since each of us is 'irremediably separate' and 'the individual's share in the overall social good achieved does not suffice to balance *for him* the harm suffered by the infringement of his right'. (7)

CONFLICTS OF RIGHTS AND DUTIES

In seeking how best to approach the question of what rights
children have and what would follow from their possession, it is
necessary to bear in mind that not only may talk of rights and
other forms of moral discourse be thought to involve different
types of moral evaluation; they also appear to function according
to a rather different logic. In a particular case, though moral
rules seem to conflict, one may never be said to actually have
two opposing duties. This apparent paradox may be illustrated
by the case of a man who has to decide between reporting his
friend's son to the police and keeping his crime secret because
the shock of his arrest would kill the father. The principle of
truth-telling may, perhaps, seem to be opposed to that of preserving life. Such a situation is often described as a conflict of
duties, but this is misleading, for the moral agony arises not
from the difficulty of deciding which duty is the more compelling
but rather from deciding where the duty actually lies. If it is a
man's duty to shield the son, it cannot also be his duty to denounce him. To say that he has two duties, his duty as a citizen
and his duty as a friend, is to use the term not prescriptively at
all, but descriptively, specifying the expectations attaching to
certain social roles. Prescriptively speaking, if the man ought to
denounce the son, it cannot also be the case that he ought to
shield him. If we concede that it is his duty to follow the first
of these courses, we cannot logically reproach him with not following the second, though others may do so if they think he has
chosen wrongly.

Whereas duties may, in principle, always be reconciled, rights
do not appear to cancel each other out in quite the same way.
This is aptly shown by a consideration of the moral issues involved in those harrowing cases of a natural mother who has had to
give up her child through no fault of her own reclaiming the
child after a number of years. Though it is no longer customary
to speak of adults' legal rights in such situations, but to look
rather to the best interests of the child,(8) it is nevertheless
possible to think of both natural mother and foster parent as
having some moral right to the custody of the child though it is
clearly impossible for both to enjoy any such right simultaneously.

The problem raised by conflicts of rights has received some
discussion by philosophers, though for the most part this is unsatisfactory or inconclusive. Some writers, supposing rights to
be derived from rules, suggest that these, by virtue of their
general character, are always to be regarded as defeasible because justified exceptions cannot always be foreseen in advance.
(9) It is difficult, however, to see how the moral claims of either
the natural mother or the foster mother in the example given may
be 'defeated' by the claims of the other. If they were to be
'defeated' - that is invalidated - this would have to be by reference to some negligence or culpability on the part of the natural
mother or some express or implied reservation at the time of the

adoption, and these we may exclude from the hypothesis.

An attempt has also been made to throw light on the problem by distinguishing between the various degrees of generality with which statements concerning rights may be expressed. These supposedly range from claims to specific rights to be accorded here and now, through discretionary rights, right packages, and right categories to the 'grand old rights to life, liberty and property and the pursuit of happiness' which it is held are to be understood as 'ideal directives to legislative aspiration',(10) which cannot always be realised, either because the means are lacking or because they conflict with some other supposed right of the same order. This interpretation of certain 'rights' as no more than ideal directives which merely 'endorse a more or less vague ideal'(11) clearly falls short of the same writer's characterisation of a right as something which may be demanded 'urgently, peremptory or insistently, something a man can stand on, something that can be demanded or insisted upon without embarrassment or shame'.(12)

If, as seems likely, specific moral rights can conflict irremediably, then we must accept that someone called upon to adjudicate between two individuals possessed of conflicting moral rights may, while recognising the indubitable existence of both rights, have to overrule one of them in favour of the other. If there is no alternative, that is, if both parties cannot enjoy their rights simultaneously so that one of the rights must be overruled whatever decision is reached, then to overrule a right cannot be censurable. However unwelcome this conclusion may be, it would seem to follow that the overruling or denial of an otherwise unimpeachable right may therefore sometimes be legitimate or even, indeed, one's duty.

Not only, furthermore, may we be obliged to concede that a right may legitimately be overruled because it clashes irremediably with another, but it also seems to be the case that a right may sometimes be overruled for the sake of some other greater good. The action of compulsory purchase or the commandeering of private property in time of war may provide a case in point. The owner of a piece of land may have acquired it by perfectly legitimate means, and may be implacably opposed to its being taken over by the public authority, however great the compensation offered. He may, for example, have strong sentimental or traditional attachments to this particular piece of land to the extent that his being unwillingly dispossessed seems morally outrageous. Yet it is difficult to argue that there may not be some circumstances (some public benefit to be gained, or perhaps, more convincingly, some great harm to be avoided) in which we should morally approve the action of the administrator who made the painful decision to appropriate it. The process of deciding whether or not it is one's duty to overrule or waive a right is, of course, no different from deciding what one's duty is in any situation. Consideration must be given to all aspects of the case. One such aspect is the existence of the right which it is proposed to overrule. It must, however, be stressed that the benefit of overruling the right is to be weighed not only against the actual loss suffered by the right-holder, but also against the further evil of overruling his right.

OVERRULING A RIGHT

A number of writers have made the point that to establish that A has a right to X is not to establish that A should be given, or allowed to do X without further question. Examples given in illustration of this claim, however, suggest that it is not always fully understood. One commonly employed instance is particularly misleading. This is the case of the landlord who has the right to evict his tenant, but ought (in view of the latter's plight) to refrain from doing so, or delay his action.(13) Such a situation would seem to involve no more than a clash between legal rights and moral considerations. This raises no great problem since it may be readily agreed that the positive laws of a country may permit actions which are morally censurable, and that even an ideal set of laws may leave much to the conscience of individuals.

The more interesting case is that in which there is a clash of undeniable moral rights, either with each other or with some other good, such that we cannot but give our moral assent to a decision by which a right is overruled. The question at issue is the status of the right (or 'right') which is overruled. Does it remain a right in the full sense, justifying the right holder in his feeling that he has in some way been 'cheated' or 'wronged', or does the 'rightness' of the decision to overrule it mean that it is in some sense to be regarded as annulled and no longer a right at all? One writer clearly thinks that to overrule or waive a right is to repudiate it, for he holds that rights to liberty, property and even life cannot be rights because situations can be imagined in which they may legitimately be denied.(14)

Significantly, however, in discussing the right to life, the writer in question fails to distinguish between the case of someone whose life may be sacrificed for reasons of state and that of someone who has forfeited his right to life, through the commission of some capital crime.(15) The view that to overrule a right is to extinguish it would appear to result from a failure to recognise the particular kinds of grounds according to which rights claims may be justified and denied. As will be seen in following chapters, rights are originated in a number of specific ways, arising from the equal freedom of individuals, certain kinds of need, and certain transactions or relationships. For rights to be extinguished, these grounds must in some way cease to apply. The individual may, for example, forfeit or alienate his equal freedom, the need may be shown to be capable of fulfilment in another way, or, in the case of a right arising from a transaction or relationship, the right may be forfeited, or renounced by the party to whom it is owed. When a right is overruled in the interests

of a greater good, none of these things need happen, so that
clearly the original justification of the right (and therefore, it is
held, the right itself) remains.

In an attempt to avoid the unwelcome conclusion that a right
may legitimately be overruled while still remaining a right, some
writers have drawn a parallel with Ross's notion of prima facie
duties,(16) and speak of prima facie rights which, after a full
examination of the moral situation and the conflicting obligations
on the parties concerned, may or may not turn out to be 'a right
proper or actual right'.(17) This, however, obscures the important difference between the logic of rights and duties, to which we
referred earlier. Significantly, Ross finds it necessary to apol-
ogise for the term 'prima facie duties' because it 'suggests that
what we are speaking of is a certain kind of duty, whereas it is,
in fact, not a duty, but something related in a special way to a
duty'(18) (i.e. a reason for a certain course of action being one's
duty). There is, however, nothing prima facie about a right
which is overruled when it conflicts with other rights, or with
some weightier consideration. The right remains, even though we
may wish to describe the duty to accord or fulfil it as a prima
facie duty (that is, the right may be a reason for a certain course
of action being someone else's duty, though other reasons may
prove overriding). To take the right in question to be merely
prima facie is to confuse the question of whether a person has a
right with that of whether he is justified in exercising it.(19)

RIGHTS AND RULES AS ALTERNATIVE WAYS OF REGULATING
CONDUCT

Since talk of rights and talk of conduct being right or wrong,
good or bad, bring to bear essentially different types of moral
evaluation and criticism, and since these two types of evaluation
may often conflict it is possible to think of ourselves as possessing not one, but two, quasi-independent systems for reconciling
claims as to what should be done. On this view, rights, on the
one hand, and other moral concepts, on the other, are not complementary parts of a single system covering the moral universe
between them, but two different systems used to do the same job
in slightly different ways. When claims have to be reconciled
this may be attempted either by reference to an all-embracing
code, which we may call 'morality', specifying what ought to be
done in individual cases, and linking this, perhaps, with some
overall good or principle, or simply by dividing up the area of
human freedom and saying who shall decide what without pre-
scribing what choices are actually to be made. Thus, in educational matters, for example, one may either do as Plato does and
lay down with supporting reasons a certain programme to be followed, or one may simply specify who shall decide how this or
that individual is to be educated.

Societies may be conceived of, furthermore, in which one system

rules alone. It is possible to imagine a totalitarian society in
which no areas of private decision exist and both moral and legal
codes are directed towards the well-being of the community.
Equally, one may imagine a society in which only the rights of
individuals are considered and the function of government is to
secure respect for these. The USSR in its early years and the
USA in the nineteenth century have been suggested as societies
approaching these extremes.(20)

Different though such societies would be, the fact remains that
one can conceive of the total task of social regulation being carried out on the basis of either rights or duties alone. One may,
indeed, go further and seek an explanation of how, in a society
which regulates its affairs according to a mixture of the two 'the
relative emphasis of the two depends on the conjunction of particular psychological, religious, social, economic and political
conditions obtaining in a given society at a given time'.(21) Thus,
for example, one might perhaps be tempted to seek an answer in
terms of psychological types corresponding to totalitarian and
laissez-faire tendencies in politics, or authoritarian and permissive
leanings in morals. Alternatively, one might, perhaps, expect to
find a more plausible account by considering men's habitual preoccupations in differing social situations. It might be thought,
for example, that in his daily life the landowner, businessman or
employee tends to regard the universe as a whole as no concern
of his and, in matters of contention, to look to his rights and to
the rights of others like himself. The priest and the administrator,
on the other hand, may tend rather to look to the whole for justification and above all seek ultimate ends and principles ensuring
consistency and simplicity.

To suggest, however, that morality falls quite so drastically
into two halves is nevertheless something of an exaggeration. The
question of whether someone's right should be implemented or
overruled on a particular occasion may, after all, be a subject of
moral evaluation. It is also a moral question why, or indeed
whether, the private desires, aspirations and interests of individuals ought to be given special weight when decisions - especially
collective decisions - are made about what ought to be done.
Ultimately rights claims have to be justified though, as will be
argued, the justifications appropriate to such claims are of a
particular kind.

One thing, however, is clear. Far from feeling obliged to
attempt to settle questions about rights by plunging into full-
scale controversy about ethical theories, we might with equal
plausibility adopt the reverse procedure. Since the rights of individuals appear to be important elements in many moral situations,
one criterion according to which the adequacy of an ethical
theory is to be judged is its ability to take account of this important moral concept.(22)

DO WE NEED THE CONCEPT OF A RIGHT?

Despite the possible logical priority of rights over duties, it was suggested earlier that the whole task of social regulation might in principle be carried out by reference not to rights, but to duties alone. Circumstances may also arise, it seems, when rights, even though they remain rights, may legitimately be overruled. This being so, it may reasonably be asked whether, for all practical purposes, we need the concept of a right at all, and whether there is any point in speaking of children, or anyone else, as possessing them.

In reply to this it is here maintained that rights do indeed have an important part to play in our moral understanding. To raise the question of rights when a particular course of action is being considered is to focus attention on the wishes, choices, and aspirations - not merely on the interests as seen by others - of those concerned. To insist that people have rights which only they may alienate is to emphasise that they are to be seen in a particular way, as beings whose wishes may not be lightly set aside, however great the benefit to be derived from so doing.

Even when a right is overruled, it is important to preserve the notion that it remains a right nevertheless. Such a view is valuable, not only in encouraging an appropriate 'spirit of reluctance, apology and respect',(23) but in emphasising that however justified the action that infringes an individual's right, the result nevertheless remains a 'wrong to *him*'(24) which calls for redress in the long run, even if this cannot be achieved immediately. Hesitation, reluctance, and redress would all be out of place if it were assumed that a right outweighed by some greater good simply ceased to be a right or had, indeed, only been a presumptive or prima facie right in the first place, or had been 'defeated'.

WHAT IS A RIGHT?

At this point the criticism might be made that no unequivocal answer to the question: 'What is a right?' has yet been given. It has been argued that rights are not powers, and the views that rights are simply the correlatives of duties or claims have been found unsatisfactory. What follows from the fact that someone has a right has also been explored in the present chapter. To date, however, no attempt has been made to define the concept in the clearly recognisable form: 'a right is ... this or that'.

Such a definition can, of course, be given without difficulty. Rights have, for example, been described as entitlements.(25) Despite a certain overtone that to be entitled implies the existence of a rule in a way which, it has been argued, is normally inappropriate to our understanding of a right, this description is not obviously false. In most contexts 'I have a right to' and 'I am entitled to' are interchangeable. The fault to be found is not that it is false, but that it is uninformative.

If we require to understand all that is meant when it is asserted or denied that someone has a certain right, this is not best achieved through the search for synonyms, but by explorations of a somewhat wider kind. One of the underlying contentions of this study is, indeed, that a most fertile source of confusion and conflict regarding the rights of individuals is the assumption that a definition of a right can be given which is at once simple and informative, and that claims to rights which do not fit such a formula are to be rejected out of hand.

In the immediately following chapters it will be suggested that the expression 'A has a right to ...' (and consequently the term 'right' itself) may be used in not one, but a number of ways. Though these uses may certainly have important features in common it will be argued that different kinds of rights claim are susceptible to different modes of justification and criticism, and that failure to distinguish between them, and demanding inappropriate justifications, is a frequent source of misunderstanding and unnecessary disagreement.

In Part IV it will be further argued that these different kinds of justification are affected differently by the fact that the right-holder or supposed right-holder is a child whose rational development may be rudimentary or incomplete, and who may be in a condition of material and personal dependence. Consideration of what kind of right is in question and what kind of justification it is appropriate to demand is therefore of prime importance when particular rights claims on behalf of children are in debate.

In chapter 4 it is proposed to begin by considering the notion of a positive right and the relationship between prescriptive and descriptive uses to which the term 'right' is subject. The following categories of moral rights will then be considered:
1 Rights of freedom in the sense of liberties (chapter 5);
2 Claim rights of freedom (chapter 6);
3 Rights of democratic participation (chapter 7);
4 Special rights (chapter 8);
5 Welfare rights (chapter 9).

The justification of different kinds of rights claims

Part III

4   Positive rights and moral rights

The most obvious and elementary distinction to be drawn between uses of the word rights is between cases where it is an ethical term and cases where it functions descriptively, or quasi-descriptively.(1) When we say that a black child has a right to the same education as a white child we may be inclined to say that if 'right' is here being used as an ethical term, the statement is true. We would also say that it is true if we were describing the legal system of Great Britain, but false if we were describing that of South Africa or any other country where the law makes separate provision for the education of white and coloured children.

The descriptive or quasi-descriptive use of 'rights' is not limited to the strictly legal field. When we say that at the court of Louis XIV, only close relatives of the king had the right to sit on a chair with a back to it in the royal presence we are describing not a law but an established social convention. Similarly, when we say that at certain public schools prefects had the 'right' to flog and fag younger pupils we certainly do not mean that this was a legal right, or even that it was anywhere laid down in any form of written school rule.

It may be thought that the distinction between ethical and descriptive uses of 'a right' is not sufficiently obscure as to be likely to cause any serious misunderstanding. Few, it may be thought, would be so obtuse in serious discussion as to answer the claim that an eighteen-year-old has the right to choose for himself whether to take part in an act of worship by referring to the 1944 Education Act, or to counter the argument that pupils have a right to self-expression in the matter of dress and appearance by reference to legal cases.

In view of this, it may seem to be of merely passing interest that usage fluctuates so easily in much of the children's rights literature. Thus the NCCL claims that 'all children should have the right to be taught in buildings with modern facilities'.(2) Though the force of the sentence as a whole is prescriptive, the term 'a right' itself is being used descriptively. A change is being recommended in regulations by which this right would in fact be conferred. Elsewhere it is said that 'children have the right to organise themselves democratically without interference', (3) the point being, as is clear from the context, that members of the SAU and other organisations should not be penalised by the educational authorities, even though pupils penalised for being members of these organisations were, in fact, unprotected by law or regulation.

RIGHTS AND RULES IN LAW AND MORALITY

The use of 'right' in moral argument no doubt has its origin in
legal discussion, and may be used in the field of morality to suggest that someone has a moral title as clear and unequivocal as
the law is supposed to be. Although we are likely to find few instances of actual confusion between the descriptive and prescriptive use of the term, we have already had occasion to allude in
passing to differences in the logic of some legal and quasi-legal
rights on the one hand and that of rights in morality on the other.
(4) As reference to this point was necessarily brief, it may seem
appropriate at this juncture to set out the argument more fully.

In the legal sphere the relationship between rights and rules
would often appear to be relatively straightforward and is commonly taken to be as follows: to assert that A has a right to X
where the right is a legal right is to claim that there is a rule,
typically to be found in written form (statute, charter, regulation,
etc.), to the effect that all persons of a certain category may do
or have X, and also to claim that A is a person of that category.
(5) Both of these claims are normally susceptible to elementary
empirical investigation and if substantiated justify the assertion
that A has a right to X without further ado.

It is true that this is a somewhat simplistic account, even of
legal rights. In common law, for example, the appeal is to the
precedent of earlier cases, rather than to the rule as such. That
the precedent instantiates a rule does not necessarily entail that
the rule is prior, for it has been held that 'the law' consists of
rules, not in the sense of prescriptions, but of generalisations
regarding past decisions of the courts, on the basis of which
solicitors, legal advisors and members of the public may make
more or less reliable predictions as to how courts are likely to
behave in the future. (6) Even when explicitly set out in legislative form, legal rules are rarely as precise as may naively be
supposed and so-called 'hard cases' may produce judgments which
modify the 'law' for the future. (7) In such cases, to which existing precedents do not seem to apply, it is not clear whether the
decisions of the courts are to be seen as the discovery of rules
which were in some way already in existence, or as the establishment of a new right on the part of one individual which will
henceforth serve as a precedent to which others may appeal. (8)
These, however, may be seen as relatively minor complications
in an account of the relationship between positive rights and a
corresponding class of rules which remains valid in the main.

In this sense alone it is possible to speak of rights which are
conferred by rules or laws. It is also necessary to this concept of
a right that either custom or some particular legislating body or
individual is credited with the authority to establish rules under
which our rights of this category are held. The analogy which
one writer appears to draw between our moral rights in general
and the right of a football team to a free kick under the offside
rule (9) would, however, be a travesty of our normal under-

standing of the term. Far from being derived from positive rules in this way, it will be argued that our most important moral rights rest on the assumption that the prior condition of Man is not one of subordination in which he has to have rights conferred on him, but one of moral independence in which he has certain rights whether they are recognised by society and its structures of authority or not.

ARE MORAL RIGHTS PARASITIC ON THE LAW?

Sometimes it is suggested that a moral right is simply something that ought to be a legal right. Talk of moral rights, it may be held, is just a way of saying that certain goods or modes of behaviour should be embodied within the 'system of rules governing the behaviour of whichever society it is that the people proclaiming the right belong to'.(10) Even the rights of life, liberty and the pursuit of happiness may be seen as mere 'ideal directives to legislative aspiration',(11) and claims to human rights no more than 'a rhetorical flourish on the part of manifesto writers'. (12)

The doctrine here being propounded closely resembles the Benthamite one that the only 'real' rights are the child of law and that use of the term to denote moral rights is little more than a metaphor. Poets, rhetoricians and other 'dealers in moral and intellectual poisons'(13) may perhaps be inclined to use the word to describe 'what it is that people's entitlements *should* be',(14) but in the last analysis 'Potential entitlements are not entitlements.'(15)

As an account of our understanding of the term 'moral rights' and the relationship between moral rights and the law, this is clearly unsatisfactory. One valid reason for saying that a certain interest ought to be protected by the law is precisely that this interest corresponds to a moral right. We may think that someone has a moral right to go about his business unmolested or not to have his property taken or destroyed without considering whether there ought to be a law to that effect or not. Indeed, we may think we have many moral rights to which the protection of the law would be quite inappropriate. One's right to the fulfilment of a promise in some minor matter (16) or the right of parents to consideration and courtesy from their children are cases in point.

Furthermore, to say that an interest ought to be protected by the law is by no means always to say that it corrresponds to a moral right. In times of economic stagnation, for example, it may be thought that the law ought to encourage production in a certain important sector of the economy by means of tax concessions. But this is not to say that the entrepreneurs in that sector have a moral right to such concessions. To justify that claim it would be necessary not to point to overall economic advantage, but to show that in some way they deserve or desperately need the concessions, have been led to expect them in the course of some transaction to which they have been a party, or should be given them because the current situation discriminates against them unjustly as compared to entrepreneurs in other fields. The public weal may provide excellent grounds for bringing a particular law or regulation into existence. It does nothing to establish that those who gain special advantages from such laws and regulations have the moral right to do so in the absence of the legislative act in question.

That legal rights are the only 'real' rights may, nevertheless, well be the use of the hard-headed layman, inclined to ridicule claims to rights not backed by the force of law. Such a view may consequently be an important source of contention and misunderstanding when the rights of individuals - including children - are disputed in an actual situation of conflict. Hardheadedness may also account for the tendency noted in chapter 1 of movements urging the rights of various groups, whether children, parents, women or others, to abandon the tactically ineffective assertion of moral rights and to concentrate in various ways on the area of positive rights. Currently the efforts of such groups may take the form of lobbying and other political activity to bring about legislative changes, or advocacy and the dissemination of information to ensure that individuals are actually able to profit from the positive rights already theirs by virtue of existing law or regulations.

Doubts about the propriety of moral use of the term 'right' may also account for the extreme scrupulousness of certain more wary children's rights authors in avoiding it. Both Holt and Berger for example strive to employ only locutions of the type 'children *should* have the right to ...' stressing that they are concerned to advocate the extension of children's legal rights.(17) In Holt's case, in particular, this appears to prevent him from doing full justice to the reasons for the changes he urges. Whatever one may think of this writer's substantive conclusions, these could in many cases be argued quite properly in terms of children's moral rights of freedom and protection from various personal indignities and degrading forms of exploitation.

WHEN IS A LEGAL RIGHT ALSO A MORAL RIGHT?

In contrast to the view that talk of moral rights is meaningless except by reference to some law, constitution, or established custom, it is sometimes suggested that to show that someone has a positive right established by reference to some unambiguous law or custom throws no light at all upon the validity of his claim to a moral right.(18) In any situation, of course, the reasons for doing and for not doing something may seem to be in conflict, and the moral agent is always bound to weigh all considerations before acting. Without bad faith we cannot say 'This the law allows or forbids and that is the end of it.' If laws are pernicious, cruel or unjust, it may be that they ought not normally to be obeyed and that the rights they confer may often justifiably be withheld and ought to be frustrated.

Barring manifest injustice, however, the fact that something is a legal right would seem to be a reason for holding that it is a moral right also. Not only does the law quite properly require us to do many things which are already morally good, but certain things, otherwise morally neutral, may become morally obligatory by virtue of being required by law. In practical undertakings such as those between landlords and tenants, for example, matters such as the extent of responsibility for maintenance and repairs, terms of notice, the payment of key money, uses to which the property may be put and so on may be morally neutral except in so far as the law apportions rights and obligations between the two parties. In entering into such an agreement each does so on the assumption that the law will be kept by the other. To this extent the law defines the nature of the agreement and in the absence of specific arrangements to the contrary creates expectations in each regarding the conduct of the other.

Turning to a right of a slightly different kind, we may doubt that in the absence of legislation there would normally be a moral right to receive formal education at the age of, say, seventeen. If, however, the law provided for all to receive education up to and beyond this age, the case of a boy of seventeen being denied education through the whim or idleness of an official would be justification for moral outrage as well as legal action. The moral rights involved in these two uses are genuinely rights due to the individuals concerned, and the moral obligation to accord them does not merely arise out of the obligation to obey the law lest the law be brought into disrepute.

Persons who forgo advantages in order to respect the law would seem to have the right to expect that others who benefit from life in a law-abiding society will do the same with regard to them. (19) Someone who does not receive his legal due while others receive theirs is unjustly discriminated against, if he himself is expected to obey the law and bear the full burden of social responsibilities.

CONCLUSION

In this chapter the elementary distinction has been noted between positive (mainly legal) rights and moral rights. It has been argued that though the notion of a right may have originated in the context of legal discussion, and although one normally has the moral right to have one's legal rights respected, moral rights in general are not parasitic on the law and may be both characterised and justified independently. Now, therefore, it is proposed to consider in turn the various kinds of moral right listed earlier and attempt to identify the kinds of justification that may be given in the case of each.

5   Rights of freedom in the sense of liberties

To claim that A has a right to do X where 'right' is used in the sense of a liberty is not to claim that A ought to be allowed to do X, that others ought to refrain from preventing him, or that society ought to protect him in the doing of X. Far less is it to claim that society or anyone else ought to help him or put him in a position to do X. It is simply to claim that A may do X if he can, and that in so doing he does no wrong. Such rights have also been termed 'rights of action' (1) and, in jurisprudence, somewhat misleadingly to the lay-man, 'privileges'.(2)

It is important to distinguish clearly the category of 'liberties' here under discussion, from that of 'claim rights' or 'protected rights' of freedom, which will be considered in chapter 6. For this purpose one may compare the situation in which two men race to take possession of an unowned object of value,(3) with that in which the object already belongs to one of them. In the first case, both men have the 'right' in the sense of a liberty to pick up and take possession of the object if they can, though each may be prevented by the other's getting there first.

In the second case, only the man who owns the object has the right to take or use it, and here the right is not simply a liberty, but also a claim right or protected right, in the sense that others ought not to prevent him. The other man does not have any right, even in the sense of a liberty, to take the object, for in so doing he would be infringing the protected right of the owner.

These two notions are sometimes conflated in the single notion of a right of freedom.(4) Doubtless this may result from the fact that possession of the two often coincides and, given the presumption normally operating in modern Western societies in favour of an individual being allowed to do whatever he wishes unless there are good reasons for hindering him, the claim that there is nothing wrong in what one is doing often serves as a claim to be allowed to do it without let or hindrance.

This sense of having the right to do something has been dismissed as 'less central' and 'less important' than other uses of the term,(5) and it has even been denied that it refers to a category of rights at all.(6) This is perhaps somewhat surprising in view of the role this concept of a right has played in the history of political theory.

The notion of a right as anything a man is under no obligation to refrain from doing is central to Hobbes's argument in both the 'Leviathan' (7) and 'De Cive'.(8) In a context in which the sovereignty of kings was justified by patently shaky arguments based

on the paternal authority of Adam and notions of divine right
which no longer commanded universal acceptance, Hobbes attempts
to do for sovereignty something analogous to what Descartes tries
to do for belief in the existence of God and the material universe.
His method is to doubt all that can reasonably be doubted about
Man's obligations and then to attempt to rebuild the edifice of
absolute sovereignty by showing how Man, given Hobbes's understanding of his nature, must of necessity trade off his initial
freedom in return for security. Hence Hobbes's initial position
that the individual is subject to no obligation to obey anyone or
refrain from doing anything whatsoever. His rights are unlimited
except by his powers, and these rights are essentially rights in
the sense of liberties.

It is not here intended to examine how Hobbes moves from this
point to that of the individual's obligation of more or less complete obedience to the sovereign on the basis of what we may
regard as erroneous assumptions about the nature of Man and the
absence of obligations other than those of self-interest. Other
writers have arrived at different conclusions having similarly
started by assuming an initial absence of obligations.

The idea of Man's initial freedom is perhaps succinctly expressed by the assertion of the Cromwellian soldier that 'no man is
bound by the law of a government which he has not in some way
voluntarily put himself under.'(9) However naively and rhetorically, the point being made is the important one that individuals
are not in any sense 'naturally' subject to authority and obligation,
and that our obligation to obey governments or desist from certain actions must be justified. This, of course, applies as much in
the case of constitutionally elected governments as it did in the
case of monarchs. Where we may now feel these writers to be mistaken is in regarding consent as the only source of obligation,
that is, in regarding our consent as providing the only limit to
our rights and the only source of (protected) rights in others.
Even this, however, may be salvaged if we accept the proposition
that the rational being must of necessity consent to the just treatment of others.

The importance of the view that we in some sense have a right
to do those things which are 'not wrong' - even if we do not have
the right to be protected in the doing of them - lies in the fact
that it contradicts any view of Man according to which he is not
in ordinary circumstances entitled to act without receiving some
form of authorisation or permission, and must regard what is not
expressly authorised as forbidden. This latter view would seem
to be implied by the practice according to which the burghers of
medieval towns had to humbly petition for a royal charter to hold
a fair or a market, or engage in certain forms of trade. It would
also appear to be implied by the need to seek a form of authorisation or imprimatur from the secular or religious authorities
before a written work, however innocuous, is published or by the
requirement that citizens should apply for a special visa with
supporting grounds before travelling outside their own country.

It is against such a view of man that Paine protests when he finds
an edict of toleration as obnoxious as religious persecution.(10)

Before leaving this historical review of writers who base their
arguments on the initial freedom of Man, attention must be drawn
to the fact that all the writers mentioned are content to assert the
mutual independence of men as 'given'. The argument is emphat-
ically not that men are equal in rights because, empirically speaking, they are approximately equal in their capacities.

Such an argument is, indeed, notoriously hard to sustain.
Problems clearly arise when we attempt to define human capacities
in such a way that they are shared by all men, but possessed by
them alone.(11) Locke notwithstanding, men appear to differ
quite widely in their various qualities and capacities and this
would seem to suggest – if the line of reasoning had any virtue
at all – that men should be not equal, but unequal, in their rights.
Even if some quality could be found which men possessed equally
and in common, this would be no reason for supposing them to be
equal in rights. To argue that it was would be to commit the naturalistic fallacy, as surely as to argue from differences of an
empirical kind to differences in rights.

The claim that individuals are equal in rights because they are
equal in some empirical sense therefore plays no part in our
present reasoning. The point is rather that 'the smallest he that
is in England (or anywhere else) has a life to lead as much as the
greatest he':(12) that individuals at least enter the world owing
no duty of subservience to any other, notwithstanding any capacities or excellences the other may happen to possess.

If, of course, the individual decides to give his allegiance to
others or entrust his fortunes to their leadership, that is a different matter. So it is if some individuals are for some reason or
other, temporarily unable to control their own lives so that others
owe it to them to give them guidance or even, under certain circumstances, coerce them. These possibilities, however, raise
further questions which will receive more thorough examination
when other categories of rights are considered.

THE JUSTIFICATION OF RIGHTS OF FREEDOM IN THE SENSE OF LIBERTIES

As regards the question of justifying the claim that A has a right
to do X where 'right' has the sense of a liberty, this must take
place at both a particular and a general level. At the particular
level, to deny that A has, in the present sense, a right to do X
is to say that X is wrong, breaking some moral principle or
unjustifiably infringing one of the various kinds of claim rights
of another individual. The nature and justification of such claim
rights will, of course, form an important part of the content of
the following pages. Where A's right (in the present sense) to do
X is in dispute, it is reasonable that the onus of demonstration
should be with whoever denies the right, for an act may be

regarded as morally neutral (and therefore not wrong) until it
has been shown to be otherwise.

At a more general level, however, the question may still be
asked as to whether it is indeed the case, as is nowadays generally assumed in western democracies, that we have the right to
do whatever has not been shown to be 'wrong', or whether we
should not rather believe, with certain nineteenth-century writers,
that we are born into a society in which a system of rights and
duties is already operative, according to which the only rights we
may be said to have are those conferred explicitly or implicitly by
laws, morality and the usages of that society,(13) or possibly by
the highest ideals of that society when they are in conflict with
its actual practice.(14) On such a view, the individual does not
exist in and for himself, but is seen as part of a greater whole,
or subordinate to a higher purpose. He may 'belong' to his society,
or be a 'member' of it in a somewhat stronger sense than that in
which these terms are normally used.

The weakness of this kind of view lies in the fact that both
wholes, particularly social wholes, and purposes imply persons.
Except for the universe itself, no whole is given in nature. Every
object is composed of smaller elements, and is part of a larger
aggregate. The perceiving of 'essences', the drawing of boundaries between discrete individuals is part of the process by
which a conscious being comes to understand the world. If this is
true in the material world, it is equally so in the social one, with
this exception that unlike physical objects, individual conscious-
nesses are irremediably separate though their viewpoint and per-
ceptions may be closely similar. At the social level there is no
indisputable way of deciding which groupings are to be regarded
as constituting 'wholes', of which individuals are 'parts', and to
the achievement of whose 'purposes' they are the means. In the
modern world the problems of defining nations and national communities are only too well known. Who is to say whether an
individual is part of and ought to serve the interests of the
British nation, the International Fraternity of Scholars, or the
Brotherhood of Kentish Secessionists? The act of definition must
be carried out by a conscious being. Since any such conscious
being must be separate from myself and since I can see no reason
for subjecting myself to his definition of the whole which I am to
serve, since I too am rational and conscious of my rationality, my
definition of the situation is at least on an equal footing with that
of others.

Like the definitions of social wholes, purposes also belong to
persons. Given the separateness of persons, there is no reason
why any one rational individual should accept another's or a group
of others' definition of the purpose he has to serve if he does not
wish or judge it right to do so, though this is not to preclude the
possibility that he will voluntarily and rationally choose to forward
the purposes of another and in so doing make them his own.

Even though an individual may not literally be a 'part' of his
society or 'belong' to it in any but the usual metaphorical sense,

may it not be argued that his indebtedness to it – particularly in
the case of young or especially helpless individuals – is so great
that any talk of his having individual rights, particularly rights
against his society is not only gross ingratitude, but arrogance?
The individual may indeed be thought to owe his very life to the
community into which he is born and in which he is reared.

This view appears to rest on two misconceptions. The first of
these concerns what is owed in terms of gratitude when one party
is able to confer a disproportionate benefit on another at relatively small cost to himself. It is a principle of the laissez-faire
view of freedom of contract that an agreement is fair and binding
provided only that it is acceptable to both parties at the time of
its making, whatever the surrounding circumstances impelling the
parties to enter into it. The relationship of slavery might be
justified on this view if it is thought that those defeated in war
prefer the life of a slave to being put to the sword.(15)

What is clearly wrong with such 'unequal contracts' is that it is
unjustifiable for one individual to profit from the contingent
extremities of another to gain an undue degree of control over
his life. In so far as repayment is appropriate in such cases at
all, the scale of this must properly relate to the effort or cost to
the provider as well as to the immediate benefit to the recipient.
When someone receives a very great benefit as a result of the
action of another, sincere expressions of gratitude and appreciation are certainly in place, but this is something different from
indebtedness in the sense of being literally obliged.(16)

The bringing of children into the world and raising them to
maturity involves some effort on the part of the adults who
immediately surround them, and perhaps also on the part of the
wider community. The raising of a new generation brings benefit
to the older generation as well as to the young and the effort
involved in caring for the young, though great, is nevertheless
finite, and any indebtedness incurred is consequently the same.
In principle at least, therefore, the individual may repay his
debts to those who raised him and still retain a measure of resources and energy to devote to purposes of his own choosing. If
it is indeed permissible to speak of repaying a debt in this context, it may be argued that the individual has some choice as
to how and when the debt is to be repaid and this would constitute an area of liberty which the case is intended to exclude.
It may further seem that the very notion of 'indebtedness' here
under consideration implies an original right of freedom as to
whether to contract into such a relationship in the first place.

A second weakness in the view here under discussion is the
assumption that it is to society that the infant owes his raising
and upbringing. Hobbes bases the duty of filial obedience on the
fact that the father has the power to destroy the infant.(17) Like
Rousseau, we may deny the right of the stronger to slay the
weaker,(18) and hence the validity of any right consequent on
this power. Possibly, we may admit the right of the adult generation not to succour the new-born infant, though even this may

be contested, as will be argued in chapter 9. To regard those
members of the adult generation who bring up the child simply as
agents of the community, however, and to argue that benefits
received from these individuals create debts to the community as
a whole is to suppose that the adults are subject to a relationship
with the community of the very kind which is here being denied.

It is possible, then, to identify the notion of having a right
simply in the sense that what one proposes to do is not wrong
and does not infringe the rights of others. It might perhaps be
thought that rights of this kind are not particularly valuable,
since if our only right to do something is a right of this kind, we
can always be prevented from doing what we wish by the actions
of others. Seen from another angle, however, the fact that we
have the right to do what is not wrong is a matter of capital
importance. To assert a right of this kind is to imply that we do
not automatically owe any general duty of obedience either to
individuals, or to established practices simply on the grounds
that they are established, or to society as a whole or those who,
for one reason or another, regard themselves as being entitled
to speak on its behalf.

Such a view of Man forms an important element in the justification of other kinds of rights which will be discussed later. The
individual's initial non-subordination to the wills and purposes of
others is also important to the value we are to set on whatever
other rights we may possess, for otherwise our rights could be
annulled by the requirement of whatever authority we are supposed to live under, that we should refrain from exercising or
even asserting them.

It may readily be anticipated that the question of whether
children may be said to possess rights, in the sense of liberties,
or whether they are to be regarded as necessarily subject to the
all-embracing command of adults will form an important question
in Part IV.

6   Claim rights of freedom and non-interference

To establish that what one wishes to do is not wrong, and that individuals are not inherently subject to the command of some sovereign lord and master or some established government, serves only to justify our rights of freedom in so far as they are liberties or rights of action. It does nothing to show why powerful groups or individuals should not use force to limit the freedom of others or interfere with them whenever it suits them to do so. To insist that others should refrain from attempting to hinder or interfere with one is to make a further claim to a 'protected' or 'claim' right of freedom.

Such claim rights of freedom are therefore substantially more valuable than mere liberties, especially to those who, like children, are weak and powerless. Since, unlike liberties, they involve constraints on others, they entail additional problems of justification. An important part of the business of justifying the claim that A has a right to X, where 'right' is used in the sense of a claim right of freedom, is to show why others should either constrain themselves or be constrained by society.

ACTIVE AND PASSIVE CLAIM RIGHTS OF FREEDOM

Rights of freedom may be both active and passive.(1) Active claim rights of freedom are rights to do this or that without let or hindrance from others and include such things as the right to freedom of movement in public places, the right to choose one's various occupations and pursuits, the right to make any one of a number of uses of things that belong to one, to seek information which others have no legitimate reasons for concealing, to disseminate information and opinion and so on.

Passive claim rights of freedom are rights to be let alone and not interfered with or harmed. They are commonly taken to include rights of security of the person, the right not to be molested, the right not to have one's belongings taken or damaged, the right not to be spied upon or have personal information communicated to others, not to have one's character blackened by slanderous reports or suffer forcible intrusion into one's home or family life.

JUSTIFYING CLAIM RIGHTS OF FREEDOM

Various attempts may be made to justify the constraints imposed
upon others by A's possession of a claim right of freedom. For
the most part, however, such attempts seem less than convincing.
1 Mill attempts a utilitarian justification of the right of freedom,
particularly in areas of thought and discussion.(2) It is not clear
whether he is concerned with liberties or with claim rights of
freedom. In either case, however, his argument is inadequate.
Rights, as we have seen, may not be deduced from the overall
good of the community, since the two sometimes conflict. At most,
the general good may serve as a reason for conferring a positive
right on someone. But the same argument may serve as a ground
for withdrawing the right if its effects cease to be beneficial.
2 An attempt may be made to account for the category of rights
here under discussion by reference to some form of consent
theory, according to which A agrees to limit his own actions in
certain respects lest B and many others unite against him, or
overpower him while he is asleep or otherwise off his guard.(3)
In this situation all may connive in perpetrating the notion of
fundamental rights which enables the strong to reconcile their
self-respect with refraining from interfering with or restricting
the freedom of others. Even the strong are able to see the mutual
respecting of rights as being in their interest.
    Such an explanation, however, fails to take account of the fact
that, Hume nothwithstanding,(4) we readily attribute rights -
including claim rights of freedom - to the powerless, even though
it would undoubtedly be in the rational self-interest of the strong
to unite in suppressing them. In any case, though such an explanation may provide some form of crude rationale as to why
certain 'rights' are, as a matter of fact, recognised in society and
why even the strong would often be well advised to respect those
of others, it does not provide us with anything that resembles
specifically moral justification.
3 Finally, one might be tempted to resort to the transcendental
argument that 'if the would-be interferer possesses freedom he
cannot legitimately deny it to others without grounds'.(5) As it
stands, however, this argument is insufficient. Powerful A who
obstructs B may be perfectly happy with a situation in which B
may obstruct him if he can or if he dares. Indeed, much of the
disrepute into which the doctrine of Natural Rights has fallen may
be attributed to the fact that it received precisely this kind of
interpretation. On such a view, certain supposed 'rights of freedom' become rights of the strong to exploit the weak without
interference.(6)
    The above argument, however, does provide something of a
framework within which protected rights of freedom may be justified. What needs to be added is that in so far as a right is a
specifically moral concept, the weak have rights as much as the
strong. To the question of how B has the right to act, A's superior strength is morally irrelevant. A may therefore be considered

to have acted wrongly if he relies on strength alone to prevent
B from acting as he wishes. The same is true if he attempts to
use moral pressure or to bamboozle B by means of sophistry. If
he wishes to prevent B from acting he may only attempt to do so
by the use of reasoned persuasion, for reasons are supposed to
be available to all and may result in B's voluntarily changing his
intention.

If the distribution of strength and the powers of rhetoric (as
opposed to reasoned persuasion) is irrelevant to the issue of
what ought to be done, the wishes of individuals are not. If B
wishes to act, this is one reason for A's not preventing him. A's
wish to prevent him and his interest in doing so is also morally
relevant in a way that his superior strength is not.

RIGHTS OF FREEDOM IN CONFLICT

A wish in itself does not establish a right. A may wish to act but
B may equally wish to stop him. A may wish to carry out an
obnoxious industrial process while his neighbour wishes to remain
undisturbed by noise and fumes. A may wish to keep facts about
his failing health, sex life or business interests secret, while his
political opponent may wish to pursue and propagate knowledge
or opinion in these areas in what he conceives to be the public
interest, or, indeed, in his own interest.

Such conflicts of interest should not be confused with the genuine and irremediable conflicts of rights described in chapter 3.
It is important for an understanding of the logic of rights and
their relation to other moral language that such conflicts may
exist. In practice, however, such irremediable conflicts of rights
are relatively rare. If this were not so, if conflicts of rights
arose whenever wishes conflicted, the concept of a right would be
useless in resolving claims.

In cases of such irremediable conflicts of rights, furthermore,
one of the rights involved is typically either a special right or a
welfare right. (See chapters 7 and 9 below.) In respect of each
other, protected rights of freedom appear to be mutually limiting
rather than capable of irremediable conflict. Where A's (passive)
right of freedom from violence to the nose begins, there B's
(active) right of free arm movement ends.(7) This does not mean
that *claims* to rights of freedom may not conflict, for not all claims
are justified. A may claim that B ought not to swing his arms
suddenly and unexpectedly without first ensuring that there are
no unprotected noses in the vicinity, while B may feel that those
with noses to injure ought only to enter a working gymnasium
with due circumspection. As this example suggests, such conflicts
of claims may to some extent be settled by reference to the reasonable expectations of individuals in the particular context in which
they arise.

AN ORDER OF PRECEDENCE AMONG RIGHTS?

To speak of different individuals' rights limiting each other never-theless appears to imply a need for some principles according to which such limits are to be set if they are not to be purely a matter of arbitrary convention.

Attempts have been made to solve this problem by suggesting an order of precedence among categories of claim rights of freedom, such that rights of one category always take priority over rights belonging to categories lower in the order. For the most part such attempts have been unsuccessful.(8)

Nevertheless, there does appear to be one very general and, as it turns out, very helpful principle according to which claim rights of freedom can be ordered. Passive claim rights of freedom, that is, rights of security of the person, property or reputation normally seem to take precedence over the right of freedom from constraint. We regard A's right not to be hurt, have his property damaged or taken away, or even be unreasonably disturbed or annoyed as limiting B's active rights of freedom, and not vice versa, and this would appear to conform to the time-honoured notion of civil society's being instigated in the first instance to provide security.

If this suggested ordering of two kinds of rights of freedom is accepted, it may seem possible to mark off the approximate boundaries of our active rights of freedom to correspond with those of other people's rights of security, even though the precise location of this boundary may in practice sometimes be a matter of contention. In this connection it will be noted that passive rights of security do not come into conflict with each other, though particular claims (for example, to the undisturbed possession of a particular piece of land) may do so. What constitutes personal injury, molestation or defamation may be fairly readily characterised and whatever the problems involved in the definition of property, acts of entering, using, damaging or taking someone's property, once it is decided that it is in fact his property, may be readily identified.

Justification for attaching such overriding priority to rights of security is clearly required. Though this may sometimes seem to be provided by the weightiness of the interests involved, this is not necessarily the case. A potential peeping Tom's right of freedom is limited by the right of others not to be peered at, even though the actual harm caused by the peeping Tom's action may be minimal, and the pleasure derived from it very great.

The fact that in establishing the proper boundaries between the rights under discussion in this chapter we look first to the interest of security of the person is no doubt explained by the fact that to injure or even to manhandle another is to commit so obvious and blatant an incursion upon his individuality as to require apology and redress. As regards the security of property, due allowance being made for the controversies by which the concept is surrounded, the taking, using or spoiling of what

someone has made or acquired for his own purposes may be regarded as a similar incursion. Much the same may be said for the
rights of reputation and privacy in so far as these are goods of
such obvious and immediate concern to the individual that to dis-
regard them would be to set his interests and point of view at
nought.

OVERRULING, RELINQUISHING AND FORFEITING RIGHTS OF SECURITY

To say that in delimiting the rights of individuals in general,
consideration is first to be given to certain important interests of
security is not to say that individuals may never be forcibly re-
strained or even, in extreme cases, subjected to injury and death.
Nor is it to say that their property may never be confiscated or
commandeered, or that pressing questions may never be asked
about private matters. As we saw in chapter 3, considerations of
great moment may, with due hesitancy and efforts at reparation,
sometimes justify acts which infringe the rights of others.

An individual may also, by his own actions, divest himself of
his rights, including his right of security. This he may do in two
ways. First, he may do so by way of forfeiture, as when he knowingly commits a crime subject to corporal or capital punishment,
or to a fine or confiscation of goods. Second, he may do so by
consent as when he confers special rights on others, for example,
if he consents to undergo a surgical operation, contracts with
others for the use or sale of his property, voluntarily takes part
in a boxing match, or stands for public office and in so doing
exposes his private life to a degree of public scrutiny.

THE RIGHT TO HAVE OUR FREEDOM PROTECTED

Finally something must be said concerning a right additional to
those discussed above, namely, the right to have one's right of
freedom and security protected from infringement when others
fail in their duty voluntarily to forbear from such infringements.
The protection of one's security and freedom usually figure among
the legal rights of the citizen and, as was argued in chapter 4, it
is, subject to certain reservations, normally one's moral right to
receive one's legal due.

In so far as there is, over and above this, a moral right to call
upon the resources of the community and therefore ultimately of
other individuals to defend one's private interests, which may
also be in the public interest but are not necessarily so, the
admittedly contentious view will be argued in chapter 9 that the
right of the weak and incapable to protection against the strong
who invade their rights is essentially the same as the right to be
protected from hunger and misfortune when one is genuinely
unable to provide such protection oneself.

7 Rights of participation

It is assumed for the purposes of this chapter that many widely shared human purposes require some degree of co-ordination, and that it is not practicable for modern individuals to imitate the Pilgrim Fathers by simply leaving all established communities. It would, however, seem to be a logical consequence of the individual's essential non-subordination to others, discussed in chapter 5, that he is not necessarily bound to accept institutions and hierarchies of control or the priorities of collective purposes which he finds established when he enters the world. This would appear to be particularly true if those hierarchies of control and priorities of purposes appeared blatantly to favour the interests of others.

In so far as one man's purposes are of paramount importance to himself, just as another man's purposes are of paramount importance to him, the individual would appear to be justified in claiming the right to equality of influence with any other in the direction of any co-ordinated social action, whether at the level of the political community as a whole or in smaller and more localised undertakings. This in turn would seem to imply that individuals are entitled to such institutions and secondary rights as are most likely to make such equality of influence a reality. Local and national government elections, together with rights of free speech, freedom of the press and other media, rights to seek and propagate information, to communicate opinion, to organise opposition and to propose and demonstrate in favour of alternative policies may be considered to be such institutions and secondary rights and judged adequate or otherwise according to how far they seem to contribute to equality of influence as an actual outcome. In western 'democracies' even adult individuals have not always had, and indeed still do not have, the opportunity of exercising equal influence on the undertakings in which they are involved and the decisions that affect their lives. For this, three reasons among others may be distinguished:
1 Suffrage has not always been universal.
2 Western democracies are characteristically representative, rather than directly participatory.
3 Many of the most important decisions affecting people's lives are taken by organisations and individuals not subject to democratic control.

Each of the above limitations on the equality of influence people have on the decisions which affect them raises questions of justification which it is proposed to consider in detail. In anticipation

of the discussion of children's rights in part IV, it may perhaps
be borne in mind that children are excluded from taking part in
elections. At best their interests – in governmental and other
matters – can be said to be represented by others. Children also
spend a great deal of their time in institutions which seldom claim
to be democratic and to which democracy is sometimes held to be
inappropriate.

1   LIMITATION OF SUFFRAGE

Although the formal equality of a vote in periodic elections in itself is far from giving the individual an equal share of influence
in the decisions which affect his life, it nevertheless goes some
way towards constraining governments to act in accordance with
the wishes of the governed. The fact that, in normal circumstances, opposing parties have an interest in competing for the
middle ground of policy ensures that elections will be closely
fought, which in turn makes it dangerous for candidates to ignore
the wishes of any particular group. If, furthermore, elections are
decided by the abstentions of the disillusioned rather than by
actual switches of allegiance, candidates have a strong interest
in avoiding unduly blatant self-seeking or expediency in the
treatment of small or powerless groups or even of individuals,
except when these can be transformed into targets of public hostility. In a society not fundamentally divided by some such feature as religion or race, political followings and interest groups
may consist of shifting aggregates of individuals fulfilling many
roles and having ties with the members of many groups and this
further makes it impossible for a successful candidate to ignore
any section of the electorate.(1)
   Historically, the right to vote has been restricted on two kinds
of grounds:
(a) incapacity;
(b) non-contribution and non-membership.
In some cases both grounds have been put forward for denying
the vote to particular groups.

(a) Incapacity
In the pursuit of common undertakings a rational man must, it is
suggested, accept equality of influence with other rational individuals whose ends are as important to them as his are to him.
This, however, is something different from accepting that outcomes should be influenced by the 'choices' of those who, for
instance:
1 do not have or cannot conceive of ends of the kind likely to be
brought about by political action;
2 cannot entertain a particular set of ends for sufficient time for
them to be attained by political means;
3 cannot be expected to distinguish between consistent and
inconsistent sets of proposed ends;

4 cannot choose (that is, cannot take experience, evidence or
argument into account in deciding) between alternative means
likely to bring particular ends about.
To give weight to the 'choices' of such individuals would be, in
some degree, to submit the outcome of the matter up for resolution to chance and to render nugatory all reasoned discussion
and criticism.

In our own country the vote is denied to those certified as
insane. Grounds of incapacity have also been urged by many who
believe that it would be wrong or irresponsible to place the burden of self-government on primitive peoples (2) or even to allow
the vote to the ignorant poor in European countries. Doubtless
the argument of incapacity will have frequently been used to
justify denying the vote to women for so long, though it appears
that difficulty in conceiving of women as having interests separate from those of their husbands or fathers also played a part.
Incapacity may also be put forward as a ground for denying the
vote to children.

As will be argued more fully in chapter 13, discussions about
the capacity or incapacity to exercise equal influence on the conditions of one's life through participation in democratic institutions
present certain difficulties:
1 Many capacities may only be acquired pari passu with their
exercise, so that to deny someone the right to participate in democratic institutions on grounds of incapacity may be to ensure
that the capacity will not be acquired, thus justifying further
denials ad infinitum.
2 For administrative purposes, such as the organisation of public
elections, certain hard and fast lines have to be drawn, for
instance, between those medically certified as insane and those
not so certified. The acquisition and loss of various human capacities, however, is to be seen as a smooth continuum, so that
the point at which official lines between capacity and incapacity
are drawn must always seem arbitrary.
3 Chronological age and the development of rational capacities do
not always keep pace, so that where lines of exclusion are drawn
in terms of age, this may seem to result in some individuals being
denied the possibility of exercising equal influence on decisions
affecting their lives even though they are able and, as will be
held, morally entitled to do so.(3)

(b) Non-contribution and non-membership
A second reason for excluding certain sections of the population
from participation in the government of the community in which
they lived has been that they had no 'stake' in that community or
made no contribution to the enterprise with which government is
supposed to be concerned. Representation has been linked with
taxation from the time of the Putney Debates,(4) not to mention
the American War of Independence. The connection has also played
an important part in the resistance to efforts to extend the fran-
chise in both Great Britain and the Southern States of America.

Although the argument that the right to vote should be conditional on the payment of taxes has not always been put forward disinterestedly, it is not entirely without plausibility and may not be dismissed without consideration.

In part, the argument appears to have been that one had justification for a say in the decisions of government because it was one's money that the government were spending. The tax-payer's right to a say in government was justified in rather the same way as that of a paid-up member in a joint stock company. When the activities of government bore less heavily and less directly on the life of the individual it may well have seemed that one's 'estate' was the main interest which one had to defend by one's right of participation, if only by resisting expensive foreign wars,(5) or lavish expenditure by the court.

The argument for limiting the suffrage on grounds of non-contribution must be linked with that based on non-membership. At Athens foreigners who attempted to interfere with the process of public business in the Forum were liable to be put to death. Since they were not citizens, the city's affairs were simply no concern of theirs. In this case, membership of the city was established by blood. In present-day Britain, the residence or business qualification for participation in local government elections, besides making a voter a 'contributor' (by means of the rates he pays) to the funds which the authority will spend, also provides a way of establishing genuine membership of the community.

The underlying moral justification for participation in government, it will be recalled, is that one's interest will be importantly affected by the government's decisions and that one therefore ought to have equal influence along with everyone else upon what those decisions should be. Membership of the community, through one's business activities or through living in it, ensures that one's interests will be genuinely affected by the decisions of government and to that extent goes some way to guarantee that one's suffrage will not be entirely subversive, corrupt or frivolous. This concern is clearly visible in the remarks of Ireton, who not only fears that the poor will sell their votes, or vote ignorantly (an argument from incapacity), but points out that they have no stake in the country in that, unlike the owner of landed estate, there is nothing to prevent them simply going elsewhere.(6) The argument might be pursued along the lines that there is therefore nothing to prevent them from emigrating when the ill consequences of the policies for which they voted become apparent and therefore no constraint upon them to vote wisely.

Conceivably, it might further be argued that since the life conditions of those who may (in theory) move from place to place do not entirely depend on decisions of particular governments, their participation is morally less urgent. There is, of course, an element of validity for arguments of this kind. Elections ought not to be affected by the whims of casual visitors, far less by the votes of outsiders brought in for no other purpose than to vote. Clearly, however, the criteria by which membership of some democratic communities in the past has been measured - in particular, the property qualification - have been unduly narrow as have the criteria according to which individuals are judged to contribute to the well-being of that community. People contribute to the society in which they live by their labour as well as by their taxes, and the level of taxation is not the only way in which the acts of government impinge upon our lives. The lives of the poor and helpless, furthermore, may be thought to be influenced by the acts of government as much as, or indeed more than, those of persons possessing wealth and estate.

2 REPRESENTATIVE DEMOCRACIES

With the exception of certain Greek city states and Swiss cantons, western democracies have characteristically been governed by representatives of the people rather than directly by the people themselves. Legitimately, therefore, the question may be asked, whether the right to participate in government is a right to have a part in choosing those who shall govern or whether, strictly speaking, this right is only satisfied by direct plebiscitary rule. It is to be understood, of course, that we are concerned with plebiscitary democracy in which all are able to propose, amend or advocate propositions to be placed before the legislating electorate, and not simply with plebiscitary dictatorship in which the electorate is merely required to vote on alternatives of another's choosing, without being able to influence either the terms or the timing of their choice.

The notion of representative democracy may be subject to two contrasting interpretations. On the one hand, it may be simply regarded as the nearest approximation to direct democracy in states too large for direct democracy itself to have been a possibility. On this view, the representative is mandated to represent the express will of his constituents in so far as this can be ascertained.(7) The alternative view is that it would be desirable for the populace to choose representatives, even if this were not necessary for reasons of practicality. On this 'aristocratic' interpretation of representative government ordinary men are capable of appreciating neither the intricacies of government nor its higher goals, but are able only to choose the best men to rule in their stead. Representatives are delegated to rule according to their own judgment rather than being mandated to pursue certain policies.

In practice we appear, in Britain, to oscillate between the delegatory and the mandatory theories of representative democracy. That the delegatory or 'aristocratic' view is no longer held in its pure form is shown by the fact that it is regarded as perfectly proper, and indeed highly desirable, for parties and candidates at election time to explain and justify their policies in some detail and not merely to extol their own talents, achievements and virtues while denigrating those of their opponents. From this it would appear that we do, in fact, recognise the ability of the electorate to choose between policies and not merely between candidates. On the other hand, we think it a criticism of a politician to say that he promotes those policies which he knows will be popular with the voters rather than following his own conscience - even though such a criticism would seem inconsistent with an unreserved acceptance of the mandatory theory in its true form, according to which the 'character' of the representative would appear unimportant, provided he faithfully pursues the policies laid upon him.

If the right to participate in government is a right to exert equal influence on that government's undertakings, it would appear that representative government as presented in this delegatory theory, according to which good men are chosen to rule according to their conscience, does not meet the case. For if a man is not born subject to others, there is no reason why he should accept others' interpretations either of the ends of governments or of his own good and that of others. We may still feel that our members of parliament should be men of principle. This, however, is no doubt because we feel that an honest man with whom we disagree on certain 'controversial' but minor issues is more likely to govern as we intend than a more flexible character whose only consideration is to remain in power.

If we accept that the mandatory view of representation is the only one consistent with the individual's right of equal influence on public affairs, we would appear committed to the view that individuals have the right to be given a maximum amount of information about the policies being proposed and pursued by their representatives. On the mandatory view, no one is entitled to pursue a policy in the name of the people without the people knowing about it. A right to equal influence on public policy implies a right to open government.

Since on this view representation is a pis-aller made necessary by practical considerations, two further things would seem to follow. First, this expedient ought to be dispensed with when the small number of individuals affected by the decision, or an improvement in communications make direct participation a possibility.(8) Second, there is a right on the part of those represented that representatives should make every effort to ascertain the views of those they represent. This in turn would seem to imply not only a right of free expression of opinion and access to representatives, but also a right of consultation and a right to institutions designed to make such consultations a reality.

It may also be asked whether the supposed right to equal influence on the course of public policy demands a Jacobin conception of democracy in which the will of the current majority is absolutely sovereign, or whether it demands what has been called a Maddisonian conception of democracy in which minorities are protected from majority power by a system of checks and balances.(9)

In so far as this latter conception implies some form of basic and not easily changeable constitution or set of ground rules, the initial generation by whom these constitutions or sets of ground rules are drawn up would appear to profit from a form of inequality between the generations of the kind vigorously attacked by Paine,(10) even though this writer himself later argued for the importance of an established constitution.(11) Attention has also been drawn to the tendencies of entrenched minorities to sit on supposed 'constitutional' rights, in order to prevent widely approved humanitarian legislation.(12)

It may, therefore, be thought that the protection of various constitutional rights ought merely to allow sufficient time for reflection before final decisions are taken, rather than provide an absolute veto to the will of the majority.

Against this, however, protection of the rights of all to an equal say in public policy would seem to entail the need for relatively permanent checks in at least certain areas. In a Jacobin or majoritarian regime the power of those in the majority is absolute, whereas that of those in the minority is nil. To mitigate this difference in power which may rob some of equal influence, indeed of any influence at all, on the conduct of the community's affairs it is therefore necessary to safeguard the right of minorities to canvass alternative policies. This in turn may seem to entail protection of certain further more specific rights on the part of minorities. These might include the right of access to the media of communication, the right to organise and campaign for alternative policies even at the cost of some inconvenience to the public authorities and the public at large, the right to draw attention to the plight of those suffering from policies currently being pursued and the right to investigate and publicise unrecognised drawbacks.

Quite apart from the possibility that such goods as 'free speech', 'freedom of association' and the 'right of resisting oppression' may themselves in some sense be basic rights they are important as a source of power in the hands of minorities enabling them to narrow the gap between themselves and the majority by persuading the unaligned to join them.

3 NOT ALL DECISIONS IMPORTANTLY AFFECTING OUR LIVES ARE TAKEN BY GOVERNMENT

A further important shortcoming attributed to the western concept of·democracy is that it fails to provide for the equal influence of all in the conduct of affairs because most of the decisions importantly affecting our lives are not taken by government at all but by other, much more autocratic, organisations and institutions. These include private firms, public corporations, and voluntary bodies, not to mention such educational institutions as schools, colleges and universities in which some individuals may spend a substantial part of their lives. To a great extent the relationship between such institutions and the individuals in them is similar to that of the 'free man' in the Hobbesian version of the initial contract, who opts into an absolutist society and makes a free and binding choice in order to avoid the greater evil of remaining outside.

It is true that the injustices of the laissez-faire 'freedom of contract' are nowadays limited by labour regulations and union agreements, but these are usually negative constraints only. Subject to certain limits the employee conforms to the instructions of his employer or the management and accepts the offered conditions of employment, or he goes elsewhere. For the great majority of people these are not, in practice, open to negotiation. Discussion with workers' representatives is normally a matter of consultation only, and may be seen as management's way of finding out what it can get away with. Employment, sales and investment policies, the level of profit taking and even policies relating to training and the staffing of departments are rarely seen as the legitimate concern of individual employees, even though these employees may spend a substantial part of their working lives on the firm's premises and devote a major part of their enthusiasm and energies to promoting its purposes. Much the same applies in educational institutions. Students in higher education, for example, may be required as a condition of their membership of universities to sign undertakings to obey regulations, or, in older institutions, swear to observe statutes which they have no power to modify and certainly had no hand in originating.

The right to equal influence would appear to be sadly infringed by institutions holding a virtual monopoly of certain important goods such as employment (hence community membership and protection from starvation) or education at certain levels (which for some individuals is the sine qua non of a satisfactory life and their making a valid contribution to society), particularly when these institutions are often largely controlled by one individual or a small number of individuals. There would, therefore, seem to be a case for saying that all such institutions importantly affecting the lives of the individuals within them should be reorganised in such a way as to ensure that those within them each have the maximum possible opportunity to influence decisions about how they are run. Needless to say, the democratisation of firms and institutions would not only involve employees and members. The community interest would also need to be protected against the 'corporate selfishness' of the institution's members. In the case of industrial or commercial undertakings this would include consumers and local interests affected by its activities, for consumers and members of local communities are also individuals with a right to equal influence on decisions that affect them. (13)

Prima facie, there would appear to be no reason to exclude educational institutions from the principle of democratisation, though, as will be argued in chapter 14, the principle may need to be applied to such institutions with particular regard to their nature, purpose and membership.

THE RIGHT OF EQUAL INFLUENCE AND UNCONSTITUTIONAL ACTION

Sometimes it is argued that although demonstrations, obstruction, disobedience to the law, and ultimately violent revolution may be legitimate in non-democratic regimes, they are not so in democracies, in which those who are discontented with the existing state of affairs may have recourse to other remedies.

It is certainly true that to act in such a way as to disturb or threaten public order is always morally hazardous. Even in undemocratic regimes the established system of law and order may protect some goods, so that even in such regimes a degree of inequality ought to be borne, if the price of overt resistance is the risk of anarchy and bloodshed.

In communities which are in any degree democratic, so the argument goes, to act unconstitutionally, particularly when this involves actual breaches of the law, is wrong precisely because it weakens or prevents from acting the very institutions which are set up to protect that equality with which those acting unconstitutionally are supposed to be concerned. Since an established constitution lays down rules which have themselves presumably been agreed democratically, any breach of these rules would seem to infringe the democratic rights of others. This argument has particular force in a democracy, where political life brings together opposing groups all sincerely convinced of the justice of their cause. Those who break the prevailing ground rules of political life in their community in their own favour can scarcely complain if their opponents do the same. Nor, indeed, have they very firm grounds of complaint if it suits their opponents to commit a slightly graver breach of the rules, for once the principle of adherence to the rules has been abandoned, the choice of this stopping point rather than that in the process of escalation is arbitrary. More seriously, to break the rules in favour of what seems to be a greater degree of equality is to make it harder to prevent others from doing the same with the opposite intention.

This said, however, it must be observed that the claim that 'in a democracy' no unconstitutional action is permissible rests on an ambiguity. On the one hand, it is possible to imagine some sort of ideal democracy in which all actually have equality of influence as far as this is compatible with such differences of ability and character as may exist between different individuals. On the other, we use the word 'democracy' to mean those states in the real world which call themselves such because they possess certain democratic institutions such as periodic elections, a degree of free speech, public ownership, workers' co-operatives or whatever, having thrown off one or another form of oppression.

No doubt in the first situation, in which all already have as near perfect equality of influence as can be contrived, any unconstitutional action would be illegitimate since, ex hypothesi, it could not increase the degree of equality between individuals, and might reduce it.

In the second situation, however, in the imperfect democracies of real life, the possibility of legitimate unconstitutional action cannot be ruled out. The right to increasingly democratic institutions has been won from its opponents progressively and it would be difficult to say that the situation as it obtains in any community at any time is the best that can be achieved. In any less than perfect democracy such ground rules as there are have been established with the most powerful individuals and groups in that community having more than their fair share of influence on their making. Barring political ineptness on their part, it is naive to suppose that the ground rules of any real political community will do other than favour existing inequalities of power.

The right with which we are concerned in the present chapter is the right of equality of influence here and now, not simply the formal right to participate in certain institutions supposedly designed to bring about such equality at some unspecified time in the future. In an incompletely democratic community, therefore, the right of unconstitutional action in favour of greater equality would seem difficult to deny absolutely. If, for reasons given above, such action is morally hazardous, this is not an argument for ruling it out altogether. It is an argument for only undertaking such action after giving due consideration to the rights of others and to the likely overall consequences of one's actions in the political situation in which one finds oneself.

8   Special rights

INTRODUCTION

In both morals and jurisprudence the contrast is frequently
drawn between so-called general rights (alternatively called 'in
rem' rights or real rights), held against everyone, and special
rights ('in personam' or personal rights), which an individual
holds against specific individuals. General rights are characteristically rights of non-interference or security of person or property, whereas special rights typically arise from transactions, or
relationships which may or may not have been voluntarily entered
into. Thus someone's general rights may include the right to
drive his car unhindered and to exclude trespassers from his
property. His special rights might include the right to receive
payment for services rendered to an individual, or to require an
employee to follow his instructions.

SPECIAL RIGHTS ARISING FROM TRANSACTIONS

Typically, rights included under this head are those arising from
debts and promises, though the category also includes rights of
reparation (for damage or injury) and rights of reciprocation or
'gratitude'.(1)
    It will be evident that the claim to a right in this category is
susceptible to justification or refutation at two levels. In the first
place, it may be asked whether the transactions did in fact take
place in the absence of invalidating conditions. Was a promise
really made? Were coercion or deception used? Was the person
entering into the transaction in his right mind, and so on? Second,
it may be asked why we should respect supposed rights of this
kind. Why should we repay our debts, keep our promises or make
reparation for injury?
    In relation to this second level of justification, various writers
draw our attention to the usefulness of the practice of keeping
our contracts. Hobbes, for example, clearly regards the possible
failure of men to do so as socially disastrous,(2) as well as self-
contradictory, while thorough-going rule utilitarians are quick to
point to the social value of the rule enjoining promise-keeping,
even though particular instances may appear to lead to more evil
than good.(3) As we say in chapter 3, however, attempts to
account for rights in terms of the good to be achieved by their
implementation are unsatisfactory.

A more viable approach to the justification of special rights at this level may be made by pointing to the inconsistency of bene- fiting from the actions of those who respect the rights created by the transactions here in question, or from living in a society in which such rights are respected, without bearing one's part by observing them oneself.(4) This is particularly obvious in the case of bargains and arrangements for mutual benefit. By such an arrangement, A is enabled to pursue his own interests by the means of doing B a service (on the understanding that B will in some way reciprocate). If B's promise is not to be kept, this changes the aspect under which A's endeavours are to be seen. The latter has been deceived and, despite the fact that he is a separate individual with purposes and aspirations of his own, is being used for purposes which are not his but B's without his necessarily having any interest in serving B's purposes. In this situation it is possible to speak of A's moral agency being sub- verted.

Superficially, the rights conferred by desert may appear some- what different from those created by promises. If we say, for example, that soldiers who have served their country well or shown conspicuous bravery in the field have a right to come home to something better than the dole, we do not imply that specific bargains were struck at the time of enlistment or at the moment when the order to charge was given. Nevertheless, when an individual's participation in the benefits of the common weal are substantially less than his efforts on its behalf an element of appropriation exists not entirely dissimilar to that present in the case of broken promises. Someone who has acted virtuously, furthermore, is manifestly a being capable of rationally choosing ends and therefore one whom it is inappropriate to mistreat or employ simply for the ends of others.

Though rights of gratitude and reciprocation are not to be con- fused with the rights and duties associated with indebtedness, for which repayment is appropriate,(5) a relationship in which one person provides favours while the other receives them with no thought that he owes duties of reciprocation would again be one in which one person exists simply for the other's benefit.

Finally, rights of restitution and reparation are created when someone's resources and purposes suffer damage, diminution or setback through someone else's deliberate or negligent acts. If someone has made legitimate progress towards the achievement of his ends or has legitimately come to possess certain resources and other objects he values, there is no justification for his arbitrarily being deprived of them by the action of another.

THE CONCEPT OF RIGHTS AND SPECIAL RIGHTS CREATED BY TRANSACTIONS

Although rights created by transactions are not obviously central to the question of the rights of children and pupils, their treatment at some length has been necessitated by the fact that this particular category of right is sometimes taken as paradigmatic of the concept of rights in general. It is true that it is not always easy to draw a hard and fast line between rights created by transactions and certain rights associated with roles and statuses, to which we shall shortly turn. It is also true that rights arising from transactions, in common with most other kinds of rights, rest ultimately upon a presumption that individual human beings are essentially separate individuals with purposes of their own.

In many instances, however, the assimilation of other kinds of rights to the transactions model may be seriously misleading in its consequences. In particular, welfare rights are, as we shall see, often interpreted as rights due in respect of either desert or undertakings given by governments to individuals, and are therefore taken to be of unduly restricted applicability.(6) Contract theories of political obligation likewise appear to arise from an attempt to construe all political and civil rights and duties as arising from the terms of undertakings exchanged between government and the governed.

The clear equivalence between rights and obligations in the case of special rights arising out of transactions of this kind has no doubt also been partly responsible for the popularity of the 'correlatives' explanation of rights discussed in chapter 2. In the educational field one well-known and, as will be suggested, conspicuously misguided attempt to account for the right to education appears to arise from undue preoccupation with rights of this pattern.(7) Finally, at a lower level of debate, the possibility that children and pupils may have rights is sometimes denied on the grounds that the young have as yet done nothing to 'earn' or 'deserve' any rights, even though the rights in question may, for example, be rights of freedom, in respect of which the question of their having been earned does not arise.

RIGHTS ARISING FROM ROLE RELATIONSHIPS AND STATUSES

It is not always possible to draw a hard and fast line to distinguish special rights arising from role relationships from those created by transactions such as bargains and contracts. Commercial and professional role relationships are often established by contract when employment is offered or accepted and many, though certainly not all, of the rights and duties of employer and employee may be set out in a written legal agreement to which each party indicates his assent. Even when the rights and duties of the parties are not so explicitly stated, they are nevertheless normally clearly understood by all concerned. We place our health in the hands of doctors and our affairs in the hands of solicitors, become customers of garages and passengers in taxis on the rarely stated assumption that certain services will be performed to a given standard of care, reliability and security. Our right to receive such services is no less a moral right because of the fact that it may also be backed by the force of law.

The rules governing the rights and duties which are implied by entering into specific relationships will doubtless vary from community to community. This in itself does not invalidate their power to bind morally, provided it is understood by both parties what the other takes the prevailing code of rights and duties to be. In entering into such a relationship one concedes the rights of the complementary role, for this is the understanding upon which the other person has entered into it. To take the advantage of such a relationship without conceding the rights would be to abuse the other person and to subvert his understanding of what he does in living up to the obligations of his role.

Although the above may account for many of the relationships which members of modern western society freely enter into, there are two kinds of role relationships whose moral implications require some further examination. These are: (1) role relationships into which we are born or about which we have no conceivable choice; (2) role relationships into which we enter as a result of 'unequal contracts'.

1 Relationships into which we are born
Relationships of this category include both family relationships and social relationships in any society in which mobility is restricted. Like it or not, one is born the son, daughter or younger sibling of such and such an individual. In the past, one may have been born the vassal of this or that lord, the subject of this or that king, the prospective landlord of these or those tenants and so on. The customary and legal rights and duties possessed by or incumbent upon the occupants of such roles constitute part of the network of positive rights operating in a given society. The question with which we are concerned, however, is whether and under what circumstances these are also moral rights. In the case of the role relationships into which we are born, the occupant of the right-holding role cannot, on the face of it, claim his right against the occupant of the complementary role on the grounds that he only accepted the role and its burdens on the understanding that his rights would be conceded. Equally, the occupant of complementary (right owing) role cannot be said to have created rights in the other person by accepting the role which he occupies, nor can we validly argue for a Hobbesian presumption that the occupants of subordinate roles accept the obligations these entail as an alternative preferable to death.(8) Even if we accept Hobbes's dubious assumptions about human nature we - unlike Hobbes perhaps - are able to imagine that the necessities of human life may be met by societies having any number of different role structures. Should it be held that the conditions of human life are such as to make the division of mankind into favoured and less favoured roles it is always open to the occupants of the latter to question the validity of the criteria according to which the roles are distributed.

Melden, though basically concerned with the important features of moral discourse in general, considers at some length the rights

of parents to particular consideration from their children.(9)
This would appear to be a special right arising from a relationship of the kind here under consideration. Melden's basic contention is that to say that A is B's father is to say that A has a
right to particular consideration from B. He is careful to point
out, however, that 'father' as he employs the term, is not merely
a biological or genealogical expression, but already a moral term,
implying that there is an existing and established moral relationship which it is the duty of B (and A) to 'serve and preserve'.
(10) In the absence of such a moral relationship, if A's conduct
had been such as to justify B's claim that 'A has not been father
to me' then A's special right to particular consideration from B
would not exist.(11) This would appear to reduce A's right to
something like a right of gratitude, due, however, not in respect
of one act of kindness, but of a series of such acts in the present
and the past together perhaps with A's continued concern for
his child's prosperity and well-being.

The view that we have certain moral rights or owe certain moral
duties for no other reason than that we happen to have been
born into a particular social slot would seem difficult to sustain.
If the set of role-relationships into which we are born is itself
unjust, there can be no reason why anyone should concede the
rights which such a set of rules requires. But the society into
which someone is born may, of itself, be relatively just.

Conceivably, a feudal society of the kind nowadays generally
regarded as grossly unjust may have had something to be said
for it. This might have been the case if, for example, the over-
lord's right of command carried with it corresponding duties of
protection and care for his vassals. In such a situation, A, who
performs his role-related duties towards B and C, may be
thought entitled to benefit from the performance of their duties
towards him. If he did not, they would be profiting from his
efforts while disappointing his legitimate expectations that he in
turn would benefit from the performance of their duties.

This would appear to be the most plausible justification for saying that the role-related rights and duties existing in a particular
society are, in fact, moral rights and duties towards the occupants of correlative roles. To give such a justification, however,
is, as in the case suggested by Melden, once again to reduce our
supposed role-related rights and duties to rights and duties
arising from tacit transactions.

It is essential to the presumption that a reciprocal arrangement
is tacitly approved by both parties that the arrangement should
be just and beneficial to both parties. This follows from the inherent separateness and non-subordination of individuals, in
consequence of which benefits obtained by one individual cannot
morally compensate for the harms suffered by another. If the
established network of rights and statutes retains any part to
play in the justification of claims to special rights it is in determining which of the (ex hypothesi) justly distributed rights and
duties are to fall to the lot of particular individuals.

From what was said above about rights in the sense of liberties, however, it will be clear that no individual is morally obliged to accept or continue to accept even a just set of rights and duties surrounding the particular social position in which he happens to find himself. He is only obliged to perform the supposed duties of his station while he enjoys its rights, or until he has worked off whatever obligation he has incurred by enjoying them in the past.

2 Rights arising from roles entered into as a result of unequal contracts
It may sometimes happen that basic needs force individuals to accept role relationships which are highly disadvantageous in that they traditionally confer inordinately extensive rights upon the other person. Thus, in the past, farm labourers may have had to choose between starvation for themselves and their families and a position in which considerable deference and subordination was required by their employers even in matters unconnected with their employment. Women are alleged often to have had to choose between comfortless spinsterhood and a surrender of freedom and individuality which no man would have found tolerable. Ill health may sometimes have constrained individuals to become party to doctor–patient relationships involving unreasonable dependence on the convenience and moods of medical personnel. Most important of all, for the purposes of this present study, young people may arguably be said sometimes to have to choose between the surrender of important educational advantages and the acceptance of the traditional pupil or student role involving a degree of obedience, vulnerability to public humiliation and obligations of respect beyond those essential to learning.

In an age of enlightened employers, husbands, doctors and teachers, not to mention militant workers, wives, patients and students, the issue may not be of great practical importance. Nevertheless, even the hypothetical existence of role relationships of this order may seem to pose at least a minor philosophical problem.

In one sense it may be said that those who enter such relationships do so freely and, if one accepts the laissez-faire notion of freedom of contract in moral matters, this is sufficient to oblige and to justify the traditional rights claims of the dominant members of such a relationship.

In so far, however, as such relationships are only made possible by an unequal and arbitrary distribution of power, on the one side, and need, on the other, it is difficult to see how moral rights can be created by them. Workers, wives, patients, students and others may still find it prudent to acquiesce in traditional role relationships, at least in so far as the external marks of respect and subservience are concerned, but would appear to be under no moral obligation to continue to do so should a shift of power occur in a particular case.

This, of course, does nothing to invalidate the rights and

obligations of gratitude for particular kindnessess or exemplary concern by individual employers, doctors, husbands or teachers. These, however, are matters over and above the rights due in respect of the traditional role relationships themselves, even though the traditional role relationship may be the medium through which such personal acts of kindness are performed.

9   Welfare rights

INTRODUCTION

When it is claimed that individuals have the right to such things
as a decent minimum level of subsistence or medical care, this is
not normally a claim to a right of freedom - a right to be unhindered in seeking these goods by their own efforts. Nor are such
rights necessarily conceived of as rights created by desert or
transactions, although as we shall see, reference to desert and
implied transactions between individuals and society is sometimes
made in support of such claims. Characteristically, claims to
rights of this kind are simply claims that individuals should be
given certain things which they need if they are unable to obtain
them by their own efforts, on the grounds of the dire consequences to the individuals concerned if these things are not provided.
Justification in terms of need is taken as definitive of claims to
welfare rights and the purpose of this chapter is to examine
whether such a justification can be made out.

WELFARE RIGHTS AND DUTIES OF IMPERFECT OBLIGATION

One view of so-called welfare rights is that they are not really
rights at all and that those who in extreme misfortune receive aid
from others or from society are not enjoying a moral right, but
merely profiting from the benevolence and charity of those who
are more fortunate. Some writers taking this view concede that
there is a duty to aid those in distress, but deny that this duty
corresponds to a right.(1) Others may even be inclined to deny
that those who fail to help others in distress infringe a duty at
all.(2)

In this vein, some writers have felt that the claims to economic
and social rights made in many post-war international charters
and similar documents simply 'do not make sense'. They are held
to lie in the 'twilight world of utopian aspirations' in contrast with
true rights which are 'demanded by the basic norms of morality
and justice'.(3) At best they are to be regarded as the expression
of 'claims' which ought to be met at some time in the future, or as
'goods or principles of guidance in national or international legislation',(4) not as 'rights proper for which there is or ought to be
some means of enforcement *hic et nunc*'.(5)

Clearly, the distinction being made here bears some resemblance
to that drawn by Kant between duties of perfect and imperfect

obligation, that is, between moral duties and acts of moral virtue. In order to avoid censure, the former must be performed without equivocation. The latter, which conduce to the agent's perfection and the happiness of others, are morally required in a general way, but may be performed either in the present instance or elsewhere and at such other times as the agent may choose.(6)

In opposition to such views it will be argued in this chapter that those who suffer extreme deprivation in respect of their basic needs in a world where resources permit these needs to be met do indeed suffer injustice, that their rights are infringed and that welfare rights are rights proprio dictu.

THREE UNSUCCESSFUL APPROACHES TO THE JUSTIFICATION OF WELFARE RIGHTS

1 The right to receive assistance in need may form part of the legal entitlement of the citizens of countries in which welfare provision is an acknowledged area of public policy. It was argued earlier that to show that there is a legal right is to show that prima facie there is a moral right also.(7) In terms of their justification, however, such moral rights are not to be seen as welfare rights at all, but as special rights. They arise not strictly from need, but as a result of transactions between governments and a particular class of individuals, namely, citizens,(8) or others to whom the government has agreed to extend certain benefits. Special rights also appear as welfare rights in the work of Paine, Babeuf and Barrington.(9) Paine, it is true, points to the general moral offensiveness of poverty and wealth side by side in the same society, but his argument for old age pensions rests partly on the claim that these would amount to no more than the normal interest on taxes the elderly have paid. Babeuf and Barrington, likewise, argue that the labourer who has been industrious in health should be provided for in sickness, and is entitled to a share in the wealth which his efforts have helped to create.

Once again, however, such arguments justify not welfare rights, but special rights due, in this case, in respect of payments made or services rendered. They justify no rights on the part of those who, however needy, have neither paid taxes nor laboured industriously.

2 The attempt may also be made to justify welfare rights in terms of men's capacities. Such rights, it may be suggested, are justified by the fact that they free a man 'from fear and want which inhibit and hinder his full development as a human being'.(10) It is the capacity to think and choose, it is sometimes argued, that gives men the political right to share in government, which one cannot exercise 'unless the basic needs of life are satisfied'. (11)

This kind of argument is unsatisfactory, or at least incomplete, on a number of counts. More needs to be said about what is meant

by 'basic needs' and about the nature of the deprivation suffered
in the event of their not being met. Reference to such ideals as
full development as a 'human being' are essentially mysterious.
Changing conceptions of humanity and human ideals, and of the
nature of Man and his place in the cosmos indicate that the term
merely serves as a front for many and various unexamined judgments of value. Man has many capacities and may exercise his
initiative in many ways. A substantial proportion of these ways
will be evil and ought therefore to be restricted. Apart from this,
however, it is difficult to see how a capacity, even if the capacity
is in itself admirable, justifies a right, either to restrict another's
freedom or, as in this case, to be given resources brought into
being by another's efforts.
3 A different approach to the question of the right to receive help
in affliction or necessity is attempted by Father Robert Johann.
Starting from a quotation from Simone Weil to the effect that no
one can say to another 'you do not interest me' without cruelty or
injustice, this writer argues that the 'bad Samaritan' who does
not respond to the need of another fails in justice as well as in
charity.(12) Fundamental to Johann's argument, however, is the
Thomist notion that 'being' is a value and that the agent who
fails to respond 'appropriately' to another betrays the value of
being in his own person.(13)
   Whatever we may think to be the force of unqualified 'being' as
a value, this particular argument has the logical disadvantage
that it specifically grounds the rights of the right-holder in the
duty of the agent and in properties inherent in the agent. Accepting Johann's underlying assumptions, it is true that the agent
fails in a duty if he does not act to help a suffering human being.
On Johann's argument, however, this duty is to the value of
'being' rather than to the victim himself. The victim is not a right-
holder but the fortunate beneficiary of another's duty.

WELFARE RIGHTS AND NEEDS

A more profitable line of approach to the problem of justifying
welfare rights may be suggested by Raphael's reference to the
'Just claims of need',(14) for it is precisely to the concepts of
need and justice that we most readily turn when the implementation of welfare rights is being advocated. It is true that the
interpretation of a need has not been entirely free of controversy
in recent years, and that in some instances it may readily be
shown that 'A needs X' is elliptical for 'A needs X for the sake of
Y'.(15) In such cases the rightness of giving A what he needs
will certainly depend on further moral judgments about the rightness of his having, or being able to do, Y. This, however, is not
quite the same as when we speak of a need as something without
which an individual suffers harm.(16) It might perhaps be said
the need here is instrumental in the sense that A needs X in order
to avoid the harm. But when we speak of someone as needy or in

need we are not really speaking elliptically, for we may have no
additional benefit in mind that will flow from his need being
relieved. When we say that a sick man needs to be cured, or that
a terrified child needs to be reassured, it would be odd to ask
what they needed these things for, or to debate the desirability
of the purposes for which they needed them.

Nevertheless, the concept of a harm is not entirely unproble-
matic. The example might be given of someone who, because of
his particular interests, regarded blindness not as a harm, but
as a benefit.(17) It is, furthermore, possible to envisage an un-
broken continuum between gross and permanent harm at one
extreme and temporary nuisance and minor inconvenience which
the individual may be expected to overcome at the other. Still, it
is rarely denied that harms are normally constituted by such
permanent misfortunes as death by starvation or illness, lasting
physical infirmity, mental derangement or impairment of the
faculties, loss of the possibility of satisfactory relationships with
others, and loss of the respect of one's fellows.

To claim a degree of objectivity in regarding some of the above
misfortunes as harms is not entirely inconsistent with conceding
that what one needs to avoid them may sometimes be socially defined and subject to expansion as society becomes more affluent.(18)
To adapt an often quoted example: in some societies and at some
times, for an individual not to be able to afford a pair of shoes or
a decent suit of clothes may constitute an acute deprivation,
whereas in others it may not seriously mark him out from his fellows or impair his relationships with them.

WELFARE RIGHTS AND JUSTICE

The main burden of the previous section was that there is at least
one sense in which to say that someone is in need, or that he
needs some specific thing is to give a reason for meeting that
need without further argument. The claim that the avoidance of
harm by having certain needs met is a right would, however, be
greatly strengthened if it could be shown that to be allowed to
suffer such harm was not only undesirable, but unjust. Though
it will later be argued that a justification of welfare rights may be
drawn from an imaginary initial contract of the kind envisaged by
Rawls, (19) it is not proposed in the present context to attempt a
fully developed investigation of the concept of justice as such.
For the present it suffices to point out that if, as was argued in
chapter 5, individuals do not enter the world in any way subordinate to others or less entitled than others to consideration, or
bound to accept any pre-existing set of social arrangements, then
any such arrangements resulting in an unequal distribution of
goods would seem to be in need of justification. This, presumably,
is the point of the so-called principle of distributive justice by
which we are enjoined to discriminate between individuals only on
relevant grounds.(20) If any unequal distribution of material goods

in the absence of relevant grounds contravenes the principle of
justice, then a fortiori the principle is infringed by any unjustified distribution so unequal that some are without the means of
avoiding gross harms of the kind mentioned above, while others
have material goods in superfluity. In the absence of corresponding differences in desert, it is therefore easy to understand
Paine's claim that wealth and wretchedness side by side in the
same society are an affront to justice and morally offensive.(21)

Whereas in the past men could attribute such inequalities to
'Nature', 'Fortune', or some higher will, this is today no longer
possible. In a world of relative affluence and powerful governments, the distribution of wealth and medical and other facilities
is at least partly subject to human control. To the degree that
starvation, sickness and illiteracy are avoidable, they only exist
as a result of men's decisions that they shall do so, that is, because powerful individuals regard their elimination as less important than the achievement of other goals.

One may hesitate to go so far as to deny the moral difference
between a decree of arbitrary execution and an administrative
decision which one knows in advance will result in death through
starvation and avoidable disease of a number of in principle
identifiable individuals. At the very least, however, the claim
that the prevention of homicide may be more important than the
prevention of starvation (22) is not obvious, for it is difficult to
see that one would prefer to be the victim of one rather than the
other.(23)

The helpless victim of a governmental or commercial decision
which, without any fault on his part, deprived him, but not
others like him, of income and left him without protection against
starvation or the means of obtaining essential medical care might
well feel that he had been discriminated against without grounds
relevant to him, and would appear to be quite justified in claiming
the right to protection against the decision's consequences.

An indication that to allow avoidable suffering has been felt to
require justification is provided by the fact that in the past,
justification for allowing the ill-effects of poverty to continue to
exist was sometimes given in terms of desert, or lack of it, on
the part of the poor. The weakness of such a justification is
readily seen if we consider the possibility of introducing death by
starvation or disease as judicial penalties. Though some might
find these acceptable in the case of serious crimes, few would
regard them as consonant with such minor offences as the incapacity or inability to find work or even improvidence or sloth. In
any case, such validity as this justification may have had disap-
pears when economic affairs are controlled by governments and
poverty may no longer be attributed to the conduct of individual
victims.

A distinction may still need to be drawn between, on the one
hand, decisions by governments or other powerful bodies which
positively direct resources or the means of gaining a living away
from individuals (enclosure acts or, in the modern context, the

closure of a factory to increase a group's profits), and, on the
other hand, the failure to allocate resources or the means of gaining them to particular individuals or groups of individuals when
this could be done without depriving others of a basic need. In
the first case, the right claimed might simply be seen as a special
right of reparation. In the second, though individuals may not be
deprived of something they already had, this would nevertheless
still be an injustice in that means which could have protected
them from gross harm are, or continue to be, directed elsewhere
in the furtherance of other purposes, without the grounds for
such an act of discrimination being present in the character or
conduct of the victims. To this extent, those who allocate the
resources of society and the society which sanctions the contin-
uance of such grossly unequal allocations that some individuals
suffer avoidable harm must bear the moral responsibility of acting
unjustly towards those individuals, and consequently of being
instrumental in the infringement of their rights.

The fact that we are here concerned with only deprivations and
consequent harms which could be avoided takes care of the objection that welfare rights cannot be considered rights because it is
often beyond the resources of governments or anyone else to
implement them.(24) A welfare right is a right to be protected
from the dire consequences of need when these are avoidable. It
is here held, however, that given the relative degree of affluence
enjoyed by certain sections of the world's population, the claim
that poverty and starvation are 'inevitable' is simply disingenuous.

WELFARE RIGHTS AND PROPERTY

In spite of the above arguments, it may still be felt that one objection remains outstanding. A reluctant tax-payer may admit that
the needs of the destitute ought to be met and even agree that it
is in some sense unjust or wrong for individuals to be allowed to
suffer gross harm when this could be avoided. At the same time
he may still ask 'But what has that to do with me?' Every penny
he owns has been earned and every possession paid for and to
this extent all his special obligations have been discharged. Can
it be shown, we may ask, that he and others like him may legitimately be deprived of some of their resources to meet the needs
of either particular individuals or the needy population of the
world as a whole?

Nozick offers one possible reply to this question when he argues
that only the so-called 'minimal state' can be justified, which
appropriates the resources of individuals for the protection of
the traditional rights of freedom and security. Such an arrangement, he claims, would be bound to arise from any plausible state
of nature. But since arrangements for the protection of individuals from need would not arise in the same way, the state is not
justified in appropriating private resources to achieve this end.(25)

Justice in holdings, that is, the just distribution of resources,

he claims, is present when goods are obtained in accordance with
the principle of justice in acquisition or justice in transfer. Justice in acquisition applies when an individual creates an object by
his own efforts or takes it from the state of nature without impoverishing others. When someone who has justly acquired an
object voluntarily transfers (gives, bequeaths, sells) it to another,
this represents justice in transfer irrespective of the deserts or
needs of those to whom it is transferred or indeed of those to
whom it is not transferred. The only other way in which an individual can legitimately come by any goods is in rectification of
previous transgressions of the principles of justice in acquisition
or justice in transfer.(26) Any further attempts at redistribution
are held to violate people's rights.

We may, of course, reject outright the dubious logic of a 'state
of nature' in which individuals are required to respect one's
rights to what one has made 'one's own' by appropriating it or
received from others in certain specified ways. Even if one were
to accept this much, however, Nozick's argument is scarcely to be
taken seriously as a case against the redistribution of resources
in the real world of today. The following palpable objections
spring to mind:

1 Nozick goes to some lengths in his attempt to come to terms with
Locke's proviso that it is only legitimate to appropriate freely
from the resources of nature provided there is enough and as
good left for others. Following Locke, Nozick takes the point of
this proviso to be that in appropriating nature's bounties, the
individual may not act so as to impoverish others. The case would
therefore be met either if he were to compensate others, or if his
appropriation instead of impoverishing the community actually
enriched it, as is often held to be the case when an individual
appropriates materials from nature and puts them to productive
use.(27) The fatal weakness of this defence, however, is that
although productive appropriation may enrich the community as a
whole, many particular individuals may be impoverished to the
point of being deprived of the very means of sustenance, particularly the common land and its productions. However much the
acts of the original appropriators may enrich rather than impoverish the community as a whole, therefore, they and their succes-
sors owe a continuing obligation to at least protect from the
extremes of starvation those, including the members of later generations, whom their acts have deprived of the means of providing for themselves.

2 Few would deny that the present distribution of goods is the
result of many acts of injustice, in both acquisition and transfer.
It is true that restitution could in principle be made, and that
this might still leave some without goods or the right to goods to
meet their basic needs. As Nozick admits, however, this would be
a highly complex operation. In the meantime, it seems reasonable
to assume that many of the very poor are the victims of earlier
acts of injustice in acquisition or transfer and that many of the
comfortably off are the beneficiaries of such acts. Until this rather

probable supposition has been shown beyond doubt to be false,
there would appear to be justification in the state's intervening
to protect the needy from starvation or other irreversible harm.
3 The justification for holding that a right of property is conferred by the act of just acquisition, even when this act of acquisition consists of no more than simply taking the object from the
state of nature, is presumably that it is precisely such an act
which confers upon the object any value which it has. As far as
market value, that is the value of other goods for which it may
be exchanged, is concerned, however, this is clearly false.

Objects rise in market value as a result of changing demand
without any further labour being invested in them. As is frequently pointed out, the market value of a piece of land may
increase not because its owner mixes more of his labour with the
soil,(28) but because of the growth of a nearby town. It is difficult to see that the owner of the piece of land has a valid moral
objection to some of this increased value being appropriated to
meet the obligations of the community from whose presence the
increase results.

WELFARE RIGHTS AND THE MORAL COMMUNITY OF MEN

The notion that those without resources have a right that they
may legitimately and unashamedly demand, to receive at least the
bare minimum of what they need receives further support from a
consideration of the moral relationship in which the various inhabitants of the world stand to each other, even in the absence
of any specific or implied undertakings being given. Raphael
considers that to justify welfare rights, the concept of need
must be linked with that of fraternity, which he identifies with
social responsibility.(29)

This, however, is obscure. Men though of the same species are
not literally brothers, and the question as to whether someone is
his brother's keeper may properly be asked. The term 'social
responsibility' also begs questions of justification and meaning.
A more tractable term might perhaps be that of 'moral community'.
The tax-payer mentioned above, who is reluctant to recognise
his responsibilities towards the destitute, would find it much
harder to deny that he stood in any moral relationship to such
persons at all, for this would be to assert a Hobbesian state of
war of all against all,(30) and in so doing destroy all justification
of his own right of property. It is indeed difficult to see how anyone can be under any obligation at all to obey the rules of a
society which holds his very life to be of such low account that its
rules allow material goods to be distributed in such a way
that he suffers death or gross harm when this could have been
avoided.

To translate the above point into Rawlsian terms, a distribution
of goods which is just and which we can rightly expect others to
respect is one which would be chosen by the rational agent in

ignorance of how such a distribution would affect him.(31) Though
one may readily accept Rawls's claim that the rational agent would
lexically order the principle of equal freedom above that of economic equality (32) it is less easy to accept, and Rawls certainly
does not hold, that he would range greater freedom including the
freedom to have absolute control of his property above that of
receiving minimal protection against gross need. If only those
inequalities are to be allowed which benefit all, including the
least fortunate,(33) then inequalities that result in deprivations
of the kind relevant to our present discussion must be ruled out.
The least fortunate cannot plausibly be said to profit from such
inequalities, for it is scarcely possible to conceive of a situation
in which they would be worse off.

WELFARE RIGHTS AND THE TRADITIONAL RIGHTS OF MAN

Most writers appear to concur in the view that welfare rights and
the traditional rights of Man are different in kind. The contrast
is frequently drawn between the first twenty or so 'traditional'
civil and political rights in the 1948 United Nations Universal
Declaration of Human Rights and the economic, social and cultural
rights of later articles.(34) It may, however, be asked whether
the traditional rights of life, liberty and property were in fact
seen as no more than rights of freedom justified by the principle
of non-interference, or whether they too support claims on others
and therefore themselves require further justification. The question would seem to turn on whether the rights to life, liberty and
property merely assert a man's right to be allowed to do what he
can to protect his own life, freedom and belongings by his own
efforts - irrespective of any command by the political authority
to acquiesce in their being taken from him, or whether the right
is being claimed to the support and protection of others, namely
the community at large. It is possible to invoke the authority of
Locke and Adam Smith for the view that traditionally these rights
were not considered merely as rights against summary execution
or the appropriation of goods by the government. At very least,
they were also rights against pillagers and 'homicidal persons',
which it was the positive duty of governments to protect as a condition of the individual's abdication of his own right of defence
and punishment of aggressors.(35) Given the very vital nature of
the interests these rights protect, Man can only be regarded as
having given up his freedom to take whatever steps he deems
necessary for their protection himself on the understanding that
adequate protection will be provided by the community as a whole.
With the collapse of the de facto authority of the government and
its ability to protect the fundamental interests concerned, the
individual's right to see to his own protection is restored.

It will be noted that this situation is not entirely without parallel in our conclusions regarding welfare rights. In relation to
these it was suggested that in so far as the political order fails

to protect a basic need, it forfeits any moral authority over the individual. As in the case of the traditional rights of Man, protection of a basic interest, if necessary with the expenditure of communal effort and resources, is the moral condition of an individual's obedience to governments. To this degree there would seem to be some similarity between the justification for paying policemen to prevent murder and the justification of paying welfare workers to prevent hunger and disease. Both are conditions of the individual's surrendering his right to shift for himself in the protection of his most vital interests.

The rights of children

Part IV

10 Rights and the concept of childhood

In previous chapters we have considered what it is in general to
have a right. We have also distinguished between various kinds
of right, and attempted to establish grounds of justification for
each of them. So far it has been assumed that the individuals with
whose rights we were concerned were adults operating in an adult
world. From now on our principal concern will be to consider how
the justification of various kinds of rights claim is affected, whether
strengthened, modified or invalidated by the fact that the
person by or for whom the right is claimed is a child, or a pupil
in an educational institution.

Our earlier discussions will facilitate this investigation of what
are to be considered the rights of children by ruling out certain
lines of enquiry which may now be seen as plainly unprofitable. It
will by now be clear, for example, that our undertaking will not
be significantly forwarded by an empirical analysis of where power
in the schools ultimately lies, or a consideration of who is in a
position to back his commands by sanctions. Since rights are not
claims against higher order moral principles, we need not begin
by enquiring what such higher order moral principles could be, or
how claims against them may be justified. Since rights are not
always, or not primarily, the correlatives of duties, we may not
think it most profitable to begin with a comprehensive theory of
duty, or a thorough-going examination of the duties of teachers,
pupils, parents, governments and others involved in education
in the hope of simply reading off the rights of those occupying
the correlative roles. Rights, as we have seen, are not simply
things which we ought to be allowed to do in the interests of certain overall social or cultural teleologies. Since they may sometimes
conflict with overall goods or duties to the point where, with hesitancy and apology, they may even be overruled, we are relieved
for the purposes of the present enquiry of the necessity of looking
too closely at the likely social and educational effects of this or
that right as a preliminary to deciding whether there is such a
right or not, though the consideration of effects becomes relevant
when the question of implementation is raised. It is to be hoped
that time spent analysing various kinds of rights claims and distinguishing between the kinds of justification which it is appropriate to demand in the case of each will enable us to avoid the
many frustrations which arise when these distinctions are not made.
In particular, it is hoped that the identification of positive rights
and special rights - especially those arising from transactions - as
two categories of rights among others will enable us to avoid the

common tendency to apply criteria appropriate to these when
rights of freedom and participation or welfare rights are being
considered.

Before entering upon a substantive discussion of whether children possess certain categories of moral rights, however, it is
necessary to remove one further ambiguity. Attention has been
drawn to two different notions of childhood which had been dubbed
'institutional' and 'normative'.(1) The institutional concept of
childhood is a legal or quasi-legal one which in modern societies
is usually defined by chronological age but may elsewhere depend
on some such consideration as whether the individual has under-
gone certain ceremonies of initiation. As regards the normative
concept of childhood, this is being employed when we say that
someone could not have been expected to know that what he was
doing was wrong, or carry a heavy weight without complaining,
or should not have been allowed to purchase a dangerous weapon
on the grounds that he was only a child. Clearly, this conception
of the child is connected with certain capacities, the acquisition
of certain elements of knowledge and experience, the possession
of certain ethical interests or reasonable expectations about a person's likely behaviour at certain stages of development.

The institutional concepts of childhood and adulthood drastically
affect or, as it may be held, are actually defined by an individual's positive rights. This raises certain problems in so far as it
is not clear why chronological age in itself should affect our moral
judgments about a person's interests or entitlements.(2) It is
obvious, however, that normative and institutional concepts of
childhood are not unconnected. The former is logically prior and
the latter only has point in the light of it.(3) When they fail to
coincide in respect of either an individual or a society as a whole,
it may be argued that the institution infringes individual moral
rights, even though there may be good practical reasons for lay-
ing down hard and fast boundaries between what are and what
are not particular individuals' rights and obligations while avoiding invidious questions about his actual capacities.

In considering an individual's moral rights, we are, therefore,
primarily concerned with such matters as his needs, interests and
capacities as may be thought to affect his legitimate expectations
and the legitimate expectations others have of him. That such
features are developmental has not failed to present problems in so
far as it has been argued that if our capacities develop progressively over the whole or even a large part of our lives, then the
placing of institutional boundaries can scarcely avoid infringing
the rights of those who mature precociously.(4) If, nevertheless,
there seem to be overriding practical reasons for recognising particular rights at a particular age there would seem to be every
reason for doing so at an age shortly after that at which most
individuals are thought to have acquired the ability to exercise
them without unreasonable risk of endangering their own interests
or those of others. Rightly or wrongly, it appears to be widely
believed that the capacity to exercise a number of important rights

in this way usually occurs during or immediately following the period known as adolescence.

In so far as an individual's moral rights, as opposed to his positive rights, depend on his actual capacities rather than on institutional assumptions about what may or may not be expected of him at a particular age, these may seem to imply difficult problems of discrimination and judgment. This much is admitted. It must, however, be pointed out that making moral judgments about anyone's rights, obligations and entitlements may require fine judgments about what could or could not be expected of him or of others in a particular set of circumstances. Such judgments are in principle no different in the case of the young than in the case of any other category of persons.

In the next chapter it is proposed to consider certain criticisms that have been made in respect of children's legal rights, or rather, their lack of them. Subsequently, consideration will be given to the question of whether and to what extent children can be said to have each of the various categories of rights discussed in part III. In examining this question, our main concern will be to see in what ways the normal justification given for a particular right is changed, modified or rendered inapplicable by certain characteristics commonly attributed to children. In this respect, the child's imperfect rationality, need for guidance and protection, and material dependence may seem particularly relevant.

11   The legal rights of children

In chapter 4 we saw that the claim 'A has a right to X' may refer to a positive right enjoyed by members of A's society. Many of the positive rights enjoyed by individuals in the modern world are those vouchsafed to them by the law. This is clearly not the place to attempt a full account of the law relating to children in this or any other modern state. Nevertheless, one of the major contentions of those writing on the subject of children's rights has been that rights are often denied children by the law which are theirs in morality. Whether this is so or not necessarily raises the prior question of what are children's moral rights, to which the remainder of this book is largely devoted. It also raises the question of what rights are, in fact, vouchsafed to children by the law. For the law may be neither as draconian nor as asinine as it is sometimes made out to be.

The following general criticisms have been made of the law as it relates to children:
1 the law which treats children differently from adults is arbitrary;
2 the law establishes unreasonable authority relations between adults and children;
3 the law treats children as property rather than as persons.(1)

In examining these propositions, reference is confined to the British context where legal provisions may approximate more or less closely to those found elsewhere. First of all, however, some remarks need to be made about the claim that in our society children have no legal rights at all.

THE LEGAL STATUS OF CHILDREN AND 'CHILDREN'S RIGHTS'

Lawyers, it appears, sometimes express doubt as to whether 'such things as children's rights actually exist', even while readily acknowledging that parents and others placed in loco parentis are subject to obligations in respect of their children, and that society as a whole has devised a system of welfare and protection for their benefit.(2)

This apparent paradox results from the fact that lawyers habitually employ the term 'rights' in the somewhat restricted or even technical sense of something which the individual is able to enforce by himself initiating legal action, or which another is able to enforce on his behalf - in the strict sense of acting for him or in his name. It is in contrast to this restricted usage that Hart speaks of himself as employing a more extended sense of the term

when he says that the criminal law may be said to protect our
rights to life and the integrity of our persons, despite the fact
that prosecutions for murder and assault are made not by the
victims of these crimes, but by the public authority.(3) In the
spirit of Hart's so-called extended usage, it is here proposed to
employ the term 'rights' to refer to advantages intentionally sec-
ured to individuals by means of the law, even though those who
frame the law may not find it expedient or practical to place the
onus of securing the advantages in question upon either the individual himself or his personal representative.

'THE LAW DISCRIMINATES ARBITRARILY BETWEEN CHILDREN AND ADULTS'

In some cases, the law clearly vouchsafes the same rights, in the
sense discussed above, to both children and adults. If, in for-
bidding murder and assault, the law may be said to protect the
citizen's rights to life and to the integrity of his person, these
rights are protected for children, just as they are for others. In
other respects, however, both in the provision of protection and
in the granting of liberty, the law distinguishes sharply between
those below a certain age and those who have attained it. In consequence, it is possible to speak of children and adults enjoying
different sets of rights, and of there existing certain inequalities
before the law.(4)

In particular, critics of the law may be inclined to point to the
arbitrariness of granting the individual full adult status at the
age of eighteen while denying him it the day before. Reference
has already been made to the real difficulties that arise when
individuals undergo a change of status or assume a new set of
rights at a particular chronological age. This, it was conceded,
may indeed lead to an infringement of the moral rights of some
young people and could only be justified by the extreme difficulty
of finding an alternative solution to certain of the practical problems of society.

In many respects, however, the law appears to be less arbitrary
and inflexible and the change from childhood to the status of an
adult less abrupt than may be thought. It is true that eighteen is
the age at which an individual finally acquires the full range of
legal rights enjoyed by an adult. At eighteen, and not before, an
individual may first make a binding legal agreement, instruct
solicitors, institute civil proceedings, and vote in elections. The
age at which the jurisdiction of the juvenile courts normally ceases,
however, is not eighteen, but seventeen. After this an alleged
offender no longer has the advantages (if advantages they are) of
the special knowledge and procedures of the juvenile courts in
dealing with young persons. Nor does he have the advantage or
otherwise of being dealt with by means of a range of orders available to those courts instead of the normally harsher and more
explicitly penal measures applied to adults. Sixteen sees the end

of compulsory schooling as well as being the age at which an
adolescent may marry. When the 1969 Children and Young Persons
Act is fully implemented, it will no longer be possible to bring a
criminal prosecution (as opposed to care proceedings under the
'offence condition') against someone under the age of fourteen,
except in cases of alleged homicide. At present a child prosecuted
for acts committed before the age of fourteen has the advantage
that the prosecution has - in addition to the normal burden of
proving that the accused committed the offence - the burden of
proving that he knew that it was wrong. Below the age of ten,
criminal responsibility cannot be ascribed at all.

In addition to these major differences in someone's legal position
according to whether he is below or above a certain age, there
are myriads of specific statutes and other regulations having the
force of law which specify a range of different ages below which a
child may not take part in certain entertainments, be employed in
certain occupations, enter certain premises, buy certain goods, or
have dealings with members of certain occupations.(5)

From the above it will be seen that the change from the legal
status of a child to that of an adult, and the varying degree of
freedom, immunity and protection each enjoys, is anything but a
sudden and complete transformation overnight. So true is this,
indeed, that the contrary criticism might seem justified, that in
the absence of any precise and formal moment of initiation into the
world of adult rights and responsibilities, the life of an adolescent
in modern western society is exceptionally confusing.

Though the wide range of ages at which certain activities are
permitted to the young and certain protections and immunities
withdrawn is sometimes represented as a schedule of arbitrary
adult tyranny, a more reasonable view might seem to be to regard
this as reflecting a certain notion of the development of human
capacities and a consequent judgment of the increase in an individual's liberty generally consistent with his own and other people's
safety, and the successful management of his own life. Critics of
the law, such as Holt and Berger, may naturally regard such a
view of human development as unduly conservative.(6) Whether or
not it is so is in part an empirical question. Holt, it will be recalled, frequently bases his arguments on the claim that children are
more competent than is generally thought, though the empirical
evidence he adduces is often of an anecdotal and impressionistic
kind.(7)

AUTHORITY RELATIONS BETWEEN ADULTS AND CHILDREN

In later chapters we shall consider, among other things, the
various moral rights of children in respect of personal freedom,
and the authority relations properly existing between them and
adults. As a preface to this examination, it may seem relevant to
consider the claim that the authority relations between children
and adults sanctioned by the law are such that children do not
enjoy any rights of freedom at all.

It certainly appears to be true that a parent or person in whom 'parental rights and duties' are vested may, up to a certain age, decide where his child shall live, how and where he is to be educated, to what religion he shall belong, with whom he shall associate, what books he shall read, what entertainments he shall attend, when he shall go out or come in, and may indeed control all the child's daily activities. It also appears to be the case that against his parent the child has no legal right of privacy and he may be punished for 'misdemeanours' of which the parent is usually the sole judge. Needless to say, such punishment may, and frequently does, include corporal punishment.(8) In Britain, parental authority over the child has the backing of the courts in that being beyond the control of his parent or guardian is one of the six conditions under which care orders may be made.(9)

This, however, is to put the case rather strongly. Parents' power to limit the freedom of their children certainly does not continue unmitigated up to the day of their eighteenth birthday. Nor is it the case that whatever children do up to that age they do only with their parents' tacit permission. Though it appears that the courts would support a parent in regulating his child's activities while living in the parental home at the parent's expense, they are not normally prepared to oblige young people over the age of sixteen to return to the parental home against their will if they are capable of supporting themselves and have somewhere to live.(10) Parents may attempt to obtain a court order obliging the local authority to institute care proceedings in respect of a recalcitrant child, but for this to succeed the court must be convinced that the child is actually in need of care and control. Failure to comply with parental wishes is apparently not in itself sufficient, particularly if these wishes were not judged to be reasonable in the light of the young person's age and ability to manage his own affairs.(11)

It is true that certain important rights of parents to restrict the freedom of children are automatically delegated to anyone in whose care a child is placed or left. To suggest that all parental rights to control the freedom of children are vested in such persons and authorities as are temporarily in loco parentis, however, is an exaggeration. Persons and institutions in loco parentis do have the right to discipline a child and may also restrict his freedom of movement. A school may, for example, forbid pupils to leave the school premises during breaks and during the lunch hour and may forbid a pupil to associate with other pupils either in the classroom or in the playground.(12) It may require certain respectful forms of address and similar compliances. Schools may, and of course do, also require their pupils to submit to all manner of educational procedures and organisational rules. The parental rights deemed to be automatically transferred to those in whose charge the child temporarily finds himself, however, are fairly closely limited to those which might be claimed to be necessary for the safety and well-being of the child, the good order of the institution in which he finds himself, and the successful achievement of that institution's purposes.

'THE LAW TREATS CHILDREN AS PROPERTY RATHER THAN AS PERSONS'

One of the most emotive assertions noted in chapter 1 was that the law governing the relations between adults and children is such as to suggest that the latter are not persons in their own right but the 'property' of someone 'if not parents then the state'.(13) It is no doubt the case that in the past, common law treated children 'as if they were the possessions of parents',(14) that 'feudal concepts of ownership permeated the family sphere' and (15) that 'the father's interest in the custody of his children was essentially a right of property' of which he could only be deprived as the result of some gross inadequacy or misdemeanour on his part.(16) The view that children were regarded as 'property not people'(17) may seem to receive support from the fact that 'children were frequently put to work by their parents to whom their wages were paid',(18) as well as from the fact that 'a parent has a right to the domestic services of his children who, being under eighteen but old enough to be capable of rendering services are living with him as members of his family'.(19) It is sometimes further argued that even though the rights of fathers are considerably less absolute now than in the past, these rights have been limited, 'not in favour of children but of other adults, whether mothers or the representatives of the public authorities.'(20)

Now, it is true that children have few legal rights of freedom which they can confidently expect a court to uphold. To claim that their status is analogous to that of possessions, however, belongs to the language of rhetoric rather than to that of sober appraisal. This is only too evident from any consideration of what the relations of property and ownership normally imply.

To say that we own an object is not, of course, to say that we may do with it exactly as we wish. We may not, for example, use it in such a way as to endanger or infringe the rights of others. An individual may be prevented from destroying or exporting a work of art which he owns, or from pulling down a historic building. Sometimes he may purchase property subject to limitations placed on its use by the seller. Such limitations, however, are imposed not in the interests of the property itself, but of other persons. Subject to such protected interests, what becomes of a piece of property depends on the wishes of its owner. The property itself has neither interests nor welfare, far less wishes, to be taken account of.

Only the law relating to animals provides difficulties for this understanding of the concept of property, for though animals are clearly property capable of being owned, the law appears to protect their interests in not being subject to 'unnecessary' pain. Whatever account is given of this fact, however, the degree of protection given to the interests of animals is very small. Though an animal may not be gratuitously tormented, it may be neutered, separated from its young or others of its kind, or humanely killed without reason other than the immediate whim of its owner. Nor is

the animal protected from suffering the most excruciating pain if
its owner can show that he has some substantial purpose in
carrying out the action by which the pain is caused which cannot
be otherwise achieved.(21)

Very clearly this does not even approximate to the relationship
in which the parent stands to his child. Even the sometimes
quoted right of the parent to the domestic services of his child
up to the age of eighteen is not, and, it appears, never has been,
enforceable against the child himself, but is simply the means
whereby parents may take action against someone who injures
him.(22)

Though parents may oblige local authorities to bring care proceedings in respect of a child whom they cannot control, it is, as
we saw, a condition of the success of such proceedings, that the
child should be shown to be in need of care. The proceedings,
therefore, must be shown to be in the interests of the child and
are intended to protect his welfare, rather than to enforce some
right of command or possession in the parent. Significantly the
feature to which the juvenile court may look in dealing with such
a case is to be found in the child, namely his capacity or otherwise to manage his own life. In deciding whether it should enforce
the claim to a right of ownership, by contrast, a court would
typically look not at a feature of the object owned but at the acts
by which possession is acquired, such as buying, discovering,
inheriting, etc., and in this case begetting or giving birth. Numerous commentators indeed make the point that 'parental rights' in
this sense no longer have any legal standing when they conflict
with the child's best interests.(23)

Even those most critical of the law relating to children are
usually prepared to admit that considerable advances have been
made in the protection of children from neglect, exploitation and
abuse and the provision of numerous welfare benefits, including
education. To see this as legislation purely to protect the state's
or employing class's property interest in future working hands,
temporarily entrusted to the care of parents until they are old
enough to be of use,(24) seems an unjustifiably jaundiced interpretation of the way things are. It is true that some advocates
of educational and child care provision find it advantageous to
employ the argument that such provision is sound economic investment, but there seems no good reason to doubt the sincerity of
others who see such protection and provisions as benefits conferred on the child. Once again, it may be stressed that to be able,
not to say entitled, to receive a benefit is a feature not of things
but of persons.

It may, of course, be that many such 'benefits' are undesired
by those who receive them. Compulsory education, control of one's
activities and associations by responsible adults, laws preventing
children from obtaining paid work or being present at strip-shows
all come into this category. In some cases, indeed, they may not
in fact be benefits at all, but superfluous or even detrimental to
the dignity, status, self-esteem and development of the child.(25)

If true, this would be a valid criticism of the law, not, however, for failing to treat children as persons but for so doing in an inept or unduly cautious manner.

If further evidence is needed that the law regards children as persons with interests of their own rather than merely as property in whom others have rights, this is provided by current legis- lation concerning custody suits in relation to which 'there is now no rule of law that the rights and wishes of unimpeachable parents must prevail over other considerations'.(26) A similar welfare principle also operates in custody suits between natural parents and others, including local authorities. In deciding such disputes it appears that courts operate on presumptions that some may find questionable. These include the presumption that it is normally in a child's best interests to be in the care of his natural parents, rather than someone else, that younger children are better off with their mothers and older ones, particularly boys, with their fathers and so on. Such presumptions are defeasible, however, and this is not necessarily on grounds of any 'fault' on the part of the parent in question.(27) As will be clear, the decision that a child should live with his father because it is supposedly in his interests to do so is morally different from a decision that he should do so because that is the father's established right which he has done nothing to forfeit.

Though the principle of the paramountcy of the child's welfare has largely superseded that of adult's 'rights', attention has been drawn to two particular areas in which it does not apply. Natural parents may still refuse consent to adoption by foster parents, though the provision that such consent may not be unreasonably withheld, together with the presumption that a reasonable parent will act in his child's best interests, has enabled the welfare prin- ciple to be introduced in this kind of case indirectly.(28)

Second, the requirement of the Children and Young Persons Act of 1948 that made it the prime duty of a local authority to use its powers to further the best interests of children in its care is expressly withdrawn by the 1969 Act of the same name which pro- vides that 'If it appears to the local authority that it is necessary, for the protection of the public, to exercise their powers in relation to a particular child in their care in a manner which may not be consistent with their general duty ... to further his best interests ... the authority may, notwithstanding that duty, act in that manner.' Berger quite rightly claims that under this pro- vision 'a child may be deprived of his liberty by the local author- ity which is under no obligation to give the child an opportunity to be protected by a court hearing and does not have to under- take the burden of proving its case'.(29)

Even if this provision does give rise to some disquiet, however, this is a far cry from showing that children are treated as mere possessions. If such were the case, children could be incarcer- ated for the mere convenience of those in charge of them without any general obligation to attend to their interests and certainly without their constituting an actual danger to the public. Of course, it may be that, as a matter of fact, children in the care of local authorities sometimes have their liberty restricted for the mere convenience of those in charge of them rather than because they constitute a danger to the public. This, however, does not show that the law fails to regard them as persons, but merely that the rights which the law clearly confers upon them are sometimes disregarded.

12 Children's rights of freedom in the sense of liberties

It was argued in chapter 5 that to claim the right to do something where 'right' is used in the sense of a liberty is simply to claim that there is nothing wrong in doing it. It may be thought that the question of whether children have rights of this kind is a relatively trifling one. When adults forbid children in their charge to do something this is, after all, usually because the action in question is in some way wrong or harmful.

Such a view of the matter is, however, to be rejected on two counts. First, there certainly are parents, teachers and others who insist on 'having things as they like them' without feeling obliged to consider whether or not the behaviour they prefer is in any substantial way preferable to that which they forbid. It might be felt that the requirement that children should wear certain clothes, engage in certain modes of speech and forms of address, adopt certain postures, avoid the company of certain other children, and so on fall into this category.

Second, it is in any case a mistake to confuse the importance of an issue with the frequency with which it arises in everyday life. Even if children were only rarely required to refrain from actions which were morally neutral, the question of whether they actually had the right to engage in them would still be of importance for it raises the further and fundamental question of children's general moral status. This is the question of whether children are separate, and to some degree morally autonomous, individuals who must remain temporarily in the care and control of others for purely practical reasons, or whether they are in some way inherently subject to an adult's authority.

Even if some may regard this issue as insignificant today, it was certainly not so regarded at the height of the children's rights controversy, either by young people themselves or by some of the adults with whom they were in conflict. Head teachers and others at that time rarely went to the trouble of empirically demonstrating the harm done by the styles of appearance, activities and affiliations they chose to forbid, and it will be recalled that the pupil expelled for publishing an article in 'Vanguard' was, at least reportedly, punished not for damaging his school's reputation or because the article itself was offensive, but because he had broken a school rule.

Parents, teachers and others may, of course, sometimes quite justifiably issue peremptory instructions without actually giving their reasons because the urgency of the situation does not admit of delay, or because the child is not old enough (or in no mood) to

be reasonable. Sometimes, indeed, it may even be appropriate to
insist on obedience in some morally neutral matter as a disciplinary expedient, because the child is currently proving too independent of adult guidance in general for his own good or the
legitimate interests of others. The adult reaction to such day to
day situations is not at issue.

The issue with which we are concerned is whether the fact that
a certain adult has chosen to forbid an otherwise unexceptionable
action to a child makes the child a proper subject of moral dis-
approval if he does it, or whether it may still be said that the
child has a right to do it, in the sense that there is nothing
wrong in it.

In this connection, it must be noted that if a child has no rights
in this sense, it is difficult to see how he can, in any meaningful sense, have various other kinds of rights such as claim rights
of freedom or rights of participation. If the child had no rights in
the sense of liberties these other kinds of rights could be annulled (and not simply suppressed) by parents' or teachers' prohibition of their exercise.

In basing our earlier justification for believing that individuals
have rights in the sense of liberties on their essential separateness from each other, it was assumed that we were concerned
with independent, mature, rational, materially self-sufficient
adults capable of looking to their own protection and choosing
their own ends. It is therefore appropriate to consider how far
the ways in which children differ from adults are morally relevant
to the question of whether they may be said to have rights in the
sense here under discussion. Various traditional arguments to
the effect that children do not have rights of this kind are considered below.

1 'CHILDREN ARE NOT RATIONAL OR CAPABLE OF MAKING
THEIR OWN DECISIONS'

Surprisingly, perhaps, the implications of the child's incomplete
rationality may be dealt with fairly summarily in the present context. To the extent that the child is not rational, the things he
does are not strictly his acts and he cannot therefore be seen as
a morally independent agent whose acts can be described as right
or wrong. In so far as we are concerned with rights of freedom
at all, we are necessarily concerned with those children only who
are capable of moral agency in the particular sphere of behaviour
in respect of which the right is claimed. The question of whether
a child (or anyone else) has or has not the right to do something
in the sense of its not being wrong when he does not understand
its implications can therefore not arise.

What can perfectly meaningfully be asked is whether someone
may or ought to be prevented from doing something, the implications of which he is incapable of grasping. The matter of the
child's incomplete rationality will therefore assume greater

importance and receive correspondingly more extensive treatment
when claim rights of freedom and certain welfare rights of the
child are discussed in the later chapters.

2 'THE CHILD IS NOT INDEPENDENT OF ADULT POWER'

Discussion of liberties, it is sometimes held, only arises when
there is a possibility of someone doing or having something to
which someone else is opposed, or of which he disapproves. Some
comment must therefore be made on the view that this category of
rights has no application in the case of children, so completely
are they in the power of adults in whose custody they happen to
find themselves. Not only are young children absolutely in the
power of adults physically, the argument might be pursued, but
even later, right into adolescence, the young are subject to
coercion by virtue of the fact that they are dependent on adults
for the achievement of their most important wishes, interests and
aspirations if not for the means of actual survival.

We saw earlier that the possession of power does not itself confer rights and that theories to the effect that it does are little
more than descriptive explanations of the system of positive rights
prevailing in the social order.(1) There may seem to be something to
be said for the view that legislators should not make laws which
circumstances, including prevailing power relations, make it impossible to enforce, but any moral justification for this view must
be expressed in terms of the importance of not bringing the law
into contempt, and of the good order which comes from uniting
positive rights with power. Such arguments, however, are subject to important limitations for good order arising from a close
alliance between positive rights and power may perfectly well
exist in just those tyrannical regimes in which undeniable moral
rights are most harshly and effectively proscribed.

3 THE BIOLOGICAL TIE ('CHILDREN HAVE A DUTY OF OBED-
IENCE TO THOSE WHO BROUGHT THEM INTO THE WORLD')

Despite attempts in the course of the so-called Age of Enlighten-
ment to derive political authority from the paternal authority of
Adam,(2) the independent citizen rarely owes his existence to the
hierarchical ruler who claims authority over him. This is not true
in the case of the child and his parents. His body is biologically
derived from theirs and his existence is the result of their act.

The mere fact of biological progenitorship cannot of itself create
or modify moral relationships of the kind expressed in statements
about rights. The artificial insemination donor appears to retain
no moral rights over the eventual product of his sperm, though
he would presumably do so if biological paternity alone were sufficient. To argue directly from progenitorship to rights of authority would be all too obvious an example of the naturalistic fallacy.

Though the child's body is biologically produced by those of his parents, he does not remain in any way a part of either of them. His consciousness is as separate from that of his parents as theirs is from that of any other human being. His pains are not their pains, though he may come to sympathise with their pains and they with his. His wishes are not their wishes, though he may come to share their wishes. Above all, their interests are not necessarily his interests, although they may often coincide.

If further proof were needed that quasi-biological arguments of the kind mentioned here cannot be used to justify absolute moral authority of parents over children and the consequent ability to annul any claims whatsoever to rights in the sense of liberties, this would be provided by the fact that such arguments make it impossible to explain how it is that the authority of parents appears to cease at maturity, the very point at which the child would begin to be useful as a possession or a servant.

One fact may seem to complicate the question of how the so-called blood tie affects the moral relationship obtaining between parents and children. This is the fact that the blood ties may sometimes seem to justify claims to moral rights on the part of natural parents when the right to the custody and upbringing of children is in question. If, for either biological reasons or as a result of socialisation, human parents tend to conceive a special affection for their own offspring and are particularly prone to suffer if deprived of their presence and the opportunity to care for them in childhood and bring them up, then it would not appear to be a matter of indifference whether parents are allowed to bring up their own offspring or whether they are by some process allocated to others. To justify depriving parents of their children it would at very least have to be shown why such a hurt should be inflicted on them. Considerations of collective good would not normally suffice. The fact that in bearing children mothers have endured an uncomfortable pregnancy and painful birth would also seem to go some way to make children 'theirs' rather than someone else's.

Arguments of this kind, however, if they justify 'parental rights' at all, justify rights against other adults. If various adults claim custody of the child, then the fact of having been the person to produce the child and liable to suffer a particular hurt if deprived of its presence, would appear to give that adult a moral advantage. It is difficult to see, however, how such arguments could create rights, especially rights of absolute moral authority, against the child itself.

4 'CHILDREN ARE NOT HELD SOLELY RESPONSIBLE FOR THE CONSEQUENCES OF THEIR OWN ACTIONS'

A further consideration which might lead us to regard the liberties of children as differing from those of adults is the fact that a free and independent adult is held responsible for the

consequences of his own actions. If such an adult engages in an
activity which damages the property of other people, he will be
held accountable to make the damage good. If he undertakes a
risky adventure which results in injury to himself, or indulges
himself in such a way as to undermine his health, or engages in
a form of social protest or eccentric behaviour which ruins his
career chances, he will have to suffer the consequences and no
one will be blamed but himself. To engage in such activities, provided they do not involve obvious risks to the interests of others,
may well, for an adult with no dependents relying upon his health
and good fortune, be things which are not wrong and of which we
should say that he had, in the present sense, a perfect right to
do them.

In the case of children, however, adults - parents, teachers
and others - are often held responsible for their conduct and may
be damaged in both their social standing and their material interests by their children's actions. This would appear to make certain actions wrong when done by children for whose acts others
were held responsible, even though they would only be regarded
as mildly eccentric or foolhardy if done by adults. In terms of
our earlier analysis of the concept of a right, such acts done by
children would infringe certain rights of security (passive claim
rights of freedom) of the adults held responsible for their well-
being and conduct. This does not show that children have no
rights of freedom in the sense of liberties, but it does show that
the liberties of children are not the same as those of adults.

5 'THE CHILD IS NOT MATERIALLY SELF-SUPPORTING OR CAPABLE OF HIS OWN PROTECTION'

Occasionally the remark may be heard that: 'when X is old enough
to support and look after himself he can do as he likes but while
he lives and takes his meals in this house and is looked after by
me, he surely owes it to me to do as I say and respect my wishes.'
Many children appear to receive extensive benefits from their
parents and it may be thought that they have few ways of repaying them other than by a show of affection, respect and obedience. The liberties of children are, of course, limited by the
transactional rights of their parents, just as the liberties of anyone else are limited by the transactional rights which others may
hold against them. The transactional rights obtaining between
parents and children will be discussed more fully in chapter 15.
For the present, the principal question with which we are concerned is whether the transactional rights of parents against their
offspring are so extensive as to leave no room for liberties on
the part of children at all.

Quite apart from the fact that transactional obligations may seem
to imply initial rights of liberty, such a view must be rejected for
two reasons. First, the advantages which older and younger generations derive from each other are not all to the advantage of the

latter. Old age may be every bit as extended and burdensome as childhood and even if most children do not eventually give their aged parents the same individual care as they have received, the burden, if such an ungracious expression can be used, is borne in other, including collective, ways. Adults, furthermore, derive considerable happiness and satisfaction from having children, and for many, life and activity only receive point from the existence of a rising generation to continue with their concerns in one form or another. If the younger generation go some way towards taking these concerns seriously, an entitlement to some degree of freedom in youth would seem a small return.

Second, the action of parents in bringing up their children may be seen as analogous to those of saving someone's life or providing succour in extreme need, to which the appropriate response is not repayment, but gratitude. What gratitude requires is not the surrender of important interests, but expressions, tokens and other marks of one's sincerely felt recognition of the importance of the service received and the risk or sacrifice on the part of the person who performed it. It may be thought a mark of ingratitude, and therefore no right of the child, to flout the wishes of a parent over a small matter and it may well be that many conflicts between parents and young children concern minor matters in which the ethical interest of the child is not great. In later adolescence, however, this may no longer be so, for conflicts may concern such weighty matters as the choice of career or mode of life, the choice of an eventual marriage partner, or close companion, the espousal and support of a social or political ideal, the practice or rejection of religious observance and so on. It may be thought that the adolescent is at least not acting wrongly in attempting to follow his own inclination in these matters, despite the expressed preference of a devoted parent. It may further be thought that the parent who, for no other reason than his own preference, attempts to coerce or pressurise his offspring to abandon his own chosen course of action in matters of such vital concern forfeits any moral claim he might otherwise have had to the latter's obedience. Such an action is, of course, to be sharply distinguished from that of an adult who coerces a child for what seems to be the latter's own good. The moral issues arising when this occurs will be explored in relation to the child's claim rights of freedom and welfare rights to guidance.

13 Children's claim rights of freedom

Claim rights of freedom, it will be recalled, are of two kinds, active and passive. Active claim rights of freedom are rights to do certain things unhindered. Passive claim rights of freedom are rights not to be interfered with or harmed. The justification of this category of rights, we saw, lay in the fact that A's preponderance of power over B did not in itself provide a reason why his wishes should prevail when they come into conflict with those of B.

Discussion of rights of this category would seem to have particular relevance to the case of children in so far as children are especially vulnerable to the exercise of power in one form or another by the adults in whose charge they find themselves. Even when adults no longer conspicuously surpass children in physical strength, they often retain the power to bring pressure to bear on them by rendering their day-to-day existence inescapably wretched or by threatening their important aspirations and long-term interests.

Where adults and children share the same proximity or are in any way affected by each other's actions their interests, wishes and convenience are bound to conflict from time to time. If rights are to be a useful way of mediating such differences between adults and children, it would seem necessary to identify principles indicating when adults may make use of their virtual monopoly of power to ensure compliance, and when they may not.

RESTRICTING THE FREEDOM OF CHILDREN FOR THEIR OWN GOOD

In considering the claim rights of freedom of adults it was argued that in principle there were no grounds for hindering people in their chosen course of action unless they infringed or were likely to infringe the rights of others. In the case of a child, however, the notion of someone's chosen course of action presents certain difficulties.

In so far as someone is truly a child and not simply deemed to be so on the basis of some such institutional criterion as age, he must be regarded as not yet fully in possession of adult capacities of rational choice. The notion of rationality, however, requires some examination, particularly as it is sometimes misleadingly spoken of as if it were some kind of badge or qualification, which one either had or had not, and which if one had it, entitled one to certain categories of moral rights without further question.(1)

The contrast may be drawn between acting rationally at the
level of prudence and acting rationally at the level of morality.(2)
To say that someone acts rationally at the level of prudence is to
say at very least that he has considered the likely outcomes of
his action and come to the conclusion that these will forward, or
at least be consistent with, his interests. It would therefore
appear to be a condition of acting rationally at the level of prudence that one has some understanding of the laws of cause and
effect operating in the field of one's proposed action, and this in
turn would appear to imply some conception of oneself and of one's
interests in the future, and a relatively settled notion of what
one's interests are and how they are likely to change. It is not
suggested that prudence is entirely a function of chronological
age. Nevertheless, its dependence on experience of life and of
the world will be evident. It is also suggested that acting rationally at the level of prudence may be particularly difficult at a
period of life such as adolescence when, for whatever reason,
the agent's aims, aspirations and desires, and therefore his
interests, are in a stage of rapid and often unpredictable change.

At what has been described as a higher level of rationality, the
agent considers his proposed act from the point of view of morality and considers the interests of others along with his own.(3)
Rationality at the level of morality, as at the level of prudence,
would also appear to imply an understanding of cause and effect
and therefore of the likely effects of the action one proposes. But
whereas prudence requires an understanding of one's own interests, rationality at the level of morality requires not only the
understanding of the often diverse interests of others, but also
an ability to see them as being of equal importance with one's own.

In a later chapter it will be argued that someone not yet rational
at the level of prudence has a welfare right to be looked after,
guided and if necessary coerced in the way of his best interests.
It may be thought that to be thus in need of guidance or even
coercion means that an individual cannot have rights, especially
protected rights of freedom. This in itself does not follow if we
accept the argument of chapter 3 that in certain circumstances
rights may conflict and that it may sometimes be morally justifiable
or even obligatory to overrule a right. Fortunately, however,
such a conflict of rights does not arise in the present case, for
we can properly speak of claim rights of freedom only in circumstances in which the actions may reasonably be deemed rational at
the level of prudence. This would seem to follow from the fact
that a claim right of freedom is a right to do something one
chooses. The notion of choice would in turn appear to imply that
of rationality, at least at the level of prudence, here under discussion.

The situation of a child bent on acting in a way which adults
have reason to think detrimental to his best interests is not without analogies with that of Mill's man attempting to cross a damaged
bridge, when bystanders are unable (Mill says 'there is not time')
to warn him.(4) In this situation, Mill says that we may forcibly

detain him from crossing, for we do not in so doing prevent him
from doing something that he wants to do. Presumably, the traveller does not want to fall into the water, which will be the most
likely consequence of allowing him to proceed. We may, however,
Mill argues, only detain him until such time as we are able to
explain the danger to him (and perhaps we might add, attempt
some rational persuasion as to why he should not attempt to cross).
If, on his own appreciation of the risk, he then chooses to proceed, that is his affair and his right.

To be able to act rationally at the level of prudence is to be
able to choose a course of action, the likely or possible consequences of that action being seen as part and parcel of it. The
traveller approaching the broken bridge cannot choose rationally
at the level of prudence whether to cross it, for he lacks the
necessary information.

The child is also prevented from acting rationally at the level
of prudence, not in this case by mere ignorance of facts - though
he may be ignorant of relevant facts - but by his inability to
appreciate such facts as may be all too readily available. Essentially, the justification for constraining him is the same as in the
case of the traveller. Coercion does not infringe his rights of
freedom for it does not prevent him from doing anything he can
be said to choose to do. By contrast with the case of the traveller,
however, there is no certainty that explaining the likely consequences of the action proposed or pointing out our own greater
experience in these matters will immediately put the child in a
position to weigh these considerations and to act prudently. It
may, therefore, be necessary to restrain him for slightly longer.
As in the case of the traveller, however, such restraint is only
excused by the child's inability to appreciate the implications of
the existing state of affairs for as long as this inability actually
lasts. It does not justify restraining him for longer, until some
institutionally determined age of discretion is reached.

Since one's interests are at least in part dependent on the
strength of personal aspirations and subjective wishes the adult
must normally be regarded as the person best able to weigh his
own conflicting interests. To judge rationally at the level of prudence, however, is not necessarily to judge correctly. All that is
required is that the agent should have as much information as can
be obtained or as he may reasonably think he needs and appreciate the link of cause and effect between the information he has
and his interests.

In the case of an adult it may, indeed, be possible to speak of
his having the right to make his own mistakes. For this three
reasons, among others, may be given:
1 To make a reasoned judgment which turns out to be mistaken
may be an important or even indispensable source of learning.
2 In so far as we are the best judges of our own interests, others
are even more likely to make mistakes on our behalf than we are.
In this way our interests are likely to suffer more damage than if
we had been allowed to decide for ourselves.

3 Even when others decide correctly on our behalf, this is humiliating because it implies that we are not their equals in rationality, do not know what we want, and have not the courage or ability to cope with the consequences of our choices.

In the case of a child not in a position to grasp the implications of alternative courses of action or follow a chain of reasoning likely to lead to the making of a correct choice, we cannot properly speak of his making a mistake at all, far less of his having a right to do so.(5) For this, once again, three reasons readily come to mind:

1 To make a mistake is to commit an error of logic or not to know or to underestimate the importance of a particular fact in an otherwise recognisable chain of reasoning. It is from this kind of failure that one stands to learn rather than from plumping with child like innocence for a particular course of action with no appreciation of likely outcomes, or of the considerations governing those outcomes.

2 Unlike an adult a child is ex hypothesi not the best authority on his own interests or the means of achieving them. It is, of course, true - since nothing is certain in human life - that on some occasions a prudent adult may choose wrongly while the child, for all his ignorance of the world, would have chosen the wiser course. If this happens, however, it is not because the child chooses more skilfully, it is an effect of chance. It is not, however, normally rational to choose to commit one's fortunes to chance. This would require a very mature understanding indeed of the implications of one's actions. A child could scarcely be said to rationally exercise the right to make such a choice.

3 Although it is humiliating for others to assume that an adult is not capable of acting rationally in his own best interest, it is no shame for a child to be guided by an adult.

In this connection, however, it must be recognised that much of the aggravation that has surrounded the so-called children's rights controversy has been not about whether a child in the sense here being used (that is, someone not capable of choosing) can have rights of freedom, but whether particular individuals or groups of individuals are in fact still children in this sense, or whether they are morally speaking adults being treated as children in conformity with misapplied institutional labels.

Where conflicts concerning the right of freedom arise between a child (in the institutional sense) and an adult in whose charge he finds himself, the invidious responsibility unfortunately falls upon the adult to decide whether the child makes the choice he does because he is not capable of acting rationally or whether there are genuine differences of rational judgment, including judgments about the choice of ends.(6) There is also the possibility that the child, though in a position to act rationally at the level of prudence, is making a mistake in the sense discussed and ought, after due remonstration, to be allowed to do so. Clearly there is a danger in this situation that the child's differing judgment may be taken as evidence that he still lacks the capacity for rational judgment and is therefore still in need of guidance and, failing that, of coercion. In this case the conclusion seems inescapable that the adult inadvertently infringes the younger person's right.

RESTRICTING THE FREEDOM OF CHILDREN TO PROTECT THE RIGHTS OF OTHERS

To date we have only considered the rights and wrongs of constraining children for their own good. This includes, of course, not only preventing them from incurring direct physical danger or damaging their long-term material prospects. As will be argued when we come to consider the welfare rights of children, it may also include imposing a certain degree of educational discipline to ensure that they become capable of living as members of society, possessing whatever degree of knowledge and social and other skills is necessary for them to survive and avoid antagonising their peers and others whose goodwill may be essential to their well-being.

On the arguments given in the previous section, constraint of this kind would seem to be legitimate and not to infringe any claim rights of freedom of children in so far as they are truly children in the normative sense, not capable of making their own rational choices in the area of activity under consideration. An equally important question, however, is how far adults may legitimately restrain children for their own (that is, the adult's) good. Under an educational ideology in which everything is supposedly done 'for the sake of the child', this question often goes unconsidered. In chapter 6 we saw that the limits of one's active claim rights of freedom are set by certain categories of the rights of others, notably by their rights of security (passive claim rights of freedom) and any special rights others may have against one. Little will be said here about the special rights that adults may have against children. This question will be considered separately in chapter 15. The following discussion largely concerns the way in which adults may properly limit children's freedom in defence of their own active and passive claim rights of freedom, or to prevent infringement of the rights of third parties.

The use of force may or may not always be appropriate if it is necessary for the exercise or protection of our rights.(7) Few, however, will think that an adult is infringing the child's right if he restrains his son who is about to fetch him or someone else a sharp blow on the ankle (or some other painful spot) with a hammer. The adult may, of course, be acting in the child's interest. For his own sake, the child must learn not to behave in this way. But a more obvious justification is that the adult is protecting his own right not to be hurt, whatever delight or instruction the child might have derived from the action he was about to perform.

It is true that adults may owe the children in their charge (especially those whom they have brought into the world) a degree of kindness, attention and interaction. This, however, is not inconsistent with adults having and protecting certain rights of security as much as other individuals, and restraining their children in order to do so, provided that no actual harm or neglect is inflicted on the children in the process. The rights which adults are entitled to protect might perhaps include such mundane things as a right to peace and quiet for at least part of the day, the right to spend some time in the unhindered pursuit of their own purposes, the right to protect prized possessions from damage and destruction, and so on.

Adults may also seem to commit no infringement of children's rights when they restrain children to protect the rights of others. These others may be members of the same family, institution or community in which the child finds himself, all of whom stand to suffer in the absence of peace and good order, or they may be members of the public at large. When a father stops his son from using his catapult, he may simultaneously be protecting his small sister's right not to risk losing her eyesight, his neighbour's right to the undisturbed enjoyment of her greenhouse and his own right not to have to pay out for shattered panes of glass.

He may also be protecting his right not to be shown up as a parent unable to control his offspring. There would, after all, seem no reason why he should suffer this indignity if the alternative is to suppress a piece of conduct, the full implications of which the child is not in a position to appreciate, and which if he were, he would, it is to be hoped, abandon.

Germane to the question of limiting the freedom of children to protect the rights of others is the issue of whether, in order to possess rights of freedom at all, it is necessary that someone should be rational at the level of morality, or whether rationality at the level of prudence will suffice. At first sight it would appear that only rationality at the level of prudence is necessary, for this is all that is required for someone to have purposes of his own. As we saw, there are no good grounds for denying that one person's purposes may be as important to him as the purposes of others are to them. It is true that someone not rational at the level of morality could not meaningfully assert his rights for he would not know what he was claiming, but this is not to say that he could not effectively use the language of right claiming to his advantage.

It may be thought that someone who is not rational at the level of morality would not recognise the moral rights of others and would, in consequence, be in constant danger of infringing them. This might seem to entitle the morally responsible section of the community to subject such an individual to constant surveillance, and restrict his activity and movement in such a way as to make such surveillance possible in order to avoid the substantial risk of their own rights being infringed. It is after all permissible to restrict dangerous or potentially right-infringing activities without waiting for the danger or infringement to eventuate, since there is no reason why anyone should be subjected to such risks from the activities of others unless he so chooses.(8)

It does not, however, strictly follow from someone's lack of moral sense that his actions may be restricted in this general way. Such an individual may quickly learn as a matter of prudence to avoid acts which bring punishment or retaliation from others. Provided a system of sanctions can be made to roughly correspond with people's moral rights and provided the individual is capable of learning from such sanctions, or in any other way, to recognise what are in fact people's rights and avoid infringing them whether from prudence, habit or any other cause, there would appear to be no grounds for restricting his liberty generally. Plausibly, it may be thought that this is the position of many law-abiding members of society, and that if such people do not, morally speaking, possess claim rights of freedom such rights are possessed by very few.

Even if we are not justified in generally restricting someone's freedom simply on the grounds that he is not rational at the level of morality, however, it is at least necessary, if he is to preserve his right to be unrestricted in his movement and activities generally, that he should as matter of fact be capable of avoiding infringement of the rights of others, however he contrives to do this and whatever his reasons for so doing may be.

There may be no reason to suppose that the acquisition of such a capacity coincides with the attainment of a particular chronological age. If, however, it were the common experience that when allowed generally unrestricted action and movement persons below a certain age or belonging to certain other institutionally defined categories, do tend to act without due consideration for the rights of others, as well as without due regard for their own well-being – this would appear to justify general restrictions on activities and movements of such groups. This would still constitute an infringement of the rights of those coming into the institutional category in question who were, as a matter of fact, capable of respecting the rights of others, but the decision to limit the freedom of members of the category as a whole might be morally justified by the prevention of the greater evil of exposing others to the risk of having important rights of security infringed by those not so capable.

THE EXTENT AND LIMITATIONS OF THE CHILD'S ACTIVE CLAIM RIGHTS OF FREEDOM

From the arguments considered above it may seem that the child has few active claim rights of freedom, since these are limited by both his incomplete rationality and by the justifiable protection of the rights of others. To suppose that he has no such rights at all, however, would be a mistake.

To begin with, though it is a precondition of someone's conceivably being able to exercise a right of freedom, that he should be rational at the level of prudence in relation to the action proposed, it is not clear whether being incompletely rational means

that an individual does not have certain rights or whether it
means that though he has them, he is not able to exercise them,
like someone who has the right to drive a car because he has
passed a driving test, but cannot do so because he now has no
arms. If this is how the situation is to be understood, then
strictly, the child would seem to have the right to choose how to
act, but simply be unable to do so. Others, it would seem to follow, must therefore choose for him and would seem to be under
an obligation to choose as he might plausibly have been expected
to choose, had he been fully rational. In so far as the child
naively shows a disposition to act in a way which would have been
rational anyway, his supposed incomplete rationality would not
justify others in interfering with him. Certainly it would not justify their interfering with him in their own interests as opposed to
his unless, of course, their interests corresponded to protected
rights.

Second, throughout our discussion of how active claim rights of
freedom are limited by the individual's limited rationality it was
stressed that by constraining someone in his own interest others
did not infringe his right to act as he chose if he were not rational
at the level of prudence in respect of the kind of decision under
consideration. One does not, however, have to be rational at the
level of prudence in all things before one can have freedom in any.
A four-year-old may not be able to choose a marriage partner or
decide for himself whether to have a polio injection, but he can
decide whether he wants to play with his toy train or his scooter.
In some choices, the issues are so straightforward that even
young children can grasp all that is involved. In others, the consequences are so insignificant that questions of imprudence and
immorality do not arise. In such cases, the only issue of signif-
icance may be the personal and immediate preference of the
chooser. Nothing may turn on what game the child plays, on
what book he reads, whether he stays in or goes out, whether
he plays alone or with others, and so on. These things are, of
course, also liberties of the kind discussed in the previous chapter. The point being made here is that, in addition, adults ought
to refrain from using their power of coercion to limit the child's
freedom in these areas without good reason, for purposeless
restrictions are as unjustified in parent-child relationships as
elsewhere.

Third, although the incomplete rationality of some individuals
may justify restrictions on their freedom when this is necessary
to avoid a clear and present danger of infringement of the rights
of others, restriction is only justified up to the point where this
protection is achieved. Beyond this a considerable area of freedom and legitimate choice may remain open to the child or young
person concerned, and it is difficult to see how one could justify
restricting this freedom for the sake of the minor convenience or
personal idiosyncrasies of adults.

THE CHILD'S PASSIVE CLAIM RIGHTS OF FREEDOM

The right of children not to be subjected to cruelty, assault or abuse is justified in essentially the same way as that of adults. Like an adult, he feels discomfort, pain, fear and, as he grows older, embarrassment and humiliation. Whereas children's active rights of freedom may be affected by their incomplete rationality, the right not to be subjected to pain and fear is not, since they have a clear interest in not being subjected to them, whether they are rational or not. Indeed, even non-rational animals may be thought to have rights of this kind.(9) Whatever special rights may exist between adults and children it is difficult to imagine that these could include a right of adults to inflict gratuitous harm, pain or unhappiness.

In the case of adults, we saw that there were certain transactions capable of negating an individual's rights of security, namely permissions and forfeitures. These transactions are attended by certain complexities when applied to children.

(a) Permissions
In our discussion of the active claim rights of children we saw that it was sometimes necessary to restrict a child's freedom for his own good. Clearly this is sometimes justifiable if not indeed owed the child as a welfare right. We were further able to argue that such a restriction was not a violation of the child's active claim rights of freedom in that it was not really preventing him from doing what he wanted to do if he could not foresee the consequences of his action or appreciate their implications for his interests.

It may be necessary sometimes to inflict on a child without his consent or against his will acts which raise the question of whether his rights of security are being infringed. Thus, for example, a child may have to undergo a surgical operation in the face of protests or likely protests if he had too clear an idea of what was to be done beforehand. If the operation is to prevent harm to the child, it is fairly clearly owed him as a welfare right even if, repugnant as this may seem, the child has to be brought to the hospital by means of coercion or deception. To do this to a sane adult would clearly be an infringement of his rights. The task of reconciling such an act with the child's right of security is not so straightforward as in the case of forcibly limiting an active expression of his freedom, for as we saw, rights of security are not modified by the child's incomplete rationality in the same way as are his active claim rights of freedom.

Two possible lines of justification, however, would seem open to us. On the one hand it might be argued that for the child to withhold his consent would be a positive act and one whose consequences he cannot appreciate. It is therefore inappropriate to speak of his having a claim right of freedom to do it. Since he does not have the right to withhold his consent, his consent may be dispensed with. Alternatively, it might be said that since the child cannot appreciate the implications of having the operation, he can neither consent nor withhold his consent. Where the operation is clearly in his interests, however, he may be presumed to consent, since, in the absence of valid indications to the contrary, it is to be presumed that someone will choose what is in his interest, if he is able.

The second line of justification would seem preferable to the first in that, with its emphasis on the act's being in the child's interest, it enables us to rule out cases where it is not clear that it is the child's interest which is being considered and in which, therefore, consent may not be presumed. Such cases might include the sterilisation of a rather unintelligent girl because the likely event of her becoming pregnant at an early age would be socially inconvenient, or the surgical straightening of a child's nose because it reminds the mother of a previous husband.

(b) Forfeitures

To say that people have a right of security is not to say that they may never be subjected to physical force. We may defend ourselves or our property against an aggressor and may even have some right of retaliation if no legal remedies are appropriate or available.(10) Criminals are arrested and incarcerated by force if necessary. People's rights of security in the possession of property may also to some extent be negated by fines or confiscation. Someone who infringes the rights of others may not lose all his own rights indiscriminately,(11) but it does not seem morally inappropriate for someone who infringes the rights of others to forfeit some of his own rights of security or active claim rights in return. An adult must be presumed to have acted knowingly and deliberately in infringing the rights of others. To assume otherwise might itself be a denial of his rights.(12)

Clearly the notion of forfeiting a right by way of punishment cannot be applied quite so straightforwardly in the case of children. In particular, we cannot deny that someone has the right to do something on the grounds that he does not fully appreciate the consequences, then punish him for doing it as if he were fully aware of what he was doing. There are, however, a number of distinctions to be drawn in relation to this question. As we saw above, the child does not become rational and responsible for his acts all at once. There may be some areas in which he is not competent to decide what he should do and in which therefore adults must assume responsibility for his actions. Simultaneously, there may be others in which he perfectly well understands the consequences and implications of his acts. In such areas it is quite in order to speak of his being punished by way of the forfeiture of certain rights when he does what he knows to be wrong. Normatively speaking, he is not a child, but an adult in respect of such acts, even though he may still be a child according to some institutional criterion such as age.

In many cases, however, the so-called 'punishment' of children is not to deter the 'offender' and others from doing things they

know to be wrong but to deter them from doing things which we
know to be wrong, dangerous or in some other way undesirable.
The so-called punishment is here simply part of the mechanism of
coercion we use either to protect the rights of others from the
acts of a child not yet rational at the level of morality, or to protect the child from the consequences of acts he would avoid if he
were rational at the level of prudence.

By contrast with punishment in the adult world, the notion of
forfeiture is here out of place in so far as a child, having done
nothing he knows to be wrong, would appear to have done nothing to justify the forfeiture of a right. In the cases mentioned
above, the act of the person who punishes must be justified by
the good achieved or the evil avoided, which, as we saw in chapter 3, is in itself no guarantee that rights have not been infringed
or that particular individuals have not been wronged.

When a child is 'punished' to prevent an infringement of the
rights of others, there may well be a genuine conflict between the
rights of the person whose rights are thus protected, and those
of the child whose rights are not forfeited, but violated. This
would appear to be one of those cases to which Nozick draws
attention, in which it may sometimes be legitimate to protect one
person's rights by violating those of some other individual who
poses an innocent threat to them.(13) Where the child is 'punished' for his own protection this is, likewise, not a case of forfeiture, but is justified by the fact that it protects the child from
the risk of harm. Rather like the surgical operation to which the
child is reluctant to submit, it may perhaps be presumed that the
child would consent to the 'punishment' if, per impossibile, he
understood how he was benefiting from it.

From the above considerations three things would appear to
follow. First, when the punishment of children avoids infringing
rights at all, this is only when it benefits the individual to whom
it is applied and may therefore be regarded as presumptively con-
sented to by him. The case is one of presumed permission, not
forfeiture. It is therefore an infringement of the right of the
person 'punished' to use exemplary punishments to deter others,
for to this he cannot reasonably be presumed to consent. When,
by contrast, an adult is punished by the withdrawal of one of his
rights of security, the right is not waived, but forfeited, so that
consent does not have to be presumed.

Second, since the child does not know that what he does is
wrong, no element of retribution may legitimately enter into the
weighting of the punishment. Only the very minimum required
for the purposes of necessary deterrence or coercion is legitimate,
and then only if no alternative can be found. If no deterrent,
reformative or other improving effect is expected no 'punishment'
is possible without infringing the child's rights. In the case of
adults, however, it may at least be argued that punishment which
corresponds to the offender's deserts does not infringe his rights,
even though no deterrent or other improving effects are expected.

Third, if the punishment of children infringes their rights or is in danger of doing so, it is proper that it should be administered with due hesitancy or regret, as is indeed normally the case when children are 'punished' by morally sensitive adults. Moral propriety, however, requires no hesitation or regret over the punishment of an adult who knowingly violates the rights of others.

RIGHTS AND PHYSICAL PUNISHMENT

Beating and the like are no longer used as judicial punishments in most parts of the British Isles and are outlawed as disciplinary measures in H. M. prisons, on board ship and in the armed forces. (14) By contrast, slapping, cuffing and sometimes even caning form part of the upbringing of children even in some relatively enlightened milieux. It may, therefore, perhaps seem reasonable to ask whether physical punishment of adults constitutes an infringement of adults' rights of security in a way that other forms of punishment such as fining or imprisonment do not. Since the abolition of corporal punishment is demanded by many of those involved in the children's rights movement, it must further be asked whether there is something which makes the physical punishment of children permissible if that of adults is not. Needless to say, we are not here concerned with gross and excessive acts of physical punishment of which opponents of these practices are able to quote such horrifying examples. Our concern is whether all physical punishment, however mild, is ipso facto excessive and a violation of the victim's rights.

Various reasons may be given for ruling out physical punishment as a legitimate means of disciplining deviant adults. To be of any deterrent value, for example, and not be treated with complete contempt by most adult offenders, physical punishment would probably need to be so severe as to be in danger of causing injury or serious harm. The use of physical force, furthermore, is now so totally foreign to the experience of most adults that even many law-breakers may justifiably claim that to suffer the infliction of pain is to be transposed from a relatively civilised plane of life to one which is shockingly unfamiliar and even terrifying.

Most adults regard the application of physical force, especially with any degree of violence or suddenness, as exceptional grounds for indignation quite disproportionate to the harm suffered from the actual jostling, buffeting, pushing or whatever experienced. In the past, it will be recalled, a symbolic slap to the face with a glove was regarded as dissolving relations between individuals to the point where the situation could only be normalised by a fight resulting in the death of one of them. The fact that the indignation surrounding accidental violence can usually be allayed by an apology indicates that its cause lies not in the hurt itself, but in the special indignity or affront involved in disregarding the physical boundary of someone's person. To act in such a way is almost literally to treat them as if they were not there and set

their interests and feelings at nought in a particularly blatant
manner.

Finally, to use the infliction of pain as a punishment is to treat
individuals as if they are not rational and not capable of desisting
from the offence in question either through being persuaded of
its wrongness or out of a prudent regard for their material interests. To be fined or imprisoned is less humiliating than to be
birched, for it implies that one is at least capable of responding
to more sophisticated motives than the mere avoidance of physical
pain at the level of an animal. To require that someone should
allow himself to be struck without retaliating may also seem to
infringe the rights of an adult human being because it implies a
relationship of submissiveness and dominance unacceptable even
in wrongdoers.

THE PHYSICAL PUNISHMENT OF CHILDREN

In drawing analogies and contrasts between the rights of adults
and children in this area, there is a danger of appearing ridicu-
lous if we seem to be comparing judicial hanging and flogging to
a swift smack on the leg administered to a three-year-old in a
tantrum. We ought, therefore, perhaps, to distinguish between a
relatively formal caning after due warning and investigation, in a
secondary school, and the more informal slaps and cuffs which
may occur elsewhere. There may seem to be a number of further
reasons why the latter, when applied to children, may not seem
to carry such serious implications of right infringement as the
corporal punishment of adults.
1 Though excessive or repeated beating may be physically even
more harmful to children than to adults, this is scarcely true of
even a sufficiently sharp slap to deter many childhood misdemeanours. Such a harmless form of physical punishment has, of
course, no possible counterpart in the adult world where it would
presumably have little effect on deliberate law-breakers.
2 Robust physical contact and a degree of rough and tumble, not
to mention occasional knocks and bumps are part of the normal
play experience of most children and are accepted by them without undue shock or lasting malice. Whereas, furthermore, the
deliberate manhandling of adults is ruled out because of the
indignity and abandonment of civilised relations involved, many
of the slaps and cuffs received in childhood take place where
dignified relations have already broken down, and may even help
restore them by bringing a child to his senses.
3 Even where such relations have not broken down a physical
punishment may be that most in the interests of the child, in that
it most promptly and effectively corrects the misdemeanour for
which it is given. No doubt constructive sanctions such as doing
a socially useful chore for irresponsible conduct are desirable,
but these are not always possible to find, or when found, effective. Other sanctions may constitute greater infringements of rights

in that they inflict greater harms and may be less effective because less readily understood by the child. The primary head
who boasts that he no longer slippers boys for throwing stones
at milk bottles, but writes 'wilful damage' on the record card
which will follow the child to secondary school and beyond can
expect few bouquets from the advocates of children's rights.

With all this we may contrast the case of the older child who is
already on his way to becoming a rational adult and is either susceptible to persuasion of the wrongness of his action, or failing
that, to the deterrence of other sanctions. In such a case, the
child is, in normative terms, an adult and the use of physical
punishment on such an individual would appear to be as much of
an indignity and infringement of his rights as if it were applied
to someone over eighteen. In this respect, the solemn and sometimes severe beatings which still occasionally take place in secondary schools partake more of the nature of judicial corporal punishment than the immediate preventive or disciplinary action
which, it has been suggested, may sometimes be justifiable in
dealing with a young child.

14

Children's rights of participation

In chapter 7 we saw that rights of democratic participation in the adult world were justified by the fact that, whatever their differences, each rational person has purposes and interests which are important to him. From the outset, therefore, there is no reason why any such individual should accept less than equal influence in the conduct of matters that concern all unless he so wishes or thinks it to his advantage to accept the rule of others.

Our present concern is to consider how far such a justification is affected by the distinctive features of childhood and in particular whether the child has rights of this kind which are violated by the all but universal practice of excluding him from participation in either the government of public affairs or in decisions which more immediately concern him.

To this end it is once again convenient to make use of the distinction between institutional and normative concepts of childhood, drawing attention to two particular features of the child which may affect his moral status, namely his condition of material dependence and his incomplete rationality.

'CHILDREN ARE MATERIALLY DEPENDENT ON THE ADULT GENERATION'

In chapter 7 we considered various arguments for excluding the materially dependent and propertyless from democratic participation. Some of these, such as the argument that the poor were subject to no constraint to participate responsibly because they could simply go away if they did not like the results of their suffrage, were clearly invalid. Others, such as the argument that the propertyless lack experience and capacity in dealing with important affairs, will be considered in their application to children below. As we saw in chapter 7, however, the most substantial argument for excluding the propertyless from the vote seemed to be that of non-contribution. Those who did not possess property and who therefore made no contribution to the maintenance of the machinery of the state through their taxes, the theory seems to have been, were not entitled to a say in its management.

As we saw, however, even in the case of adults this argument is rather shaky. One does not only contribute to the well-being of one's community by paying taxes. One also contributes by means of one's labour and possibly also by the support and encouragement one gives to the labour of others. In any case, the argument from

non-contribution does not really strike at the root of the justification of rights of participation, which is that one is subject to
government and is therefore entitled to a share of influence on
its decisions, whether one contributes to its maintenance or not.
The right is a right of equality, not a special right to be bought
or earned.

Even, however, if the non-contribution argument were valid in
principle, it is not clear that it would enable us to reject the
notion of children's rights of participation out of hand. It is true
that children do not usually contribute to the community's material wealth either financially, or directly by their labour. Nevertheless, they do contribute in one important way to the well-being
of the community. In the absence of a rising generation to take
over our concerns after us the life of the adult generation would
be wretched and, despite talk of intrinsically worthwhile activities,
in many respects pointless.

If it is thought that this is a purely existential and not very
meritorious contribution on the part of children, it may further
be pointed out that children contribute to the well-being of the
community not only through what they are, but also through what
they do. Not only does the younger generation eventually take
over the older generation's concerns and afford the latter some
satisfaction by so doing. Members of the younger generation also
make considerable efforts to learn what it is necessary for them
to know in order to be able to take over our concerns. In this
respect, the young may be said to have and to accept, often with
great idealism and earnestness, considerable responsibilities, in
respect of the well-being of the community as a whole. If this is
doubted, we may consider the plight of a community in which the
younger generation as a whole, and not just a few disaffected
individuals, refused to concern themselves with the preoccupations
of their elders.

There is a further way in which someone might attempt to argue
from children's material dependence on adults to justify their
exclusion from the democratic process. This would be to say that
as children are entirely dependent on adults, their interests coincide, so that they do not need an independent voice in the management of the community's affairs, much as it might have been
argued in the past that women did not need the vote because their
material interests were inseparable from those of their husbands.

The argument is vulnerable on two counts. First, if children's
interests are identical with those of adults, this is in itself no
more an argument for excluding the former from participation in
favour of the latter than vice versa. Something further has to be
said to show why it is the children who are to be excluded, or,
indeed, why anyone need be.

Second, material dependence does not equal identity of interests.
Whether children ought to be materially dependent and subject to
adult discretion and generosity is itself capable of being disputed,
(1) and might well divide members of the younger and older generations if the issue were put to a universal vote. In more general

terms, the distribution of resources, facilities and freedoms between young and old also provide areas in which interests might
diverge. Those who have longer to live have an interest in more
progressive long-term undertakings involving some immediate
hardship which others might not regard as worthwhile. What
people regard as desirable ends may differ also between young
and old. In short, we do not always vote the same way as those
whose purely material interests are the same as our own.

'CHILDREN ARE NOT FULLY RATIONAL'

To some extent the conditions under which it makes sense to
speak of rights of participation are similar to those implied by the
assumption of rights of freedom. There are, however, two important differences. First, exercising rights of freedom may sometimes involve taking steps to fulfil short-term, immediate purposes,
which may change from day to day. Sometimes very little may hang
on the choice made. Indeed, it may be no more than the expression of personal preference or individual taste, so that the degree
of rationality required before it makes sense to discuss whether the
child can have such a right or not may be relatively limited. It
was therefore argued in the previous chapter that even a young
child may be thought of as having a limited range of rights of
freedom in appropriate circumstances.

Participation in the affairs of one's community, however, normally has effects which are far from immediate, so that the activity
would seem to imply a degree of steadfastness in one's conception
of a desirable state of affairs over time, for one could scarcely be
said to be capable of choosing rationally if it were likely that one
would no longer desire or be interested in the results of one's
choice by the time those results began to be achieved. Possibly it
may be thought that such stability of purpose and intention is
neither likely nor desirable in a developing child. It may further
be doubted whether the normative concept of childhood is consistent with having any serious understanding of what would be
involved in choosing between various candidates for office, programmes of legislation or even specific legislative provisions.

It may perhaps be countered that few adults have any such
understanding either, and vote on the strength of such things as
habit, the candidate's personal appearance and peer group
fashion. This, however, may be seen as part of the general attack
on democracy or an elitist argument for restricting the suffrage
more closely. It certainly has not been shown that where serious
issues are at stake adults are not usually capable of choosing responsibly, even though they may subsequently come to regard
their choice as mistaken.

There is a further difference between rights of freedom and
rights of participation. When someone exercises a right of freedom, the outcomes of his action are largely confined to himself or,
if they affect others it is in relation to interests which are not

protected by rights. In exercising a right of participation, by
contrast, one is not only choosing representatives, programmes
or measures for oneself, but also for others. The conditions of
other people's lives may be importantly changed by how an individual and those like him may decide to vote and it is suggested
that this fact may place more stringent limits on rights of participation than are applicable in the case of rights of freedom.

Clearly, someone who is a member of a democratic society must
concede that his rights are not infringed every time a decision
is taken to which he is opposed, for if he accepts that others
whose views and interests differ from his own are to have equal
influence with himself, then he must envisage that this may sometimes happen. Only on the basis of such a concession can he
require others to accept democratically taken decisions when it
does not suit them to do so.

To have one's wishes constrained and one's purposes and interests adversely affected through the exercise of equal influence by
others whom one is obliged to regard as rational like oneself and
having interests and purposes identical in status to one's own is
one thing. It would, however, be quite different for one's important interests to be made subjects of chance, or for them to be
adversely affected by the relatively minor whims of a group exceptionally vulnerable to demagogy or deception. This, it is sub-
mitted, would be the state of things if the electorate included a
substantial number of individuals who, whatever their chronological age, were in respect of their purposes and capacities,
normatively speaking, children. Such an arrangement would give
the interests and purposes of fully rational adults less consideration than those adults might reasonably expect.

Even though it may be thought that in view of the arguments
above, children do not have a right to an equal share in the actual
power to influence how things are done, nothing has been said to
suggest that they do not have the right to have their wishes,
preferences and point of view taken into consideration as far as
possible when important decisions are taken. This, in turn, would
seem to imply that every effort should be made to find out what
are the wishes and preferences of children of various ages and at
various times, particularly in matters that closely concern them,
and that attempts should be made to devise institutions for this
purpose. It would further seem to follow that (subject to safe-
guards against libel, malicious damage to character and the in-
vasion of privacy) the fullest expression of children's opinions and
the spread of information by them about the conditions of their
lives should be protected and that attempts, however clumsy, on
the part of children approaching the condition of adults to organise themselves for the purpose of expressing opinions should not
be frowned upon or persecuted, but positively encouraged and
aided.

It is true that consultation, however full and conscientious, may
not be as effective as full-blooded participation in ensuring that
one's point of view receives due consideration. Nevertheless, such

arrangements for ascertaining the point of view of children may
be something more than a mere public relations exercise. It may
be thought that in a liberal democracy voters are often fair-minded
in matters not directly affecting their own interests. Most children, furthermore, will reach the voting age sooner or later and
are perfectly capable of rewarding or punishing those politicians
who have treated them well or badly in the recent past.(2) It
therefore seems possible that some people in public life might find
it not only rewarding, but also advantageous to support the
obviously reasonable preferences of children even though these
were not yet able to immediately repay their champions with direct
electoral support.

THE RIGHTS OF THOSE WHO ARE CHILDREN IN AN INSTITUTIONAL SENSE ONLY

We saw earlier that for a number of reasons any attempt to accord
rights on the basis of some institutional criterion such as chronological age was bound to be somewhat arbitrary and was likely to
result in rights being accorded to many who in normative terms
did not qualify and in depriving of such rights many who did.(3)
Any attempt to accord positive rights on normative grounds, however, involves insoluble difficulties of a practical kind. In the
case of rights of participation, these difficulties are rendered
particularly acute by the fact that any proposed normative criterion is itself likely to prove a subject of political contention and
is susceptible to gerrymandering and manipulation.(4)

Almost certainly, therefore, considerations of overall good make
it necessary to accord positive rights of participation on the basis
of some such objective institutional criterion as chronological age.
What this age should be will no doubt depend in part on empirical
information about the younger members of particular societies,
and perhaps about the nature of the issues democratically decided
in that society and the nature of the democratic procedures employed. Clearly, however, the appropriate age must be one at
which the majority of individuals are judged to have attained the
relevant capacities in view of the need to exclude from participation any significant numbers of those who have not.

Even though a society may be justified in denying rights of participation to some who are normatively speaking 'adults' because
any alternative procedure would be even more undesirable, it is
still a matter of debate whether this practice infringes the rights
of the individuals concerned. It might be argued that if all obtain
positive rights of participation at the same age there is no injustice since all members of the community have the chance to exert
an influence on public affairs for an equal amount of time. Against
this, however, it must be conceded that rights are indeed being
infringed in that the individuals are being denied the right of
equal influence enjoyed by others who do not differ from them in
any morally relevant way. Possibly the infringement may seem to

be of no great moment, since destined to be of relatively short duration unless the age of participation is set absurdly high. Still, it might result in burdens being laid upon those just below the relevant age which would not otherwise come their way. The legal requirement to serve a period of military service between the ages of eighteen and twenty with the voting age held at twenty-one used once to be quoted as an example of such a situation. If substantial numbers of young people were normatively speaking adults at the age of, say, fourteen and would reject the idea of compulsory schooling up to the age of sixteen, this would be a further example, especially if the requirement were maintained in the interests of preventing adult unemployment.

If the practice of according rights of participation on a basis of institutional rather than normative criteria does, in fact, result in an infringement of the rights of certain individuals, it would appear that such individuals are owed a collective debt of apology, deference and compensation appropriate to someone whose rights are being infringed. More importantly, it would seem that they are owed a particular duty to ensure that, as far as possible, the views of such individuals are ascertained, allowed expression, and taken into account to a point as closely as possible approaching that at which equality of influence with others who are normatively speaking adults is restored.

PARTICIPATION IN SCHOOL AND FAMILY DECISIONS

In our original discussion of rights of participation it was suggested that these are not only applicable in the community as a whole but also in institutions and particularly places of employment in which individuals spend a substantial part of their time or which importantly affect their lives. If this is true, it would seem that rights of participation are also due to those who spend a substantial part of their time in schools and whose lives are importantly affected by what goes on there. In the discussions mentioned, however, it was also suggested that in individual institutions as opposed to the community as a whole, rights of participation were subject to a number of legitimate limitations. First, it was suggested, membership of or entry into certain institutions might imply transactions creating special rights of authority and corresponding duties of compliance. It was also seen, however, that if such an agreement were manifestly unjust, taking advantage of some contingent monopoly of power to impose an unreasonable degree of subordination, it would not be morally valid.

Second, it was suggested that rights of participation might be limited if a certain degree of direction and compliance were required by the purposes of an institution which those in it might reasonably be assumed to approve. Thus, soldiers might be expected to accept that wars were more likely to be won if orders on the battlefield were obeyed without question and employees,

perhaps, that firms were more likely to stay in business if certain policy matters were left to the managing director and his
accountant. Arguably, however, the legitimate extent of this
limitation is less than would be suggested by actual practice. Not
all the autocratic decisions taken by military commanders concern
such urgent matters as winning battles, and the question of how
much of a firm's income should be taken as profit and how much
directed to providing employees with a reasonable wage or tolerable working conditions are not necessarily best made by
accountants.

Third, institutions, unlike sovereign communities, have obligations to persons other than their members. Armies and police
forces have duties to the community, firms to shareholders, consumers and members of the public whose environment is likely to
be polluted by noxious processes, and so on. Rights may be conferred and obligations imposed on some members of institutions by
the wider community and persons other than its members.

THE SUPPOSED NON-CONTRIBUTION OF CHILDREN IN SCHOOLS

If we accept a model of education in which teachers labour and
children merely receive the benefit of their efforts, then it might
be arguable that children make no contribution to the school's
work, and have no right to a say in the management of it. If,
however, the school is regarded as a community in which all work
together for certain ends; if, for example, the pupil's progress is
an end for both teacher and pupil, then it is not so clear that the
pupil makes no contribution. In many cases the community as well
as the pupils themselves eventually benefits from the knowledge
and skill they acquire.

An alternative version of the argument from non-contribution
against democracy in schools is that as the sole provider of
resources which the school requires, the community quite legitimately deals hierarchically with the school and is entitled for this
purpose to establish a hierarchical and non-democratic structure
within it. This, however, does not accord with the observed
features of schools and education systems, in this country at
least. Though society provides the material substance of most
schools, much of what goes on in them seems to be decided in the
schools themselves, by the head teacher in more or less close consultation with the staff. Provided what goes on in schools meets
certain conditions, it is not clear that a hierarchical structure is
required by society. In any case, it may be argued that society's
provision of the resources of the school would not entitle it to
deny all rights of participation to those within it, for this would
be an example of an unequal contract.

Allied to the argument from non-contribution is the argument
that democracy would be inappropriate in schools because pupils
have a relatively limited stake in what is done there. Compared to
some of the staff, their membership is relatively transitory and

like Ireton's poor they will probably go away before the effects of
any long-term policy are felt.

Clearly, institutions do differ from the community as a whole in
that in the community we all have essentially the same stake, since
what the community undertakes may affect all our purposes. In
institutions, by contrast, individuals may be involved in a greater
or lesser degree. Some may be permanently and totally involved,
while others only come within its influence temporarily. Some may
be involved with one institution, others with many and so on.

The value of this argument should, however, not be overestimated. Though this and other considerations may make it
inappropriate for children (or any other transitory member) to
exercise undue influence upon long-term decisions, the pupil's
point of view is an abiding one even though individuals change.
From the pupil's own point of view, the importance of his stake in
the school cannot be overestimated. While he is at the school, he
is a member of it in the fullest sense. Many of the decisions taken
in a school are immediate and short-lived in their effect and if the
child's involvement and stake in the school were the only consideration it would provide slender grounds indeed for denying him
rights of participation in its management.

THE IMPERFECT RATIONALITY OF CHILDREN AND THE MANAGEMENT OF EDUCATIONAL INSTITUTIONS

The argument that it makes no sense to speak of the right to participate in the management of affairs one does not have the capacity to understand would appear to apply as much in the school
as in the community at large. In a later section, furthermore, the
argument will be considered, that there are logical reasons why
pupils cannot be supposed to understand certain decisions of
central importance to the conduct of schools.

All the same, many of the things that go on in schools are far
less inscrutable than affairs of state. It will further be recalled
that even in the community at large, the child would seem to have
a right of full and serious consultation. Adults, it was argued,
are under an obligation to bring about the closest possible
approach to equality of influence compatible with the child's limitations and the rights of others. This would also appear to apply
in schools, particularly in the case of those who are 'children' in
an institutional sense only.

'THE SCHOOL IS NOT AN INDEPENDENT SOVEREIGN COMMUNITY'

Schools are required by the community to provide education to
the definition of which certain admittedly broad, but none the
less real, limits are set. Although this may not entitle the community to extinguish all rights of participation within the school,
it is entitled as a special right arising from its provision of

resources to require that these resources should be spent for the purpose for which they are intended, irrespective of the 'democratic' decisions of those within the school.

The community holds those in charge of schools responsible for the safety and acceptable conduct of those in them. Clearly, pupils cannot collectively have the right to overrule requirements made to this end unless they also have the power to absolve those in charge from this responsibility. The community is justified in requiring those in charge of schools as their agents to ensure the safety and acceptable behaviour of pupils because of the welfare rights of protection and education they owe the children and because of the duty they owe members of the public to protect their rights (usually rights of security) from being infringed by the irresponsible acts of children temporarily in their charge.

Finally, the providing authority has legal and moral obligations to school staff as employees. The school community cannot, therefore, be entitled as a right of participation to demote, discipline or humiliate a teacher unless it is also able to shoulder the authorities' responsibilities to him. It is, of course, in theory possible to think of a school community employing its own teachers, but this would entail the school community having responsibility for its own financial arrangements, which may be regarded as beyond the capabilities of children as normatively defined.

These considerations would appear to impose considerable limits on what pupils may be said to have the right to decide collectively for themselves. As we saw in chapter 7, similar limits may apply to the rights of participation in many institutions which are not themselves sovereign communities but are designed to fulfil specified purposes within society at large. To note that certain ranges of decision are ultra vires, however, is not to concede that members of the institution concerned have no rights of democratic participation at all. In the case of schools there would appear to be many matters affecting the lives of both staff and pupils which are currently settled by tradition, habit, or the personal predilection of individuals. Such matters, it is suggested, could be arranged differently without detriment to society's educational requirements or to the providing authority's responsibilities either to the general public or to its employees.

IS TALK OF RIGHTS INAPPROPRIATE TO THE TEACHER-PUPIL RELATIONSHIP?

According to some educational models, becoming a pupil is an act of complete subordination to one's teachers, incompatible with any notion of rights of participation in the control of the institution in which both find themselves.(5) Even today, some remnants of this model are still to be found in both schools and institutions of higher education. Students, as we have seen, may be required to undertake to obey regulations which they have had no part in making. The parents of pupils in some selective schools are still

required to promise in advance that their children will respect
rules regarding the wearing of school uniform and participation
in matches out of school time.

Ideally, no doubt, the teacher-pupil relationship is one in which
pupil and teacher strive together for a conception of the good
they both share. Both may enter into the relationship freely and
either may terminate it at any time. In such a relationship there
is no need to consider rights, for there are no conflicts of interest. The pupil takes the ends envisaged by the teacher as his
own. In real life, however, things are different. The interests of
pupils and teachers do conflict or there would be no need for
oaths to be sworn or written undertakings to be given. Here the
situation is clearly one in which talk of rights is applicable. Education is being treated as a good, given in return for the surrender of part of the pupil's freedoms. No doubt there is much to
be said for the view that the pupil who receives the benefit
accruing from the role of pupil ought to accept such reasonable
obligations of the role as may exist in practice. As we saw in our
discussion of special rights, however, this is something quite different from the laissez-faire conception of freedom of contract
according to which someone who controls a good in scarce supply
may exchange it for any coercion he cares to demand. This practice it was argued may be challenged if it constitutes an unequal
contract in which one party exploits his control of a highly desirable or necessary good to extract unreasonable commitments from
another.(6) Arguably, the trading of a good so necessary to the
fulfilment of some individuals as education for a surrender of all
rights to a say in decisions significantly affecting one's daily life
would be an example of such a contract.

PARTICIPATION AND THE PURPOSE OF SCHOOLS

Although schools and other educational institutions may be unjustified in trading the benefit of education against excessive
compliances, it may be thought that pupils could reasonably be
assumed to assent to whatever degree of direction and compliance
is necessary for the achievement of the purposes for which they
are there. This is somewhat similar to the case of persons in
other kinds of institutions, but there are certain differences.
1 Unlike some soldiers and factory workers the child may not
actually be in school willingly. Therefore, it has to be shown that
the purpose for which he is there is sufficiently in his interest
for it to be plausible that he would assent to it if he were fully
rational, otherwise the compulsion to attend would be itself an
infringement of his right and his presence could not serve as justification for a further degree of compulsion once he is inside. That
compulsion to attend school does not, in fact, infringe the right of
someone who is in a normative sense a child will be argued when
the welfare rights of children are considered in chapter 16.
2 The ends for which armies and factories exist are fairly clear

and widely agreed. This is not so in the case of schools, for educational aims are properly the subject of value judgments and would therefore appear to be particularly appropriate to democratic control. Unfortunately, however, there appear to be good reasons for supposing that the democratic control of the specifically educational aspects of school policy by pupils is inappropriate. The teacher-pupil relationship, it has been argued, is essentially asymmetrical. In advance of learning, pupils cannot choose what they ought to learn or even know what they want to learn. They cannot know what standards are appropriate, in what order their studies should be approached, what schedules of work should be followed or what exercises and other activities performed. Nor can they decide who should be their teachers. The argument is not based on contingent incapacities of the young, but derives from what it is to be a pupil. Just as it makes no sense to speak of children having rights of freedom to decide for themselves how they shall individually be educated, so it makes no sense to speak of them collectively having rights of participation in this choice. (7)

In response to this latter argument certain distinctions have to be drawn within the area of what might be called educational decisions. First, it may be held that all decisions taken in a school are educational decisions, since all elements in the environment are potentially educative or miseducative in their effect. This may be true, but may only validly be employed as an argument against pupil participation in an institution in which all decisions are indeed taken on educational rather than administrative grounds. Second, educational decisions may be decisions about pedagogy. Here it may contingently be the case that the teacher's greater experience ensures that his judgment will in most cases be superior, and to that extent perhaps pupils may be presumed to delegate the choice of teaching methods to him. On the other hand, however, it may be thought that pupils' own knowledge and experience of how they learn most effectively means that they have a valid contribution to make in the question of teaching methods and have each in relation to one another an equal right to influence teaching methods in the way that best suits themselves. In any case, reasons of this kind for limiting the participation of pupils are to be clearly distinguished from that considered immediately below, which logically follows from their ignorance of the subjects they are taught and which alone may be deduced from their status as pupils.

In schools, judgments are to be made concerning the point and standards of the particular discipline the pupils are engaged in learning. Clearly, it would seem, there can be no question of democratic decisions by pupils as to whether it much matters if Russian inflections are wrong provided the writer's meaning is clear, or if historical evidence suggests or does not suggest a certain conclusion provided that conclusion is in line with preferred ideologies. If these things are at all matters for democratic decision, they are matters for democratic decision by those who at least have some understanding of the alternatives involved.

Before leaving this subject, the point should be made, however, that the term 'pupil' is susceptible to much the same ambiguity as that to which we have drawn attention in the case of the word 'child'. One may be a pupil in the normative sense that one is ignorant of a subject and desires to learn it, or in the institutional sense that, willy-nilly, one daily goes to school. That a pupil in the normative sense is in no position to decide what he ought to study follows analytically. Pupils in the institutional sense on the other hand may be more or less ignorant or not very ignorant at all about the central standards of the disciplines they study. Likewise, 'teachers' in the institutional sense may be more or less knowledgeable or not very knowledgeable at all about the subjects they teach. If it is with actual pupils and teachers in the institutional sense that we are concerned, the former having already, perhaps, some knowledge of their subject, then it is difficult to see why they could not be said to have some rights of participation, at least at the level of serious and genuine consultation, even in matters directly relating to their studies.

15   Children and special rights

Although special rights do not figure importantly among the
rights publicly demanded for children, consideration of this category cannot be passed over without mention for a number of
reasons. To begin with, it is important to make the negative
point that special rights are but one category of rights among
others. If there is, as was suggested in chapter 8, a common tendency to assimilate all rights to this category, and particularly to
special rights arising from transactions, this may prove particularly misleading when attempting to assess the validity of claims
on behalf of children to rights of other kinds.

If it is assumed, for example, that rights in general have to be
earned, as if all rights conformed to the model of transactional
rights to payment for services rendered, it might seem easy to
deny all rights to children, or at least to those who seem particularly undeserving in relation to their conduct or studies. Equally,
if it is thought that rights are characteristically created by some
such transaction as promises or undertakings, then many adults
might be disposed to think that children had no rights against
them, since they at least have made children no promises and
given them no undertakings.

Against such hardline opposition to children's rights claims it
is, of course, possible to argue that children do indeed have
special rights in respect of both their deserts and their contribution to the well-being of the adult world, as well as in respect
of certain more specific transactions. More importantly, however,
the point is to be made that the rights most widely and most con-
tentiously claimed for children are not special rights but rights of
freedom, rights of participation and certain welfare rights.

In so far as such rights are possessed by adults they are, as
has been seen, justified not by deserts or transactions but by the
independence, separateness and non-subordination of individuals
or in the case of welfare rights, by need. To the investigation of
corresponding rights claims on behalf of children, therefore, the
question of desert and adult transactions in their favour is irrelevant. In the main the proper approach to such claims would appear
to be that followed in chapters 12, 13, 14 and 16, namely, consideration of how far children may, like adults, be regarded as
separate, non-subordinate beings with ends and purposes of their
own, or whether they, like adults, also have important needs
which they cannot satisfy by their own efforts.

It should not, however, be thought that consideration of special
rights is irrelevant to the question of children's rights in general.

Children themselves do have special rights of both role-related
and transactional kinds and these will be considered below. Adults
may also be thought to have more or less extensive special rights
against them. As was noted in chapter 6, the extent of someone's
rights of freedom, both in the sense of liberties and of active
claim rights of freedom is defined by the rights of others. These
rights of others are often rights of security (passive claim rights
of freedom) but they may also be special rights.

Many of the special rights thought to be held by adults against
children have in consequence already been dealt with incidentally
while discussing the extent of children's rights of freedom and
participation in earlier chapters. Thus, for example, the notion
that the benefit conferred by the act of begetting the child was
so great as to preclude the possibility of the child's having liberties of his own was disposed of in chapter 11, while the special
right of adults to restrict the freedom of children in return for
material and other benefits conferred during childhood and youth
were shown to be considerably less extensive than might have
been assumed.

THE SPECIAL RIGHTS OF CHILDREN

(a) Transactional rights
Turning to the special rights of children themselves, it would
appear that for the most part the justification of rights arising
from transactions is not seriously modified by the fact that the
beneficiary of the right is a child. It is true that before a certain
age a child may not be able to understand what a promise is and
it may therefore be thought meaningless to speak of making a
promise to him and therefore to speak of his having a right to the
fulfilment of that promise. Apart from the case of a very young
child, however, there seems no reason to regard promises to the
young as any less binding than those made to anyone else. Certainly there seems no reason why children should not be thought
of as having rights of recompense, gratitude and recognition for
services and kindnesses done or rights of reparation for harms
resulting from negligence or malice.

It may be thought that the children's interests involved in these
transactions are often relatively unimportant in material terms and
that the wrongs involved in failing to keep promises and so on to
children are of a relatively minor kind, shortlived in their effects
and soon forgotten. Such an act may indeed frequently be justified by conflicting interests of greater moment including weightier
interests of the child himself. Nevertheless, the overruling of a
right remains a wrong and due hesitancy, deference and respect
would normally seem to remain appropriate.(1) The parent or
teacher who puts himself (or others) to some trouble in order to
seek alternatives to infringing such a right on the part of the
child is therefore showing a quite proper degree of moral sensitivity and is not simply being soft or weak-minded.

Though the view was rejected that the act of begetting the child creates substantial rights against him on the part of his parents, it may more reasonably be argued that the act of pro-creation creates substantial responsibilities in parents and cor-responding rights in the child.(2) It is true that, as we saw, many lawyers, using a narrowly professional sense of the term, might be inclined to say that though parents are responsible for the material support and upbringing of their children, this does not mean that children strictly have a right to these things.

Nevertheless, by intentionally or negligently bringing the child into the world, parents expose him to the danger of pain, star-vation, humiliation, and many other vicissitudes. It therefore seems not entirely unreasonable to hold that, morally speaking, the duties of support, protection, guidance and, as will be argued later, education, to which parents may seem committed are owed not merely in respect of the child but to him.(3) Children are not simply incidental beneficiaries in respect of this obligation, but right-holders. The right is a transactional right of reparation.

The possible legalistic quibble that the child was not in exist-ence at the time of its conception and thus can have derived no rights from it may surely be ignored. Even the law now recog-nises responsibilities to the unborn (4) though not, it must be admitted, to the unconceived! Nevertheless, it is possible to think of any number of instances in which someone has a moral right of reparation in respect of acts done before they were born or con-ceived. Anyone injured through the malfunction of an artefact negligently made before his conception would be in this position.

(b) Role-related rights
Not only may the benefits mentioned above be regarded as due to children in respect of (transactional) rights of reparation. They may also be regarded as their due in respect of the role-relationship in which they stand to their parents and those in whose care they find themselves.

It was argued in chapter 8 that role-related rights arising out of a particular set of social relationships are morally valid only if the network of rights and duties of which they form part is itself relatively equitable. Whether the network of established rights and duties currently existing between children and adults is equitable or not is, of course, very much a matter of contention and is an issue central to this study as a whole. Those contesting the justice of adult-child relationships in the modern, western world, however, have for the most part claimed that any injust-ices are on the side of the older generation towards the younger rather than vice versa. Role-related rights of the younger gener-ation against the older may therefore seem not to be invalidated on this score.

Apart from the possible undue restriction of children's rights of freedom and participation noted in previous chapters the relation-ship between older and younger generations may indeed seem relatively just, at least to the extent that both generations appear to derive substantial benefits from it and make substantial contributions in return. In the future the child will be required to make his own material contribution to the society in which this relationship is embodied. Already, as a child, he will, by his very existence, normally contribute to the well-being and happiness of his parents and to the meaningfulness of their lives, as well as striving to learn many things necessary to the continued life of his community. The benefits of material support, guidance and so on which he received from the older generation may therefore perhaps be seen as a not entirely gratuitous benefaction.

As with certain other interpersonal relationships, there may seem to be some impropriety in introducing the contentious language of rights into the discussion of relations between parents and children. Certainly, to see these purely as a form of exchange with each party constantly on the watch to make sure that the other does not receive more than he gives would be absurd, and a relationship in which individuals only get and concede each other their rights, or see all they receive as no more than their rights would in many respects be an impoverished on.(5) One's relationships with one's children, as indeed with one's friends, colleagues, teachers and pupils are something to which, over and above one's obligations, one commits a good deal of one's idealism and generosity. Constant reference to the rights of the other party or indeed to one's own rights suggests that they are, and may indeed lead to their becoming, relationships of a less edifying kind.

To say, however, that one should, in sensitivity, not refer to people's rights is not to say that rights do not exist within a certain relationship or that it is not important to respect them. The pretext that a relationship is especially noble or elevated is no reason for not according someone his rights. This indeed is the minimum one owes to others and any morally superior relationship implies that this at least is done.

SPECIAL RIGHTS OF CHILDREN AND THE TEACHER-PUPIL RELATIONSHIP

Unless one takes an exceptionally negative view of the value of education one must admit that the child derives considerable benefit from his role as a pupil and his relationship with his teachers. It will later be argued that the benefit of education would in any case be the child's right as a welfare right because of the wretched condition of someone left entirely unprovided for in this way. The child, however, also has special rights in this regard on account of his involvement in the pupil-teacher relationship.

Not only pupils, but also teachers gain from the existence of this relationship and both have their contribution to make to its maintenance. Not only does the teacher acquire an income and social position as a result of standing in this relationship to others. He also has the opportunity of remaining in contact at however

rudimentary a level with the intrinsically worthwhile and absorbing activities that constitute the school curriculum.

The adult world in general also gains from the fact that teaching and learning goes on and that some individuals stand in
relation to others as pupils to teachers. It is through schools and
similar institutions that many of our traditions of awareness,
worthwhile activities and values are kept alive. Indeed it is to a
large extent through schools and indirectly therefore via the
medium of an incalculable number of individual teacher-pupil
relationships that society preserves and renews itself, passing on
not only its traditions and values but also the skills by virtue of
which its material viability is ensured.

To all this the contribution of the pupil, his positive efforts as
well as his willing compliance are essential. Though the adult
world undeniably commits effort and resources to the business of
teaching and learning, the child in addition to making often very
strenuous efforts to learn, gives up or rather sees others give up
on his behalf, a substantial part of his freedom for some eleven
years and the possibility of exploring the world in his own way,
however unprofitable and inefficient such an enterprise may be
thought to be.

The teacher is also placed in a position of trust not only in
relation to the authorities who employ him and parents who entrust
their children to him, but also in relation to the pupils themselves.
It would seem to be a breach of that trust and an infringement of
the child's right if, instead of being educated, he is abused, humiliated, subjected to needless and stultifying boredom, made to
learn things which are of no value or to engage in sloppily inefficient learning procedures, as a result of which he eventually
emerges from school having learned little of value.

Little need be added concerning the case of pupils being more
or less deliberately indoctrinated for in this case the infringement of the pupils' rights is too obvious to require labouring. In
such a case, the child innocently submits himself to the teacher's
authority on the assumption that what he is taught is good or
true, and is systematically given to believe things that suit the
purposes of others.

16 Children's welfare rights and the right to education

A welfare right, it will be recalled, is a right to receive help or goods from others in circumstances of extreme need, when one is unable to obtain these things by one's own efforts. Unlike some other kinds of rights there would appear to be no difficulty concerning the application of welfare rights to children. Rights of this category do not depend on one's legal status. The point of their attribution is not diminished by the absence of rationality. They do not have to be earned, nor do they result from the particular acts or negligences of others, or from the roles in which one stands in relation to them. All that is required is that an individual should have present or future interests capable of harm through neglect or deprivation.

There are, however, certain differences between the welfare rights of adults and those of children. When adults become the subject of welfare rights this is usually the result of circumstances of a contingent or accidental kind, such as illness, loss of employment or some other adverse change of fortune. The child, by contrast, is in a position of dependence by his very nature and has certain needs which adults do not.

THE CHILD'S RIGHT TO MATERIAL SUPPORT

The human child, unlike the young of some other species, is not born in a medium or environment which provides a ready abundance of whatever he needs to survive. Adults are also afflicted by this difficulty, but the adult's position differs from that of a child in two respects:
1 Partly by virtue of his physical strength, but more particularly by virtue of the knowledge and skills which he will almost inevitably have acquired in reaching adulthood, the adult is able to obtain or create sustenance from the resources of his environment. Significantly, in cases where welfare rights apply to adults these characteristics are in some way impaired, as when someone loses his physical strength and mobility as a result of illness or injury or when changes in external conditions render the survival skills he has acquired inapplicable. Climatic change may turn an agricultural region into a desert, rendering the farming skills of the inhabitants as materially useless as the unguided movements of a child. Technological advance may have the same effect, by rendering a particular mode of gaining a livelihood uneconomic. Conceivably, the victims of such misfortunes may be held to be to

blame for their own plight through their failure to avoid accident,
preserve their health or adapt to changing conditions. Some might
even feel that this fact invalidates an adult's moral claim to welfare rights. By no stretch of the imagination, however, could such
an argument be applied to children. They can do nothing about
their lack of robustness. Nor can they be held responsible for
their initial lack of knowledge and skill, for in human beings the
knowledge of what is good to eat and skill in finding or making it
are not innate or developmental, but can only be learned from
others. In particular, the ability to be provident may seem to be
one of the least natural of human achievements, only to be acquired
by the experience either of an individual or a whole community.
2 In more advanced states of society, where it is not possible for
the individual, whatever his personal skills, to obtain sufficient
nourishment from his environment, the adult is in a position to
gain a stake in the resources of the community by negotiating
special rights for himself. This he is able to do by making a contribution to the ends of the community as a whole, or to the purpose of particular individuals. One way or another the adult is
usually able to earn a living. His knowledge of the needs of others
and of prevailing social practices and his solidarity with those in
the same position as himself often enable him to drive a bargain
which, if not actually equitable, will at least enable him to survive.
Once again, a typical case in which welfare rights are claimed for
adults is that in which this situation breaks down, in which the
contribution the adult is able to make is not required, or when
those who might require it have not the resources to provide
benefits in exchange, or when the prevailing social conditions or
ethos are not conducive to maintaining solidarity in bargaining.
   That the child is not able to create special rights for himself in
this way is again inherent in his nature and condition. In his
early years the child may not have a material contribution to make
either to the ends of society or the purposes of other individuals.
Even if they had such a contribution to make, they could not
themselves initially have the knowledge or skills necessary to
wring corresponding benefits from an unsympathetic community or
individuals, far less organise solidarity with others, for such
possibilities rely heavily on skill in communication and the ability
to predict the reactions of others. Both of these are essentially
learned.

THE CHILD'S RIGHT TO PROTECTION

The individual is threatened by gross and substantial harms not
only by the physical and animal world, but also by the malevo-
lence or self-interest of his fellows. In considering the child's
welfare rights to protection from such harms, much applies that
was said on the question of his right to material support on account
of his lack of physical strength, knowledge of the world and understanding of others. Consequently, the child is necessarily thrown

on the aid of his elders, not only for his material support, but
also for his protection. If this is not forthcoming from those
against whom he has special rights, it must be provided by the
community as a whole.

THE CHILD'S WELFARE RIGHT TO GUIDANCE

From infancy to a point well beyond that at which the child is
still dependent on others for material support and protection, the
child may act in such a way as to endanger himself or his substantial interests through ignorance of the material world or the
likely conduct of others, or through failure to predict what his
best interests are or are likely to be in the future. Guidance is
therefore something of which the child necessarily stands in need,
for at the point at which he first begins to act independently he
is, without guidance, inevitably ignorant of what the consequences of those acts will be and how they will affect him.

Adults too, of course, may damage their interests through
making mistakes about the world or about the intentions or likely
actions of others. They may also come to regret opportunities
missed or decisions made about how to lead their lives. Adults,
however, in addition to a substantial body of experience from
which to extrapolate in new situations, have also acquired habits
of caution and reflection before entering new situations and of
premeditation before abandoning present aims and seeking new
ones. It may also be thought a condition of being an adult that
one has some sense of which aims are mutually consistent and
which are mutually exclusive and an understanding that among
various in themselves attractive aims, some must be given priority
over others.

In these respects the situation of a child differs markedly. The
child is a progressively developing being, and the range of his
activities and movements is constantly widening. The experience
of being in new situations, in unknown places and among unfamiliar objects is therefore an especially frequent one. Habits of
reflection and prudence, furthermore, may be thought to be
learned rather than innate. Lacking the advantage of the kind of
instinct or sixth sense sometimes attributed to animals, and con-
fronting a more varied and in some respects more hazardous
environment than many animals, human beings can without guidance only find out about the world by testing and investigating it
for themselves. Unguided and unsuperintended investigation is
likely to be a risky procedure.

Not only, furthermore, must the child learn to move about
physically in an unfamiliar world, but certain of his actions and
acquired patterns of behaviour will importantly affect his later
interests and ways which the child himself cannot be expected to
foresee.

In addition to avoiding immediate and particular harms, furthermore, the child, unless he is to remain permanently dependent, or

live a relatively brief and accident-ridden life, needs to learn the
general principles upon which prudent conduct and a satisfactory
life may be based. As such knowledge belongs to the cumulative
wisdom of a society, these things can of necessity only be learned
from others.

THE RIGHT TO GUIDANCE, AND COMPULSION

Children do not always heed the warnings, advice and guidance
of their parents and may come to substantial harm if not actually
prevented from doing some things or obliged to do others. Para-
doxically it would, therefore, seem reasonable to speak of the
child as having a welfare right to compulsion and of adults failing
in their obligation to the child if they do not supply it when this
is necessary to protect him from the consequences of his ill-
considered acts. This is most obviously applicable to the case of
exposing himself to the danger of injury or ill-health. In a society
of any complexity like our own, however, many decisions concerning the child and importantly affecting his future may need
to be made at an age when the child himself is not only incapable
of making them, but may resist decisions which are clearly in his
interests when they run contrary to his more immediate wishes.
Choices relating to educational matters and in particular the
choice of whether or not the child is to undergo a process of formal education, or whether or not he should continue to do so after
a certain age may often fall into this category.(1)
   It may be thought that to speak of the right to be compelled to
do something is self-contradictory. This would certainly appear to
be the case if one holds with Hart that to be a right-holder is to be
one who may at his option choose or decline to do the thing specified by the right in question.(2) Such a view, however, appears
to result from a confusion between 'A has a right to X if he
chooses' and 'A has a right to X unless he chooses otherwise'. A
positive act of choice as a condition of having a right is only necessary to the first interpretation, yet it is the second which enables us to make the best sense of the notion of waiving, that is
choosing not to enjoy, a right already established.(3)
   Though the child may later be expected to become a fully
rational being, he cannot as yet divest himself of a right on which
his well-being depends, for to be a child in a normative sense is
precisely not to be able to make such choices. If a child is not in
a position to waive a right, be it to guidance, education, protection
or whatever, then the right must be considered not waived, and
therefore still in being.(4) Consequently the obligation to implement the right is undiminished by any words, signs or movements
ostensibly indicating waivure or protest which the right-holder
may be seen to make.

THE RIGHT TO EDUCATION

To claim a welfare right to education is to claim that an individual cannot provide for his own education and that if he does not receive education from others including those against whom he may have special rights, then he is liable to substantial harm. The claim that there is a right to education has, however, been made in various contexts and its justification has been discussed in terms of a number of different categories of rights. It is convenient to consider all of these discussions together at this point, though it will be argued that by far the most convincing and satisfactory justification of the right to education is when it is considered as a welfare right.

In addition to its most famous statement in Article 26 of the United Nations Universal Declaration of Human Rights (1948) and the Declaration of the Rights of the Child (1959) this right, or supposed right, is also mentioned in the International Covenant of Economic, Social and Cultural Rights (1966) and the American Declaration of the Rights and Duties of Man (1948). The European Social Charter (1961) contains no specific mention of the right to education. The first part of the Convention, however, mentions a right to vocational training and Article 7 clearly implies recognition of the right by the signatories and contains limits on the employment and other activities of young people which would interfere with their education. The right to education is specifically recognised in the basic law or constitution of Russia, China, Egypt, Venezuela and a number of other states. It can therefore be said that the right to education is in some sense recognised as a legal right in those countries, as it is in such countries as West Germany, which specifically recognise Human Rights as part of their national law.(5)

It is sometimes held that there is not strictly a legal right to ` education in Great Britain. Though local authorities are obliged to provide school places for all children in their area unless a satisfactory alternative is provided by the parent, the child himself cannot legally claim this right, while parents taking action against local authorities or local authorities taking action against parents do not strictly do so on the child's behalf.(6) In a wider sense of the word right discussed in chapter 11, however, it may reasonably be said that the law protects the child's right to education, just as it protects his right not to be molested or ill-treated.(7)

As we saw in chapter 4, the individual has a prima facie right to the implementation of his legal rights unless the law in question is unjust. It would, therefore, appear that possession of a legal right to education - even in the wider sense mentioned above - provides some substance for the claim that one is morally entitled to receive it.

GREGORY'S CLAIM THAT WE SHOULD DISPENSE WITH THE RIGHT TO EDUCATION

Rejecting the notion of a right to education other than in the descriptive sense as it appears 'in particular constitutional set-ups'
(8) Gregory suggests that adequate reasons for providing education are furnished by considerations of public interest and the
needs and interests of individuals.(9) It should be said from the
outset that Gregory's position appears subject to a certain inconsistency. His underlying ethical view is that there is an 'element
of personal decision in one's moral commitments'(10) and that talk
of rights is essentially a matter of making proposals or recommendations for action. Consequently, much current talk of moral
rights is, as he puts it, 'ontologically mysterious' and 'would be
unconvincing to men and societies who do not embrace the particular morality or vision of society that enables one to talk of the
right to education'(11) or did not 'even possess the concept of
moral and human rights'.(12) Though this kind of view may, in
itself, be internally coherent, it is difficult to reconcile with his
later claim that public interest and, in particular, the needs and
interests of individuals are 'good reasons' for providing education
in a straightforward and unmysterious way.(13) A particular
society's conception of 'the public interest', not to mention the
importance such a society attached to the needs and interests of
individuals as reasons for action, would appear to be as much
subject to the contingencies of time and place as the moral vision
which permitted such a society to talk of the right to education or
its possession of the concept of a human right.
    The objection to basing individuals' claims to the provision of
education simply on needs, however extreme, or interests, however vital, is that the grounds they provide are insufficient unless it is first conceded that extreme need and vital interest justify
claims of right. If someone's need does not create a right one only
has a reason for meeting it if, as a matter of psychological fact,
one is moved by the spirit of sympathy or benevolence. Even if it
is conceded that there is a general duty of benevolence, one would
be doing no wrong by electing not to fulfil it on this particular
occasion or in respect of this particular individual.

THE RIGHT TO EDUCATION AS THE CORRELATIVE OF PARENTAL DUTIES

Assuming that to possess a right is simply to stand to benefit from
the performance of another's duty (14) Olafson takes his task in
justifying the right to education to be the discovery of grounds
for holding that the older generation has, by virtue of various
acts and acceptances, incurred the obligation of providing education for the young. In essence, his arguments are the following:
1 It is the parents' act which brings the child into the world.
2 Members of the older generation owe restitution for the education

they themselves have received.
3 They also owe restitution for the benefits they receive from the
fact that people in general are educated.

Olafson also suggests a possible fourth argument that, in due
course, members of the younger generation will have to perform
certain civic duties, which they cannot do without certain minimal
educational attainments which Olafson specifies.(15)

To comment on Olafson's arguments in order:
1 Despite Melden's counter-example of the man who causes a litter
of kittens to be brought helpless into the world (by placing the
parents together in the mating season)(16) Olafson's first argument would not appear to be entirely without substance. Even in
the case of the kittens Melden recognises the duty to dispose of
them humanely. Any unwillingness - if unwilling we are - to describe this as a right of the kittens to humane treatment stems from
our doubts about the status of animals as possible right holders
rather than about Melden's responsibility for his act and its consequences. Proof of the invalidity of Melden's counter-example is
the fact that if it were valid it would prove too much. Not only
would it show that a couple are under no obligation to feed and
care for the children they bring into the world. It would also suggest that no one was obliged to make reparation for any harm or
injury resulting from his acts.

It is no doubt true as Melden claims that not all couples have
sexual intercourse with the intention of bringing a child into the
world. We are, however, responsible for our negligences as
well as our intentional actions. It may also seem that in not only
conceiving the child but in allowing it to be born and nourishing
it so that it survives beyond immediate infancy the couple, or
those members of the older generation who bring it up, enter into
some form of parent-child relationship with it, thereby progressively incurring role-related obligations towards it. In so far as
Olafson is concerned to show that a particular child may, in the
first instance, have a special right to education against particular
adults, his argument would therefore appear to be well founded.
It fails, however, to show that there is a universal right to education, since it establishes rights for neither orphans nor those
whose parents are, for one reason or another, unable to provide
education for them.
2 Olafson's second argument represents an attempt to extend the
range of individuals to whom an education is owed. Melden objects
to the logic of the present older generation attempting to repay
the younger generation for benefits they have received from their
seniors.(17) This, however, is to take the argument too literally.
A sensible interpretation of Olafson's argument would seem to be
that when the members of an older generation educate the younger
it is because they are interested in the well-being of their des-
cendants, and it would not be legitimate for any group (e.g. the
present 'older generation') to profit from this practice without
bearing their part in due course.

A stronger point in Melden's criticism is that though Olafson's argument explains the obligation of the older generation it does not, in fact, justify the right of the younger. The older generation do not on this argument have obligations to particular members of the younger generation. The obligation they are under is to make a contribution to the educational enterprise as a whole. Members of the younger generation would not have rights on this count but would simply be the fortunate beneficiaries of the older generation's fulfilment of its duties. No injustice would be shown if one or more members of the younger generation were to miss out on their education. All members of the older generation, having benefited from education, have an obligation to contribute to the enterprise, but no right has as yet been shown on the part of individual members of the younger generation to benefit from it. The argument that they have a right by virtue of the contribution they will later make to society's well-being is tenuous. Those who are destined to die young, and those who fail to develop their talents because of parental neglect of their education will make no such contribution. They will not earn their right and neglect of their education would, therefore, seem no injustice.

3 Olafson's third argument, like the second, establishes an obligation to contribute to the enterprise of education but not a distinctive obligation to members of the younger generation who, if they are lucky enough to receive an education, once again find themselves in the position of third party beneficiaries.

4 At first sight it would seem that such individual rights as are created under Olafson's fourth argument may be negated by the state or community simply deciding that this or that individual will not be asked to perform such civic duties as voting or taking part in government. In chapter 7, however, we saw that this would infringe the individual's rights of participation, for involvement in 'civic duties' is not only an obligation but itself a right. More, however, will be said later on about the relationship between an individual's democratic rights of participation and his right to education.(18)

A UNIVERSAL RIGHT TO EDUCATION

If we seek to establish a right to education on the part of all human beings, or indeed all rational or potentially rational beings independent of particular constitutional arrangements or any given transactions or actively incurred responsibilities, this may be either as a right of freedom or as a welfare right. The right to education as a right of freedom would, of course, be a right to obtain education or to educate oneself by one's own efforts without interference. This is perhaps not what most people are concerned about when the right to education is discussed in a modern context. Even this right, however, is not, and certainly has not always been, universally respected. One has only to think of the control exercised over the processes of teaching and learning by religious and political authorities at various times and in various

places, not to mention the narrow limits to which the educational
experience of many women has been and still is restricted. Yet to
pursue knowledge and develop an understanding of oneself and
the world is clearly an end which the individual may desire, and
which would not normally conflict with what can be regarded as
rights of others. It is therefore difficult to see how one individual
or group of individuals could be justified in attempting to frustrate
the pursuit of this end by others. On a general level it may be
argued that in so far as the individual is not born subject to the
purposes of others, he has the right to decide his own destiny in
the exercise of his free decisions. At the very least, therefore, he
would appear to have the right not to be positively prevented
from developing the necessary understanding to do these things
on equal terms with others.

This does not imply that there is a right of free access to all
knowledge or even that it is in the best interests of the individual
to have unrestricted access to knowledge at all stages of his development. It does, however, rule out such interferences with the
development of understanding as are represented by indoctrination and systematic censorship, which give the individual a misleading picture of the universe and his place in it.

That rights are infringed by the placing of deliberate impedi-
ments in the way of those who want to learn may seem only too
obvious. What may be less so is that if adults infringe this right
through negligence, through their words and actions accidentally
causing error, ignorance and irrationality to develop, they owe a
duty of reparation for the harm done, thereby creating a corresponding special right on the part of the individual harmed. This
obligation is the more incontestable in so far as the individual concerned has been actively encouraged in the belief that adults are
in some way an authority in respect of belief and reliable sources
of information about the world.

The young and immature would therefore appear to have the
right to expect that adults will be at some pains to correct errors
and misconceptions which arise from their utterances and the manner in which they conduct their affairs and, indeed, that they
will strive to avoid misleading the young in the first place. This,
in turn, would seem to imply the provision at very least of a non-
miseducative environment for the young. This is something which
cannot be achieved without a certain expenditure of effort and
resources. Given the natural propensity of the human young to
learn, a non-miseducative environment is, in many respects,
indistinguishable from a positively educative one. Needless to say,
the adult generation cannot escape the obligation of striving to
provide a non-miseducative environment and painfully correcting
misconceptions to which they inadvertently give rise by excluding
the young from human contact altogether or even by confining
them to a sheltered environment away from the hurly-burly of real
adult human affairs. This, besides itself creating a positively misleading picture of the world, would be a restriction of the liberty
of the young of the grossest kind.

If we were conscientious in fulfilling our obligation to avoid misleading the young, and in correcting any seriously misleading
impressions to which our conduct might give rise, it is not altogether clear that we should not be going a long way towards meeting the supposed right to education as it is usually understood,
particularly if the right is given a fairly limited, conservative
interpretation. Each form of knowledge implies the possibility of
a corresponding area of ignorance and error. Unless we greatly
changed our ways, we should need to forewarn the young against
the illogicalities and exaggerations of persuasion which we custom-
arily employ. Misstatements of fact are sometimes made, deliberately or inadvertently, so that we are obliged to put the young
human being in a position to distinguish between truth and false-
hood. There is need to undo such moral corruption and insensit-
ivity as will be learned through contact with adults in the conduct
of their daily affairs. We do not always strive to understand others,
or their point of view and are therefore prone to refer to them
misleadingly in a way likely to impoverish the understanding of
those who happen to hear us, but as yet lack their own canons of
judgment. Our general lack of concern for aesthetic matters and
the 'spiritual' dimension of human life (if such there be) may also
be said to create a distorted impression of the potentialities of the
human condition which only a careful programme of education can
prevent.

THE RIGHT TO EDUCATION AS A WELFARE RIGHT

It is one criterion of successfully claiming a welfare right that the
good claimed should be something without which the individual
sustains some relatively serious or permanent harm. If we are to
claim education as such a right, it is necessary to consider at
some length just what it is that the individual would be deprived
of if he did not have the benefit of education.

It is not proposed here to attempt any independent analysis of
the concept of education. In this context it is convenient to refer
to Oakeshott's eloquent and lucid account of the educational engagement,(19) in so far as many of the basic features of his
position would command widespread acceptance. The notion of a
'right' to education would no doubt be totally foreign to Oakeshott's way of thinking, as is amply shown by his reference to
those being educated as 'postulants' to the human condition. His
account of the educational engagement is nevertheless valuable,
for the emphasis it places on the extent to which being a human
being is dependent on learning.

Learning, Oakeshott argues, is to be distinguished from the
'spontaneous flowering of settled potentialities' and from 'the organ-
ism's natural and continuing accommodation to its environment'.(20)
For Oakeshott, the human world is composed not of things, but of
meanings. 'Human beings are what they understand themselves to
be; they are composed entirely of beliefs about themselves and

about the world they inhabit. They inhabit the world of intellig-
ibles, that is the world composed, not of physical objects, but of
occurrences which have meanings and are recognised in manners
to which they are alternatives'.(21) As such, human beings are
essentially dependent on teaching by someone who is already
initiated in the tradition of those meanings, and therefore inevitably dependent on the resources and efforts of others for their
education.

In considering what loss is entailed when someone simply receives
no initiation into the realms of human meaning, we may be provoked
by Oakeshott's constant references to excellences and subtleties of
thought and imagination and by his rejection of vocational learning
and socialisation into the present-day world,(22) into believing
that he is concerned with a kind of education which the majority
of the world's population have never received, but without which
many of them manage to live what is arguably a fully human life.
This may indeed be Oakeshott's intention. It is nevertheless true
that human beings are dependent on what is learned not only for
an understanding of the higher regions of mathematics, science
and literature, but also for such homely things as the use of
language, the grasp of such institutions as personal property, the
rudiments of courtesy and moral agency and an elementary factual
knowledge of things outside their immediate experience. Human
beings are also dependent on learning for such basic things as the
conventions relating to elementary functions such as eating, excret-
ing and mating, which some educationalists may be inclined to
dismiss as elementary socialisation. To receive no education at all
is to be initiated into none of these matters, at however elementary
a level and consequently not to learn them, for no one can achieve
any degree of competence in these areas without constant guidance
and direction. Failure to receive education is not simply to be left
with a restricted view and distorted understanding of the universe
and our place in it. It is to have no understanding at all. It is also
to have no possibility of independent existence among other human
beings.

At the very least it would seem arguable that though the individual who receives no education does not necessarily perish as he
does if his physical needs are not met, the deprivation and injustice, the degradation of an individual and the setting of his vital
interests at nought would at least approach in gravity the act of
allowing him to die for want of food or elementary care, protection
and guidance.

TO HOW MUCH EDUCATION IS THERE A RIGHT?

So far it is not clear that a right has been established to anything
very positive in the way of educational content. It has been argued
that the child has a right not to be misled, or as a right of reparation, the right to be disabused when this has taken place. It has
also been shown that he has a welfare right not to be left to

languish in a state of gross ignorance such that he is unable to communicate with others or lead an independent human life among his fellows. It is not evident, however, that this entitles each and every individual to such things as an introduction to the complexities of mathematics or to any systematic exposition of empirical data about the world outside his immediate experience.

Clearly, we cannot here list the minimum curricular requirements to be met before the individual's welfare right to education can be said to have been implemented. It is, however, possible to indicate some considerations to be taken into account in defining this right more precisely.

(1) Education and the right to protection from gross material need
Education may be regarded as a good to which one might have a right both as an end and as a means. In some countries basic literacy and numeracy may become the sine qua non of employment, and therefore necessary if the individual is to meet his basic needs by his own efforts. The provision of education to the required level – which may vary from time to time and place to place – may therefore be the necessary means to the implementation of the welfare right to be protected from material deprivation. It may be thought that this does not establish a right to any particular level of education since the individual's material needs can be met in other ways, such as community support or charitable benefactions. To be reduced to life-long dependence on the support of others, however, – even supposing this to be forthcoming – might itself be regarded as an unacceptable humiliation and therefore as a harm from which the individual is entitled to be protected.

(2) Education and the right of democratic participation
Olafson, as we saw, declines to enter upon a justification of the right to education in terms of other, superordinate civil and political rights on the grounds that such other rights themselves need to be justified.(23) In the present study, however, arguments have already been presented to establish that the individual has rights of democratic participation. It is therefore of interest to consider whether it can be shown that the effective exercise of rights of participation implies a certain level of education, and also whether inability to participate in the political life of one's community is to be seen as a harm of such magnitude that protection from such a disability constitutes a welfare right.

In this connection, it has been argued that in addition to certain specifically economic and political knowledge, political participation in a democracy implies the ability to choose between courses of action not only intelligently but wisely. This entails the ability to 'weight' various conflicting considerations, and consequently requires a broadly based range of understandings in all the available forms of knowledge.(24) It has also been argued that if individuals are to participate effectively in democratic processes their educational experience must be such as to create the disposition to do so.(25)

To show that the right to sufficient education to take part in the political life of a democracy is specifically a welfare right, two possible lines of argument appear to be available. On the one hand, it might be possible to argue that someone who is, individually or as a member of a class, not able to do this is liable to find himself the victim of acute material disadvantage as the result of political manipulation and exploitation by others. This would seem a far from implausible claim. It might also be possible to show that to be unable to play a part in the political life of one's community was itself a major deprivation. This argument certainly opens up a promising line of speculation, but must necessarily remain inconclusive within the scope of the present study. Such an approach would seem to require the establishment of some kind of ideal of the whole or complete human being, failure to achieve which was to be regarded as in some way intolerable or morally unacceptable. This argument, if it could be made out, would no doubt bring not only political education into the ambit of the welfare right to education, but also many other specific educational achievements without which the individual was to be seen as suffering harm or deprivation. This might, however, also have the highly undesirable consequence of diluting the concept of a welfare right to the point where it was useless in urging the prompt fulfilment of certain needs and the provision of important protections.

(3) Education and the good life
Turning to arguments more closely connected with the justification of education as an end, it has been suggested that an individual has at least an interest in devoting a great deal of his time to the pursuit of knowledge and understanding. One ground given for this is that any increase in knowledge and understanding throws further light on the question of what he ought to do,(26) even though it may eventually leave him little time in which to do it. Given this strong interest which the individual has in maximising his knowledge and understanding, might it not be held that he has the right to receive as much education as he desires, or at least the right to be educated to the full extent of his capacities?

In considering this view, however, it must be borne in mind that we are concerned to make out a claim for education as a welfare right, for which the main justification is the avoidance of gross or irremediable harm. The failure to realise to the full a capacity for acquiring knowledge and understanding or indeed any other legitimate capacity is certainly a matter for regret. It is, however, scarcely on a par with suffering death from starvation or disease.

It may be further recalled that one of the elements in the justification of a welfare right is that certain gross misfortunes take place in a world of relative affluence, in which resources are available to prevent them. The victim's moral indignation at being deprived of the resources he needs is justified in part by the fact that while he suffers gross harm or misfortune others do not, and indeed have their relatively minor wants met. The person who is prevented from fully realising his capacities is by no means in an analogous position. Far from being singled out for exceptional misfortune, the person who does not realise his capacities to the full is in no different position from the remainder of humanity, for not to realise to the full those capacities which are important to one is an all but universal part of the human condition. We saw earlier that there were difficulties in arguing from capacities to welfare rights, and it may well be thought that in so far as capacities should influence the allocation of resources at all, each of us has unextended capacities of his own which might be developed with whatever surplus resources are at his disposal.

This is not to deny that the right to develop one's capacities by one's own effort and at the expense of one's own resources is an important right of freedom and that it therefore is desirable that the general arrangements of the community to achieve other important ends such as security or political stability should not needlessly inhibit or forbid this. It may also well be that as a matter of public policy it is considered expedient to allow some individuals to develop their capacities more fully than is possible to everyone. This, however, would not strictly be a moral right, but a positive right instituted in the interests of achieving a certain socially desirable end.(27)

Even if we do not have the right to be educated to the full extent of our capacities, we may still be inclined to ask whether the individual has not some right to receive more education than may seem to be implied by the notion of a welfare right. This right might seem to be fully met if the individual were placed in a position in which he was capable of leading a simple existence of limited perspective, either among others like himself or in company with more enlightened people who treated him with consideration. Such a person's condition, it might be thought, could not seriously be compared to that of someone dying from hunger or disease or ignorant to the point of bestiality.

As a compromise between the right to be educated to the full extent of one's capacities, on the one hand, and the minimal level of educational attainment indicated above, it may be suggested that the individual is entitled to receive education from the community, at least until he has gained sufficient insight into the pursuit of knowledge and the various modes of human understanding to decide for himself whether to continue this pursuit by his own efforts and at the expense of whatever resources of his own he may possess.(28)

This possibility may seem to raise further questions about the point at which someone may be said to be in a position to choose whether or not to continue the pursuit of an activity which is intrinsically worthwhile. It may, for example, be thought that to understand an activity sufficiently to make choices concerning it is, among other things, to see the reasons for pursuing it and therefore to be in some degree committed to it. On this view it would appear that one is never really in a position to make such a choice, for either one acts in ignorance, or one is already committed and the choice no longer open.

This conclusion, however, is unjustified. The reasons for
choosing to pursue one worthwhile activity rather than another
include not only reasons intrinsic to the activities themselves, but
also reasons connected with one's own capacities, predilections
and other commitments. There is, therefore, no difficulty about
understanding the intrinsic reasons for pursuing this activity
rather than that, and at the same time deciding to do something
else in the light of reasons of a different kind.

A more substantial question is whether there is indeed a distinction to be made between the degree of education required by
an individual's welfare right and that required by his being able
to choose to continue his pursuit of knowledge and understanding
by his own efforts. In so far as the more elementary degree of
education envisaged contains a genuine element of understanding,
the recipient must already be in a position to undertake positive
efforts to extend his understanding if only by means of his private
reflections. Such, indeed, is bound to be the case in so far as his
understanding is properly so called and not merely a misleading
form of consciousness which suggests that there is nothing more
of importance for him to learn, or that it is in some sense not
appropriate or feasible for him to do so. That an individual should
be placed in a position to choose whether to continue his pursuit
of knowledge and understanding may therefore seem to be not
something additional to the implementation of his welfare right to
education, but an unavoidable consequence of it.

One final point should be made. Since welfare rights are based
on need, the amount of education to which there is a right is a
matter not of inputs but of outcomes. The right to education as a
welfare right is therefore not to be seen in terms of a number of
years of education, but of a level of knowledge and understanding to be reached, or in some cases, perhaps, a level beyond
which no further progress may be made and after which only custodial care remains possible. This consideration provides support
for Principle 5 of the United Nations Declaration of Rights of the
Child (1959) that: 'The child who is physically, mentally or
socially handicapped shall be given the treatment, education and
care required by his particular condition.'(29) Such a child has
no less of a right to education because the social cost of imple-
menting this right is higher than in the case of others, or because
the material return for attempting to do so may be relatively
limited.

17 Children's rights and the children's rights controversy

Although the main philosophical issues which it was proposed to consider in this study have now been dealt with, it may seem appropriate to reconsider, by way of example and in a necessarily summary form, some of the children's rights claims noted in chapter 1. In so doing it is proposed to make clear how the theoretical considerations advanced earlier have relevance to an important difference of view which had, and may continue to have, obvious practical consequences for many schools and other educational institutions.

Whatever may now be thought of the claims made in the course of that controversy, it must be recognised that when they were first made they were capable of arousing excitement, not to say passion, in many of those closely involved. It will equally be evident from the account of events at the height of the controversy that a number of busy and relatively senior individuals in the educational world expended much time and energy in the process of containing what threatened to become a tense and difficult situation. Though there appear to have been no serious acts of violence or personal injuries and no extensive damage to buildings and equipment it is difficult to estimate the educational harm entailed by the loss of goodwill and mutual hostility between school authorities and pupils.

No amount of philosophical analysis can resolve genuine conflicts of interest and in some situations there may be such a genuine conflict of interests between young people who wish to live in a freer and more adult manner, and adults who feel that their good standing in the eyes of their peers depends on their ability to prevent such a change taking place. Towards the end of this chapter, however, ways will be suggested in which acrimony over children's rights claims may be engendered not by such conflicts of interest at all, but by misunderstanding. As result of misunderstandings about what is implied by the assertion or denial of a right, each side, it will be argued, may feel obliged to demand more than the other can honourably concede. Consequently, each may find the other unreasonable or oppressive and himself over-react accordingly.

As may also become clear from our brief reconsideration of some of the rights claims noted in chapter 1, many of these, often expressed in the form of short, peremptory demands, actually involve claims not to a single right, but to rights belonging to a number of the categories of rights explored in earlier chapters. As was seen, different kinds of rights claims involve different

approaches to the question of justification. Assertions and denials
of many claims will therefore inevitably have been at cross-
purposes, not to say subject to rhetorical misrepresentation in
the heat of debate.

In this final chapter an attempt will be made to unravel the
various rights claims involved in particular demands and, with
due hesitation, to suggest under what circumstances and in what
senses the claims might be regarded as valid. By referring to
earlier chapters an attempt will also be made to clarify what is
being said, and perhaps more importantly, what is not being said
when claims to particular rights are asserted or denied.

'THE CHILD IS ENTITLED TO BE CONSIDERED AS A PERSON IN HIS OWN RIGHT'

This is the first, and in some respects the most important of the
supposed rights of children. Unlike other rights it is not a right
to do or have a particular thing or category of things and it may
even be doubted whether it is properly seen as itself a right and
not rather a precondition of having any rights at all. To assert
that someone is a person is to claim not only that he has interests,
but that his interests may not be simply set aside if the only
reasons for so doing are the wishes or advantages of others. It is
to claim, for example, that his liberty may not be restricted or his
point of view ignored simply for the sake of other people's convenience, and that he may not be shown off or humiliated for the
sake of other people's vanity.

From what has been said in chapters 11-16 it will be clear that
children are persons with rights, and not simply future persons
or potential right-holders who will eventually possess the full
range of adult rights, but at present have none at all. If children's rights differ from those of adults, it is not because children
are any less persons or entitled to any less consideration but
because their needs and capacities, and consequently their interests, differ from those of adults in ways that have important consequences for their rights of freedom and democratic participation
as well as for their welfare rights.

To be entitled to be treated as a person is certainly to have the
right to equal consideration with other persons, for as we saw,(1)
no reason can be found for generally giving the interests of one
person priority over those of others. The right to equal consideration, however, is not simply a right to be treated identically
with others, but, on the contrary, a right to different treatment
in the light of one's differing interests and circumstances. The
right to be treated as a person is therefore not to be construed
as the right never to be treated paternally and certainly not as
the right never to be coerced. All may be coerced into respecting
the rights of others, and some, particularly the young, may without infringement of their rights be coerced for their own good.
That the law and various social practices allow the child to be

treated differently from adults and may, in particular, impose
restrictions on the child which adults do not suffer is therefore
not ipso facto a reason for saying that society fails to treat children as persons. There is indeed no inherent absurdity in saying
that, as Berger puts it: 'there is one code of civil liberty for
adults and another for children'.(2) Differences of treatment only
become grounds for the complaint that someone is not being treated
as a person when they reflect inequalities of consideration or show
that the interests of one category of individuals are simply disregarded.

'CHILDREN HAVE CERTAIN RIGHTS OF FREEDOM'

Earlier it was shown that the claim to a right of freedom may con-
ceal an ambiguity between the claim that what one does is not
wrong, and the claim that others ought not to prevent one from
doing it. Subsequently it was held that not all prohibitions by
adults (including parents and teachers) render the action prohibited a wrong, and not all attempts by those adults to restrict
the liberty of the young are justified. An individual may nevertheless be prevented from undertaking what he proposes if the
action in question would infringe the rights of others, or in the
case of a child or someone not fully rational, be damaging to his
own best interests. These considerations would seem relevant to
claims that children, including school pupils, have rights of freedom in relation to (1) personal appearance, (2) the use of drugs,
alcohol and tobacco and the exercise of sexual freedom, (3) publication and expression of opinion subject to no greater degree of
restriction than is encountered in the adult world.(3)

(1) Personal appearance
At a certain stage the child clearly has an interest in exercising
freedom in the matter of personal appearance, for in some degree
what one appears to be is what one is. One's appearance pro-
foundly affects the way one is seen by others and above all the
esteem in which one is held by one's peers. It may also be thought
that children should be allowed some limited freedom of choice in
this area in order to acquire a sense of taste and appropriateness
while still in the protected and educative environment of the family or school.

In the light of arguments considered in earlier chapters, however, it would seem that the child's freedom in this matter may
without infringement of his rights be restricted on two kinds of
grounds. First, the child can only be thought of as having this
right in so far as he actually has an interest in being allowed freedom, that is in so far as he is able to choose in such a way as not
to harm his own interests. The child has a welfare right (of guidance and protection) vis-à-vis his elders to be prevented from
flouting conventions which he may not fully understand, to the
extent of attracting ridicule or hostility, particularly on the part

of those in a position to affect his substantial material interests.

Second, children's freedom may legitimately be restricted by the rights of others. While the child does not provide his own clothes, his choice may seem quite properly to be limited by what his parents are prepared to pay for. If it is thought, furthermore, that the outlandish appearance of children reflects badly on their parents and damages the latter's interests, it would seem to follow that children do not normally have the right to dress outlandishly. Not only would this infringe any rights of gratitude and deference which parents may be thought to possess. It also infringes their right of security and parents would seem justified in exercising a degree of coercion in order to protect their own interests from damage of this kind. This, however, does not mean that parents are entitled to absolute control over the child's appearance, for to dress him in such a way as to attract ridicule or humiliation would be to infringe the rights of security to which he too is entitled. Nor would it entitle parents to control the dress of their children simply in accordance with their own tastes. This argument depends on there being an actual likelihood that the parents' interests will suffer from the bad opinion others will gain of them and their children.

The rights of the child vis-à-vis the school in such matters is subject to slightly different considerations. No infringement of the child's rights of freedom is committed if the school forbids the wearing of certain things in order to protect the rights of others. Pupils may therefore quite reasonably be obliged to dress in conformity with the requirements of decency and hygiene, or in such a way as to avoid damage to property (stiletto heels), injury to persons (metal studded jackets) or destruction of good order and a viable educational atmosphere. Pupils in a multi-racial school, for example, might therefore be reasonably forbidden to wear Black Power or National Front insignia. Such prohibitions, however, may seem relatively uncontroversial – the real issue arises when a school insists that its pupils are to wear 'uniform' and forbids the wearing of other, otherwise unexceptionable, articles.

Private schools may, of course, make whatever stipulations they like as a condition of entry, though parents who concurred in any particularly humiliating requirements, if such they were, would, with the school, be guilty of infringing their children's rights of security. Normally, however, schools, unlike parents, do not provide the pupils' clothing or hairdresser's fees. The educational resources which they have at their disposal belong to the community and are not the property of the school to withhold or bestow in return for a special right to control the child's appearance. There would therefore be no moral justification for popular schools in an area (selective or otherwise) making this a condition of entry, to satisfy the idiosyncratic and personal aspirations of heads or governors. The justification usually given for the uniform rule is that it improves morale and enhances the school's reputation, as a result of which all pupils in the school benefit. This, however, would not show that pupils' rights are not infringed, for, as has been seen, the collective good and individual rights often conflict without contradiction. It might perhaps be argued that pupils may be presumed to accept the requirements since, education being an important good, all may be presumed to consent to what is necessary for its achievement, but this is unconvincing. Few would suppose that the wearing of school uniform is actually essential to the achievement of education, for this would be to deny that education could take place in the schools of many countries overseas. The most that can plausibly be claimed is that education is rather more effectively or more easily achieved in schools where children wear clothes of uniform appearance, and even this, though widely and perhaps rightly believed, has scarcely been shown. It would therefore seem difficult to deny that the school which attempts to coerce children into wearing uniform and punishes or withholds educational benefits from them if they do not, infringes their rights of freedom.

If the heads or governors of a school wish pupils to wear certain clothes and not others, their only recourse consistent with respect for pupils' rights of freedom would seem to be to attempt to persuade children and their parents of the benefits they believe to flow from being a uniform school and of the desirability of pupils who are inclined to prefer mufti waiving their rights for the good of all. This, of course, does not alter the fact that if a school thinks that the benefits of being a uniform school are very great to some or all pupils, it may act rightly in ignoring the rights of those who wish to wear other clothes and in using whatever means of coercion it possesses in order to enforce its rule. As we saw in chapter 3, however, the morally appropriate attitude when one finds oneself obliged to override a right for the sake of the greater good is one of reluctance, apology and deference towards those whose right is overruled.

(2) Tobacco, alcohol and sexual freedom
That the prohibition of tobacco, alcohol and sexual activity should be a focus of children's rights activity is not surprising given that these things are commonly regarded by the immature as a mark of adult status. To see such prohibitions as purely arbitrary symbols of domination like the prohibition on all who are not prefects to walk about with their hands in their pockets, however, is scarcely justified.

Adults on whom children are materially dependent would seem to have the right to take steps to avoid the additional burden and damage to their reputation arising from their children's ill-health, drunkenness or pregnancy. Children capable of appreciating the consequences of their acts would also seem to act wrongly (that is, to be exercising no rights of freedom in the sense of liberties) if they involved their parents in such risks. Since, furthermore, the use of tobacco and alcohol and untimely sexual activity may reasonably be thought to have consequences which are in various ways undesirable to the agent and sometimes irreversible, it may also be thought that adults owe it to young people as a right of

guidance and protection to prevent them engaging in any of these
activities until they are unmistakably in a position to appreciate
the consequences of their actions and make their own decisions.
The only serious moral dilemma would appear to arise from the fact
that some educational institutions contain pupils of such an age
that no one would think it necessary or right to forbid them to
drink, smoke or have sexual intercourse if they had left school.
Clearly, it would be an infringement of the rights of such pupils
to forbid them to engage in such activities or make their benefiting from the school's resources conditional on their abstention if
this were a purely arbitrary preference of educators and other
adults. If there are morally acceptable grounds for such a prohibition, this would seem to be the protection of younger children
in the same institution who might be influenced by their elders
and who ought to be prevented from engaging in such activities
for their own good.

(3) Publication
When the right is claimed for pupils to publish views, opinions
and literary productions without more restrictions than are operative in the adult world, certain distinctions are to be made.
(a) School magazines and suchlike are often produced with the
aid of school staff and resources. There seems no reason why the
school should make such resources available for publishing material which is anti-educational in its effects or blatantly at odds
with the standards the school ought to be seen to uphold. This
would be to allow the misappropriation of resources provided by
society at large for educational ends.
(b) Denial of the right to criticise the school via the public media
is all too readily confused with denial of the civil rights of the
individual to criticise the political authority under which he lives.
This, however, is not the relationship in which the pupil stands
to his teachers. The relationship between the pupil and his
teachers is a working, professional relationship in which each side
has access to privileged information about the other. Gross incom-
petence or abuse ought not, of course, to be protected from criticism, but it is reasonable that the teacher who strives to do his
best for the child should be able to expect not to be publicly
lampooned for his foibles, momentary lapses and minor short-
comings. Likewise, it is quite proper for pupils to be protected
from public comment by teachers who have special access to
information about them.
  There is a further consideration. There are certain professional
relationships in which the duties of those involved cannot be
clearly defined in terms of specific outcomes. The relations of
doctors with their patients and barristers with their clients are
both of this kind. Barring gross lapses of professional conduct
and competence all that can be demanded is the good will and best
efforts of the professional in the interests of his client, without
any guarantee that these efforts will actually result in success.
The client, for his part, is required to give his confidence and

trust to the professional and to show that he has trust and confidence publicly. It is unreasonable to expect to benefit from
someone's good will and best efforts while publicly expressing
criticism and dissent. Arguably, the relationships between teachers and pupils may be role-relationships of this kind, creating
special rights and obligations of the sort discussed in chapter
8. Such a relationship would meet the criterion of being just
in the sense specified in that chapter, in so far as it may be supposed to benefit both parties.
(c) It may happen that a pupil publishes through the media literary material or opinion and comment on general matters (politics,
morals, religion, adolescent activities) and that the school feels
that such a publication by someone known to be one of its pupils
brings the school into disrepute. The school is not (usually) a
private organisation like a political party or club, which may discipline or expel its members as it thinks fit, but an organ of
public provision. Pupils, furthermore, are not employees or sub-
ordinates who may be subjected to certain constraints as conditions
of employment, and it is dubious whether even employees may
properly be prohibited from general expressions of views not
touching their organisation's aims or interests. It is therefore difficult to see how the school can forbid publications in this third
category without infringing the pupil's rights. Once again, however, this is not to deny that in certain tense situations the school
authorities may sometimes quite legitimately override pupils' rights
and attempt to lay down and enforce hard and fast rules in an
attempt to prevent what they conceive to be a greater evil.

THE RIGHT OF PUPILS TO PARTICIPATE IN THE MANAGEMENT OF THEIR SCHOOLS

As was argued in chapter 14, the school is not an independent
polity and the community at large is entitled to set limits on how
its resources are employed and to some extent to lay down the
limits of responsibility and power. Pupils' rights of democratic
participation are further limited by what they can, as a matter of
fact, be expected to decide prudently for themselves or responsibly for others. Within these admittedly fairly narrow limits, however, there were held to be no grounds for denying pupils the
right to the nearest approach possible to equality of influence in
matters affecting their daily lives. From this it would seem to
follow (a) that pupils have a right to take democratically decisions
upon which nothing of great moment hangs (but which may seem
to be of importance to them), (b) that maximum opportunity ought
to be given for pupils' preferences to be made known directly by
their chosen representatives to those by whom school decisions
concerning them are made. This would appear to imply a right to
such institutions as consultative school councils and representation
at the meetings of governors and others.
    It may be thought that there is a further reason why people have

a right to such consultative institutions at the point of decision. This is that the provision of such institutions may help them to understand how and why certain decisions which concern them are made. To act or be required to act without understanding why one does so or is required to do so is an extreme form of the negation of the right of freedom, for if one does not even know why one acts as one does, the purposes for which one acts cannot in any sense be said to be one's own. Children may not, of course, be in a position to understand the reason for all the things they are required to do. All that is being claimed is the right that all practicable steps should be taken to reduce the area of their ignorance and the consequent heteronomy of their actions.

THE RIGHT TO ORGANISE DEMOCRATICALLY

It is difficult to see how a school can rightly forbid pupils to join a particular organisation or even to act as a responsible and law-abiding officer of such organisations provided they do not personally foment disruption or other anti-educational activities among their fellow pupils.

A more interesting question is how seriously pupils' organisations are to be taken and how far their 'official' pronouncements are to be treated as more than an expression of the personal views of those who make them. Certainly, such 'spokesmen' cannot claim to speak for pupils or adolescents in general, but only for their own members, and this only after some democratic process which can be regarded as consultation or the conferring of a mandate. Such representatives can, furthermore, only seriously be regarded as such if it is thought that they have some understanding of what is involved in speaking on behalf of others collectively and that pupils who in some sense authorise the officers of such organisations to speak on their behalf understand what it is they do when they confer such authority.

To take a purely imaginary example, it would be absurd for a group to demand the rights of pupils to study the history of their own class (rather than upper-class history of kings and generals) and to claim the right to speak on behalf of 1,000 members if a substantial proportion of those members were very young.

THE RIGHTS OF DEMONSTRATION AND PROTEST

At the height of the pupils' rights movement much heat was generated over whether school strikes were really strikes or mere truancy and whether demonstrations were not mere disruption and protest mere disobedience. Upon the answer to this question depended the further one of whether pupils engaged in such activities were to be summarily punished along with those caught flicking ink pellets, or engaged in serious dialogue like adults who down tools and temporarily withdraw their co-operation when they feel they have a genuine grievance which is not being dealt with through the normal constitutional channels.

Adult protesters, of course, may put themselves to considerable inconvenience and may be presumed to be fully aware of the implications of their actions. Adult strikers may be presumed to know that their strike may put their employers out of business and themselves out of a job, as well as endangering the economic viability of the country as a whole. To at least some children, however, a school strike or protest march through the streets of the town may be no more than a jape and it cannot seriously be held that they are in a position to weigh the fun of taking part in such an escapade against the loss of a day's schooling and its possibly more lasting effect on their own and others' education.

At the height of the pupils' rights controversy attempts appear to have been made by both sides to define all incidents in either one way or the other.(4) This was clearly inappropriate. It would be surprising if all protests deserved to be taken seriously. Equally obviously, it is morally impermissible to punish sincere (even misguided) protest as if it were simply childish disobedience. Clearly, it is wrong (that is, an infringement of his rights of security) to punish someone for doing one thing when he is intending to do another. This is analogous to the occasionally encountered practice of defining unauthorised borrowing as theft or an accidental double entendre as uttering an obscenity. One form of double-think seems particularly reprehensible. This is when an incident is denied the dignity of an adult protest on the grounds that the pupils are not able to understand the implications of such an act, and then punished with all the severity due to an act of calculated rebellion.

THE RIGHT TO REPRESENTATION AND DUE PROCESS

(1) Administrative decisions
Administrative decisions about the curriculum and school organisation generally, as well as about individual children, may greatly affect both their immediate happiness and their future life chances.

Teachers, including head teachers, may sincerely feel professionally bound to act in the best interests of individual children and believe this to be sufficient safeguard for those children. Such people are, however, no more immune from error, pressure from above or the seduction of their own interests and convenience than those in other walks of life.

Adults would seem to have at least a moral right to consultation regarding decisions that affect them and this right increasingly finds implementation in the everyday world. If it is true, as has been suggested, that children cannot be expected to judge their own interests, then it would seem that they have the right that such decisions should be preceded by consultation with someone else who can be regarded as being committed to their best interests. Such consultation does indeed often take place on parents'

evenings and similar occasions and many schools undoubtedly
encourage parents to consult the head and staff about their children's educational careers.

The point to be made, however, is that such consultation is a
right of the child, not a mere public relations exercise to be dispensed with when it is expedient to do so. Since, furthermore,
not all parents are sufficiently competent or concerned to ensure
that decisions affecting their children are in the latter's best
interests, the right to fair and proper treatment would seem to
imply a right on the part of children to some form of pupil advocacy by someone of professional standing, whose interests are
sufficiently independent of the school and its hierarchy to be
plausibly regarded as representing the child.

(2) Discipline
As we saw, the moral issues concerned with punishment are complicated by the child's diminished responsibility for his actions,
so that the punishment of children ought to aim at reform rather
than retribution.(5) In so far as punishments in educational
institutions are decided upon and administered by teachers who
are in theory principally concerned with the best interests of
individual pupils, there would appear to be no conflict of interests.
If the child is being punished for his own good, talk of representation and due process appropriate to the adversary conditions
of the law court would appear to be out of place.

This, however, represents an ideal situation. Real teachers,
besides being capable of making mistakes, are also capable of
acting harshly and unreasonably, of submitting to pressure from
colleagues, of undue attachment to such interests as good order
and survival in the classroom and, just like anyone else, of seeking easy solutions to immediate problems.

No doubt, in the case of trivial offences the pupil's interest is
best served by the present system under which the teacher acts
promptly and summarily and then strives to rehabilitate the
offender and re-establish a good positive working relationship
with him. If mistakes are sometimes made, this is well understood
by most pupils and no great harm is done. Certainly, this would
appear to be more in the interest of pupils than the teachers
having to prove every incident of classroom high spirits before
judge and jury with the option of a complicated system of appeals.

There is nevertheless no reason why even in small matters one
individual should find himself in a position in which he has no
option but to accept injustice from another. Even in trivial matters, repeated or systematic injustice can be cumulatively disagree-
able, not to say damaging, and there would seem to be a case for
having as a right of the child someone to whom he could appeal if
need be without running foul of professional etiquette or exposing
himself to reprisals. It is true that most children have such a person in the shape of a sympathetic parent. Not all parents are sympathetic, however, and not all are able to take up even genuine
grievances or clashes of personality with the school in the way
most helpful to the child.

Trivial matters aside, relatively severe sanctions are still sometimes carried out in many schools. Sometimes a punishment may
involve exceptional public disgrace as when a child is known to
have been punished for stealing, even though the punishment itself may be relatively light. Sometimes the sanction may involve
the interruption or termination of schooling or risk damaging the
pupil's long-term interests by being entered on official records or
reports. Where substantial interests of the child are involved,
arguments for the rights of representation, due process and
appeal would appear to be as irrefutable as in the case of adults.

RIGHTS AND OTHER MORAL CONSIDERATIONS IN SCHOOL

In chapter 3 we saw that rights and obligations did not always fit
neatly together in a single system of guiding discourse. The
rights of different individuals, we saw, might conflict not only
with each other, but with actions which it was genuinely incumbent upon others to perform. That rights ought sometimes to be
waived or might even on occasion legitimately be ignored, it was
argued, did not mean that they were any the less rights for that.
At this juncture, therefore, it may seem appropriate briefly to
suggest how failure to understand this point may have contributed
to some of the misunderstandings common at the height of pupil's
rights controversy.

We may, for example, consider a situation in which a particular
group of pupils feel themselves to have a certain grievance. They
have, for example, been forbidden to wear (perfectly respectable)
sports jackets instead of school blazers. We may assume that the
head teacher is under considerable pressure from someone whose
goodwill brings considerable benefit to the school and its pupils,
to maintain the school's status as a 'uniform school' at all costs.

It is plausible to suppose that at some point in the resultant
interview between head and pupils one of the latter may be so
incautious as to refer to the individual's 'rights' of freedom in
matters relating to his personal appearance. In absence of an
understanding that there is a distinction between conceding that
there is a right and conceding the obligation to allow its implementation, the head may feel obliged to deny that there is such a
right, giving as his grounds either that such a right would conflict with the general good, or that the pupils qua pupils or children could not possess rights at all. Alternatively, being unaware
that conflicting rights may perfectly possibly co-exist, he may
seek refuge in the argument that he alone has the right to control
what takes place in the school (since he will be held responsible
for it), and that consequently no one else in the institution can
have any rights at all. Indeed, the claim to rights by other individuals must on this understanding of the logic of rights talk, be
seen as a challenge to his legitimate control of matters for which
he would be held to account. In any case, the more or less peremptory assertion that the pupils have no rights is likely to

provoke a hostile reaction from those pupils who feel quite under-
standably that there must be something wrong with an argument
that leads to so unreasonable a conclusion.

If, however, the head is more sophisticated and concedes that
there is a right, but that for reasons he may or may not feel able
to disclose he cannot allow it to be exercised, this too is capable of
misunderstanding by those who see 'you have the right to' as the
equivalent of 'you ought to be allowed to' or 'I ought not to prevent you'. In this situation the admission of a right coupled with
a refusal to allow its exercise must seem like sheer cynicism, or
an exercise of naked power.

The analysis of the concept of a right and its relation to other
kinds of obligation would not, of course, entirely resolve this particular problem, for no amount of conceptual analysis can remove
genuine conflicts of interest. Nevertheless, a satisfactory resolution of the highly charged question of whether the pupils can
have any rights at all allows attention to be concentrated on the
substantive issues. In the present case these are:

(a) Whether the head is right to overrule the pupils' rights if
such they are for the sake of this particular greater good or
whether he should rather put it to them that they simply ought to
waive their rights in the interests of the school as a whole.

(b) Whether a particular individual should be able to confer benefits on a particular school or withhold them on grounds of arbitrary
preference, supposing these benefits to be provided by his own
efforts or from his own resources.

If it is thought that this case well illustrates the view that if
rights may legitimately be overruled there is no point in having
them and that instead of raising the issue of rights at all it would
have been better to deal with these substantive moral obligations
from the outset, reference may again be made to our analysis in
chapter 3. On the basis of this it may be suggested that there is
indeed point in giving consideration to the pupils' rights in the
matter, for three reasons.

First, to concede that the pupils have a right is to concede that
their wishes and not merely considerations of the general good
have to be weighed in the decision-making process. If their right
is seriously weighed, there is at least a chance that their wishes
may prevail. If it is denied that there is a right, on the other
hand, the only issue to be considered is the political one of how
much inconvenience or detriment to the general good is likely to
be caused by the expression of their discontent. The consideration risks ceasing to be a moral one and becomes instead one of
expediency.

Second, to recognise that the pupils may have rights is to see
them as persons not only whose interests but also whose wishes,
aspirations and point of view are to be taken seriously. This must
necessarily influence the tone of any discussion of what is to be
done and, if rightly understood, greatly enhance the self-esteem
of those whose rights are overruled or who are required to waive
their undeniable rights in the interests of the greater good.

Third, to recognise that a right has been overruled is to recognise that though the decision taken may be the best in the
present circumstances the situation is far from being morally satisfactory. In the example here considered, the head who recognised that pupils have a right might feel obliged to work towards
a situation in which pupils at some stage in their careers would
choose their own dress without damaging the interests of the
school as a whole. He might, for example, seek to persuade the
school's crusty benefactor of the desirability, or at least the
harmlessness, of this. Or he might perhaps try to introduce a
more up-to-date style of uniform or a variety of uniform styles
among which pupils might choose. There would be no obligation on
him to try to do any of these things if the pupils' rights were
simply extinguished by considerations of greater good.

CONCLUDING REMARKS

As our enquiry has proceeded, it has become evident that if talk of
moral rights is meaningful at all, then some such rights are possessed not only by adults, but also by young people and children.
If the grounds on which rights are attributed to others are applied
consistently, the rights of children are modified by such considerations as their limited capacity and experience, their need for
protection, and their condition of material and social dependence.
They are not, however, entirely negated.

As has been amply shown, it does not follow from this that all
the demands made by and on behalf of children are to be met
straight away. Some, indeed, are not to be met at all. What does
follow is that it is at least sometimes morally obligatory to consider the interests, wishes and point of view of the young with the
same degree of seriousness as those of adults who are in a position
to assert their rights more effectively and forcibly.

That children have rights is not to be seen as a matter of purely
academic interest. In a democracy public officials - and this may
be thought to apply to private individuals and organisations also -
may be held to account not only for acting efficiently and legally,
but for acting in a way which is morally defensible as well. That
one's activities and decisions blatantly infringe the moral rights
of individuals is a proper ground of public criticism. That one
acted thus and not otherwise out of consideration for someone's
rights, even though one would have infringed no law or regulation,
may often provide a comprehensible account of what one does in
the course of one's official, professional or social life. To this
degree moral rights of individuals for which coherent, rational
and publicly defensible grounds can be shown acquire something
of the quality of social realities which one ignores at one's peril.
Consequently, those moral rights which children possess are a
matter of undeniable practical concern for parents, officials,
teachers and others upon whose activities and responses the happiness, fortunes and well-being of children depend.

Notes

1 THE CHILDREN'S RIGHTS MOVEMENT

1 Many of the events mentioned in the following pages are reported and discussed in contemporary issues of the 'Times Educational Supplement' (TES),
   as well as in the daily press.
2 TES, 30.1.70, p. 5.
3 TES, 13.2.70, pp. 2-3.
4 TES, 27.2.70, p. 6.
5 TES, 17.7.70, p. 5.
6 TES, 13.11.70, p. 6.
7 Ibid.
8 TES, 11.12.79, p. 9.
9 TES, 8.10.71, p. 11.
10 TES, 19.5.72, p. 6.
11 TES, 14.4.72, p. 9; 28.4.72, p. 9; and 26.5.72, p. 6.
12 Loc. cit. no. 10.
13 TES, 19.5.72, p. 6.
14 TES, 28.4.72, p. 9.
15 S. Hansen and J. Jensen, 'The Little Red School Book', London, Stage I,
   1971.
16 Edited by J. Hall and published by Childrens Rights Publications, Ltd,
   London, 1971-2.
17 L. Berg, Bust Book 'feed back', 'Children's Rights', no. 6, July - August
   1972, pp. 4 and 8.
18 Notice board, 'Children's Rights', no. 5, May - June 1972, pp. 22-9.
19 P. Adams et al., 'Childrens Rights', London, Elek Books, 1971.
20 TES, 2.10.70, p. 6.
21 S. Swerling, 'Who's Getting at Our Kids?', London, The Monday Club,
   1972, pp. 22-3.
22 National Council for Civil Liberties, 'Children in School', Discussion Paper
   no. 1 in the series 'Children Have Rights', London, National Council for
   Civil Liberties, 1970-1.
23 TES, 13.3.72, p. 9.
24 TES, 5.5.72, pp. 9 and 14.
25 TES, 22.9.72, p. 14.
26 Advisory Centre for Education, A draft charter of children's rights, 'Where',
   no. 56, April 1971, pp. 105-8.
27 TES, 13.3.72, p. 9.
28 TES, 5.5.72, p. 8.
29 TES, 19.5.72, p. 7.
30 TES, 29.12.72, p. 3.
31 See particularly the notorious Children's Bust Book, 'Children's Rights',
   no. 5, May - June 1972, pp. 14-23.
32 N. Berger, The child, the law and the state, in Adams et al., op. cit.,
   pp. 153-79.
33 National Council for Civil Liberties, op. cit.
34 TES, 14.4.72, p. 9; 28.4.72, p. 9; 19.5.72, p. 6; 26.5.72, p. 6.
35 National Council for Civil Liberties, op. cit.
36 Advisory Centre for Education, op. cit.
37 Berg, op. cit.
38 Advisory Centre for Education, op. cit., p. 108.
39 TES, 28.4.72, p. 9.
40 Swerling, loc. cit.

41 Berger, op. cit., p. 163.
42 National Council for Civil Liberties, op. cit., p. 3.
43 Ibid.
44 Berger, op. cit., p. 158.
45 Advisory Centre for Education, op. cit., p. 105.
46 Ibid., p. 107.
47 National Council for Civil Liberties, op. cit., p. 3.
48 TES, 14.5.72, p. 6.
49 Berger, op. cit., p. 172.
50 National Council for Civil Liberties, op. cit., pp. 4-5.
51 TES, 14.5.72, p. 6.
52 TES, 26.5.72, p. 6.
53 TES, 26.5.72, p. 3.
54 R. Ollendorff, The rights of adolescents, in Adams et al., op. cit.
55 TES, 26.5.72, p. 6.
56 TES, 19.5.72, p. 6.
57 Advisory Centre for Education, op. cit., p. 105.
58 National Council for Civil Liberties, op. cit., p. 4.
59 Advisory Centre for Education, op. cit., p. 105.
60 Berger, op. cit., pp. 158-9
61 Ibid., p. 172.
62 National Council for Civil Liberties, op. cit., p. 4.
63 Advisory Council for Education, op. cit., p. 107.
64 National Council for Civil Liberties, op. cit., p. 6.
65 Berger, op. cit., p. 173.
66 Advisory Council for Education, p. 107.
67 TES, 26.5.72, p. 6.
68 TES, 19.5.72, p. 6.
69 TES, 26.5.72, p. 6.
70 National Council for Civil Liberties, op. cit.
71 Advisory Council for Education, op. cit., p. 107.
72 Advisory Council for Education, op. cit., p. 105.
73 TES, 26.5.72, p. 6.
74 Advisory Centre for Education, op. cit., p. 107.
75 National Council for Civil Liberties, op. cit., p. 5.
76 Ollendorff, op. cit., p. 120.
77 Berger, op. cit., p. 173.
78 Advisory Centre for Education, op. cit., p. 105 and National Council for
    Civil Liberties, op. cit., p. 6.
79 TES, 26.5.72, p. 6.
80 Advisory Centre for Education, op. cit., p. 107.
81 Ollendorff, op. cit., p. 120.
82 P. Adams, The Infant, the family and society, in Adams et al., op. cit.,
    p. 84.
83 Advisory Centre for Education, op. cit., p. 107.
84 Ollendorff, op. cit., pp. 120-1.
85 Adams, op. cit., pp. 88-9.
86 TES, 26.5.72, p. 6.
87 Advisory Centre for Education, op. cit., p. 106.
88 C. Bereiter, 'Must We Educate?', Englewood Cliffs, N. J., Prentice-Hall,
    1973, pp. 38-54.
89 J. Holt, 'Escape from Childhood', Harmondsworth, Penguin, 1974, pp.
    114-205.
90 See, for example, M. D. A. Freeman, 'The Rights of Children', London,
    Pinter, 1980, and also the brief discussion paper by J. Bradford, 'The
    Spiritual Rights of the Child', London, Church of England Children's
    Society, 1979.
91 W. Guy and P. Chambers, Public examinations and pupils' rights, 'Cam-
    bridge Journal of Education', vol. 3, no. 2, 1973, p. 15.
92 E. M. Moore, Human rights and home-school communications, 'Educational
    Review', vol. 26, no. 1, 1973, pp. 56-66.

93 See, for example, J. Kleinig, Mill, children and rights, 'Educational Philosophy and Theory', vol. 8, no. 1, April 1976, pp. 1-15, F. Schrag, The child's status in the democratic state, 'Political Theory', vol. 3, no. 4, 1975, pp. 441-57 and The child in the moral order, 'Philosophy', vol. 52, no. 200, April 1977, pp. 167-77.
94 G. Haydon, The 'right to education' and compulsory schooling, 'Educational Philosophy and Theory', vol. 9, no. 1, 1977, p. 1.
95 N. Maccormick, Children's rights: a test case for theories of right, 'Archiv für Rechts- und Sozialphilosophie', vol. 62, no. 3, 1976, pp. 305-17.
96 'Harvard Educational Review', vol. 43, no. 4, November 1973, and vol. 44, no. 1, February 1974.
97 J. L. Paul, G. R. Newfield and J. W. Pelosi (eds), 'Child Advocacy Within the System', New York, Syracuse University Press, 1977.
98 G. Godfrey, 'Parental Rights and Duties and Custody Suits', London, Stevens, 1975, pp. 39-46.
99 N. Bagnall, 'Parent Power', London, Routledge & Kegan Paul, 1974; J. Stone and F. Taylor, 'The Parents' Schoolbook', Harmondsworth, Penguin, 1976.
100 Department of Education and Science and the Welsh Office, 'A New Partnership for our Schools', Report of the Committee of Enquiry appointed jointly by the Secretary of State for Education and Science and the Secretary of State for Wales under the chairmanship of Mr Tom Taylor, C.B.E., London, HMSO. 1977. pp. 21-34.
101 National Council for Civil Liberties, op. cit., pp. 4-5.
102 B. Brophy, Children have rights, in M. Vaughan (ed), 'Rights of Children', London, National Council for Civil Liberties, 1971, p. 5.
103 H. J. Gamm, 'Kritische Schule', Munich, List-Verlag, 1970.

2 THREE TRADITIONAL THEORIES OF RIGHTS

1 See, for example, T. Hobbes, 'De Cive', I, 14, 'English Works', ed. Sir W. Molesworth, London, John Bohn, 1839-45, vol. II, p. 13, and B. de Spinoza, 'Tractatus Politicus', II, 4, 'Works of Spinoza', trans. R. H. M. Elwes, London, Bell, 1887, p. 292.
2 D. Hume, 'Enquiry Concerning the Principles of Morals', Indianapolis, Bobbs Merrill, 1957, sect. 3, p. 23.
3 W. N. Hohfeld, 'Fundamental Legal Conceptions', New Haven and London, Yale University Press, 1919, p. 36.
4 See, for example, T. E. Holland, 'Jurisprudence', Oxford, Clarendon Press, 1888, p. 69; T. H. Green, 'Political Obligation', London, Longmans, 1966, p. 41, and J. Plamenatz, 'Consent, Freedom and Political Obligation', Oxford University Press, 1938, p. 82.
5 H. L. A. Hart, Definition in theory and jurisprudence, 'Law Quarterly Review', vol. 70, 1954, p. 43.
6 H. J. McClosky, Rights, 'Philosophical Quarterly', vol. 15, no. 59, 1965, p. 115.
7 S. I. Benn and R. S. Peters, 'Social Principles and the Democratic State', London, Allen & Unwin, 1959, p. 91.
8 McClosky, op. cit., p. 116.
9 See Hobbes, op. cit., II, p. 17, also 'Leviathan', II, 20, 'English Works', op. cit., vol. III, p. 188.
10 R. Brandt, 'Ethical Theory', Englewood Cliffs, N. J., Prentice-Hall, 1959, p. 433.
11 D. Lyons, Rights, claimants and beneficiaries, 'American Philosophical Quarterly', vol. 6, no. 3, July 1969, p. 173.
12 H. L. A. Hart, Bentham, 'Proceedings of the British Academy', vol. 48, 1962, p. 312.
13 See, for example, D. Lloyd, 'The Idea of Law', Harmondsworth, Penguin, 1964, p. 312; J. Hospers, 'Human Conduct', New York, Harcourt Brace & World, 1961, p. 409; F. A. Olafson, Rights and duties in education, in J. F. Doyle (ed.), 'Educational Judgments', London, Routledge & Kegan Paul, 1973, p. 173.

14 Benn and Peters, op. cit., p. 89.
15 See, for example, H. B. Acton, Rights, 'Proceedings of the Aristotelian Society', Supplementary Volume 24, 1950, and H. L. A. Hart, Are there any natural rights?, 'Philosophical Review', vol. 64, 1955.
16 D. D. Raphael, Human rights, old and new, p. 56, and The rights of Man and the rights of the citizen, pp. 102-3, both in 'Political Theory and the Rights of Man', ed. D. D. Raphael, London, Macmillan, 1967.
17 Hohfeld, loc. cit.
18 Raphael, op. cit., pp. 56-8.
19 H. Morris, Persons and punishment, 'The Monist', vol. 52, no. 4, October 1968, p. 499.
20 See Melden's comments in A. I. Melden, 'Rights and Right Conduct', Oxford, Blackwell, 1959, p. 13.
21 B. Mayo, What are human rights?, in D. D. Raphael (ed.), op. cit., p. 75.
22 J. Feinberg, 'Social Philosophy', Englewood Cliffs, N. J., Prentice-Hall, 1973, p. 64.
23 Cf. Feinberg, op. cit., p. 58.
24 See below, p. 42.

3   RIGHTS AND OTHER FORMS OF MORAL LANGUAGE

1 Some parts of this chapter are drawn from my article, Pupils' rights, 'Proceedings of the Philosophy of Education Society of Great Britain', vol. 7, no. 1, January 1973, and are included by kind permission of the Society.
2 J. Plamenatz, 'Consent, Freedom and Political Obligation', Oxford University Press, 1938, p. 83.
3 See, for example, J. Bentham, Anarchical Fallacies, 'Works', ed. J. Bowring, Edinburgh, 1843, vol. 2, p. 506; J. S. Mill, 'Utilitarianism, On Liberty, Representative Government', London, Dent, 1910, p. 50: D. G. Ritchie, 'Natural Rights', London, Allen & Unwin, 1916, p. 144; F. H. Bradley, 'Ethical Studies', Oxford University Press, 1927, p. 208; L. T. Hobhouse, 'The Elements of Social Justice', London, Allen & Unwin, 1922, p. 39.
4 R. Barrow, 'Moral Philosophy for Education', London, Allen & Unwin, 1975, p. 145.
5 H. L. A. Hart, Are there any natural rights?, 'Philosophical Review', vol. 64, 1955, p. 190.
6 H. L. A. Hart, Bentham, 'Proceedings of the British Academy', vol. 48, 1962, p. 315.
7 R. Nozick, 'Anarchy, State and Utopia', Oxford, Blackwell, 1974, p. 33.
8 G. Godfrey, 'Parental Rights and Duties and Custody Suits', London, Stevens, 1975, pp. 6-7.
9 S. I. Benn and R. S. Peters, 'Social Principles and the Democratic State', London, Allen & Unwin, 1959, p. 100.
10 J. Feinberg, 'Social Philosophy', Englewood Cliffs, N. J., Prentice-Hall, 1973, pp. 68-83.
11 Feinberg, op. cit., p. 58.
12 Ibid.
13 See, for example, H. T. Sockett, Parents' rights, in 'Values and Authority in Schools', ed. D. Bridges and P. Scrimshaw, London, Hodder & Stoughton, 1975, p. 41.
14 S. M. Brown, Inalienable rights, 'Philosophical Review', vol. 64, 1955, p. 208.
15 Brown, op. cit., p. 209.
16 See W. D. Ross, 'The Right and the Good', Oxford University Press, 1930, p. 20.
17 W. K. Frankena, Natural and inalienable rights, 'Philosophical Review', vol. 64, 1955, pp. 228-9. See also R. Brandt, 'Ethical Theory', Englewood Cliffs, N. J., Prentice-Hall, 1959, pp. 438-9.
18 Ross, loc. cit.
19 A. I. Melden, 'Rights and Right Conduct', Oxford, Blackwell, 1959, p. 19.
20 W. D. Lamont, Rights, 'Proceedings of the Aristotelian Society', Supplementary Volume 24, 1950, p. 91.

21 Ibid.
22 See, in particular, Hart's comments regarding Bentham's dawning realisation that the concept of rights cannot be wholly explained within the framework of his utilitarian philosophy. Hart, Bentham, p. 312.
23 Feinberg, op. cit., p. 75.
24 H. Morris, Persons and punishment, 'The Monist', vol. 52, no. 4, October 1968, p. 499, Morris's emphasis.
25 H. J. McClosky, Rights, 'Philosophical Quarterly', vol. 15, no. 59, 1965, p. 123.

4 POSITIVE RIGHTS AND MORAL RIGHTS
1 S. I. Benn and R. S. Peters, 'Social Principles and the Democratic State', London, Allen & Unwin, 1959, p. 92.
2 National Council for Civil Liberties, 'Children in Schools', London, National Council for Civil Liberties, 1970, p. 7.
3 Ibid., p. 5.
4 See above, p. 28.
5 J. Feinberg, 'Social Philosophy', Englewood Cliffs, N. J., Prentice-Hall, 1973, pp. 64-5.
6 See H. L. A. Hart, 'The Concept of Law', Oxford University Press, 1961, p. 8.
7 D. Miller, 'Social Justice', Oxford University Press, 1976, p. 54.
8 R. Dworkin, 'Taking Rights Seriously', London, Duckworth, 1977, p. 81.
9 R. Barrow, 'Moral Philosophy for Education', London, Allen & Unwin, 1975, p. 142.
10 Feinberg, op. cit., p. 71.
11 Ibid.
12 Ibid., p. 67.
13 J. Bentham, Anarchical Fallacies, 'Works', ed. J. Bowring, Edinburgh, 1843, p. 523.
14 Gregory, op. cit., p. 99. Gregory's emphasis.
15 Ibid.
16 Miller, op. cit., p. 55.
17 N. Berger, The child, the law and the state, in P. Adams et al., 'Children's Rights', London, Elek Books, 1971; J. Holt, 'Escape from Childhood', Harmondsworth, Penguin, 1975, pp. 114-205.
18 See, for example, H. T. Sockett, Parents' rights, in D. Bridges and P. Scrimshaw (eds), 'Values and Authority in Schools', London, Hodder & Stoughton, 1975, p. 41.
19 H. L. A. Hart, Are there any natural rights?, 'Philosophical Review', vol. 64, 1955, pp. 185-6.

5 RIGHTS OF FREEDOM IN THE SENSE OF LIBERTIES
1 D. D. Raphael, Human rights, old and new, in 'Political Theory and the Rights of Man', ed. D. D. Raphael, London, Macmillan, 1967, p. 56.
2 W. N. Hohfeld, 'Fundamental Legal Conceptions', New Haven, Yale University Press, 1964, p. 5.
3 H. L. A. Hart, Are there any natural rights?, 'Philosophical Review', vol. 64, 1955.
4 See, for example, H. J. McClosky, Rights, 'Philosophical Quarterly', vol. 15, no. 59, 1965, p. 120.
5 Hart, loc. cit.
6 B. Mayo, What are human rights?, in D. D. Raphael (ed.), 'Political Theory and the Rights of Man', London, Macmillan, 1967, p. 71.
7 T. Hobbes, 'English Works', ed. Sir W. Molesworth, London, John Bohn, 1841, vol. III, pt. I, ch. 14, p. 117.
8 Ibid., vol. II, pt. I, ch. I, pp. 10-11.
9 Sir W. Clarke, The Clarke papers, ed. C. H. Firth, vol. I, 'Camden Society Publications', New Series 49, 1901, p. 301.
10 T. Paine, 'The Rights of Man', London, Dent, 1915, p. 65.
11 M. Macdonald, Natural rights, in P. Laslett (ed.), 'Philosophy, Politics and

Society', First Series, Oxford, Blackwell, 1956, p. 44.
12 Clarke, loc. cit.
13 See, for example, F. H. Bradley, 'Ethical Studies', Oxford University Press, 1876, pp. 165-85.
14 T. H. Green, 'Political Obligation', London, Longmans, 1927, pp. 146-8.
15 Hobbes, op. cit., vol. III, p. 126.
16 J. Feinberg, Duties, rights and claims, 'American Philosophical Quarterly', vol. 3, no. 2, April 1966, p. 139.
17 Hobbes, op. cit., vol. III, p. 188.
18 J-J. Rousseau, 'The Social Contract', London, Dent, 1913, p. 6.

6   CLAIM RIGHTS OF FREEDOM AND NON-INTERFERENCE
1 J. Feinberg, 'Social Philosophy', Englewood Cliffs, N. J., Prentice-Hall, 1973, pp. 59-61.
2 J. S. Mill, 'On Liberty', 'Utilitarianism, On Liberty, Representative Government', London, Dent, 1910.
3 H. L. A. Hart, 'The Concept of Law', Oxford University Press, 1961, p. 191.
4 See above, p. 23.
5 R. S. Peters, 'Ethics and Education', London, Allen & Unwin, 1966, p. 182.
6 J. P. Mabbott, 'The State and the Citizen', London, Hutchinson, 1947, pp. 62-3.
7 Feinberg, op. cit., pp. 72-3.
8 See ibid., p. 77.

7   RIGHTS OF PARTICIPATION
1 S. I. Benn and R. S. Peters, 'Social Principles and the Democratic State', London, Allen & Unwin, 1959, pp. 350-3.
2 See, for example, J. S. Mill, Representative Government, in 'Utilitarianism, On Liberty, Representative Government', London, Dent, 1910, ch. 1, pp. 177-9.
3 See below, pp. 88-9.
4 Sir W. Clarke, The Clarke papers, ed. C. H. Firth, vol. I, 'Camden Society Publications', New Series 49, 1901, p. 316.
5 T. Paine, 'The Rights of Man', London, Dent, 1915, pp. 118-19.
6 Clarke, op. cit., p. 319.
7 G. Tullock, 'Private Wants, Public Means', New York, Basic Books, 1970, pp. 79-80.
8 Tullock, op. cit., p. 81.
9 R. A. Dahl, 'A Preface to Democratic Theory', Chicago University Press, 1956, pp. 105-7.
10 Paine, op. cit., pp. 14-17.
11 Ibid., p. 198.
12 Benn and Peters, op. cit., p. 103.
13 P. A. White, Work-place democracy, and political education, 'Journal of Philosophy of Education', vol. 13, July 1979, p. 11.

8   SPECIAL RIGHTS
1 J. Feinberg, Duties, rights and claims, 'American Philosophical Quarterly', vol. 3, no. 2, April 1966, pp. 138-9.
2 T. Hobbes, 'Leviathan', in 'English Works', ed. Sir W. Molesworth, London, John Bohn, 1839, pt. I, ch. 13, p. 113.
3 J. Hospers, 'Human Conduct', New York, Harcourt, Brace & World, 1961, p. 316.
4 H. L. A. Hart, Are there any natural rights?, 'Philosophical Review', vol. 64, 1955, pp. 185-6.
5 Feinberg, loc. cit.
6 See below, p. 75.
7 F. A. Olafson, Rights and duties in education, in J. F. Doyle (ed.), 'Educational Judgments', London, Routledge & Kegan Paul, 1973, pp. 173-95. See below, pp. 140-2.
8 Hobbes, op. cit., pp. 189-90.
9 A. I. Melden, 'Rights and Right Conduct', Oxford, Blackwell, 1959.

10 Ibid., pp. 38-42.
11 Ibid., p. 42.

9 WELFARE RIGHTS
  1 B. Mayo, What are human rights?, in D. D. Raphael (ed.) 'Political Theory and the Rights of Man', London, Macmillan, 1967, p. 73.
  2 R. O. Johann, Love and justice, in R. T. De George (ed.), 'Ethics and Society', London, Macmillan, 1968, p. 25.
  3 M. Cranston, Human rights, real and supposed, in Raphael (ed.), op. cit., p. 53.
  4 Q. Wright, Relationship between different categories of human rights, in UNESCO 'Symposium on Human Rights', London, Wingate, 1949, p. 47.
  5 J. E. S. Fawcett, The international protection of human rights, in Raphael, (ed.), op. cit., p. 125.
  6 I. Kant, Preface to the metaphysical elements of ethics, in 'Kant's Critique of Practical Reason and Other Works on the Theory of Ethics', trans. T. K. Abbott, London, Longmans, 1909, pp. 301-3.
  7 See above, pp. 44-5.
  8 M. Cranston, Human rights, a reply to Professor Raphael in Raphael (ed.) op. cit., p. 97.
  9 D. D. Raphael, The rights of Man and the rights of the citizen, in Raphael (ed.), op. cit., pp. 113-14.
 10 C. J. Friedrich, Rights, liberties and freedoms; a reappraisal, 'American Political Science Review', vol. 57, no. 4, December 1963, p. 843.
 11 Raphael, op. cit., p. 115.
 12 Johann, op. cit., p. 26.
 13 Ibid., p. 32.
 14 D. D. Raphael, Human rights, old and new, in Raphael (ed.), op. cit., p. 63.
 15 B. Barry, 'Political Argument', London, Routledge & Kegan Paul, 1965, p. 48. See also A. R. White, Needs and wants, 'Proceedings of the Philosophy of Education Society of Great Britain', vol. 8, no. 2, July 1974, pp. 159-80.
 16 D. Miller, 'Social Justice', Oxford University Press, 1976, p. 130.
 17 Ibid., p. 131.
 18 Ibid., pp. 136-43.
 19 See below, pp. 81-2.
 20 S. I. Benn and R. S. Peters, 'Social Principles and the Democratic State', London, Allen & Unwin, 1959, p. 49.
 21 Raphael, The rights of Man and the rights of the citizen, p. 114.
 22 Raphael, Human rights, old and new.
 23 See Honderich's sceptical remarks about our reasons for regarding violence with so much more aversion than inequality. T. Honderich, 'Three Essays on Political Violence', Oxford, Blackwell, 1976, Essay I, pp. 1-44.
 24 See, for example, Cranston, op. cit., pp. 50-1.
 25 R. Nozick, 'Anarchy, State and Utopia', Oxford, Blackwell, 1974.
 26 Ibid., pp. 149-231.
 27 Ibid., pp. 178-82.
 28 Cf. J. Locke, 'Two Treatises of Government', ed., P. Laslett, Cambridge University Press, 1960, Second Treatise, ch. 5, para. 27, p. 329.
 29 Raphael, The rights of Man and the rights of the citizen, p. 113.
 30 See T. Hobbes, 'Leviathan', 'English Works', ed. Sir W. Molesworth, London, John Bohn, 1839-45, vol. III, pt. I. ch. 13, p. 115.
 31 J. Rawls, 'A Theory of Justice', Oxford University Press, 1972, pp. 11-21.
 32 Rawls, op. cit., pp. 60-1.
 33 Ibid.
 34 See, for example, Cranston, op. cit., p. 46, and Raphael, Human rights, old and new, p. 59.
 35 Raphael, The rights of Man and the rights of the citizen, p. 109.

10 RIGHTS AND THE CONCEPT OF CHILDHOOD

1 J. Kleinig, Mill, children and rights, 'Educational Philosophy and Theory', vol. 8, no. 1, April 1976, pp. 3-5.
2 F. Schrag, The child's status in the democratic state, 'Political Theory', vol. 3, no. 4, November 1975, pp. 443-52.
3 Kleinig, op. cit., pp. 3-4.
4 Schrag, op. cit., p. 452, Kleinig, op. cit., p. 7.

11 THE LEGAL RIGHTS OF CHILDREN

1 These claims are made repeatedly in the polemical literature of the children's rights controversy between 1968 and 1972. (See above, pp. 5-16). All these are to be found in N. Berger, The child, the law and the state, in P. Adams et al., 'Children's Rights', London, Elek Books, 1971, pp. 153-79.
2 C. J. R. Sachs, Children's rights, in J. W. Bridge et al. (eds), 'Fundamental Rights', London, Sweet & Maxwell, 1973, p. 31.
3 H. L. A. Hart, Bentham, 'Proceedings of the British Academy', vol. 48, 1962, p. 315.
4 Berger, op. cit. p. 161.
5 The legal information in this section is taken from H. K. Bevan, 'The Law Relating to Children', London, Butterworth, 1973.
6 N. Berger, 'Rights', Harmondsworth, Penguin, 1974; J. Holt, 'Escape from Childhood', Harmondsworth, Penguin, 1975, pp. 118-211.
7 See, for example, ibid., pp. 154-5.
8 G. Godfrey, 'Parental Rights and Duties and Custody Suits', London, Stevens, 1975, pp. 8-25.
9 Bevan, op. cit., p. 23.
10 B. M. Hoggett, 'Parents and Children', London, Sweet and Maxwell, 1977, p. 11.
11 Ibid., p. 125.
12 J. Stone and F. Taylor, 'The Parents' Schoolbook', Harmondsworth, Penguin, 1976, pp. 68-72.
13 National Council for Civil Liberties, 'Children in School', Discussion Paper No. 1 in the series: 'Children Have Rights', London, National Council for Civil Liberties, 1970, p. 3.
14 Berger, The child, the law and the state, p. 154.
15 Godfrey, op. cit., p. 5.
16 Ibid.
17 Berger, The child, the law and the state, p. 154.
18 Ibid.
19 Bevan, op. cit., p. 45.
20 Hoggett, op. cit., p. 10.
21 S. R. L. Clark, 'The Moral Status of Animals', Oxford University Press, 1977, pp. 34-50.
22 Bevan, op. cit., p. 451.
23 See, for example, Godfrey, op. cit., pp. 6-7.
24 Berger, The child, the law and the state, p. 154.
25 Ibid., p. 25.
26 Godfrey, op. cit., p. 7.
27 Bevan, op. cit., p. 262.
28 Ibid., pp. 242-9.
29 Berger, The child, the law and the state, p. 166.

12 CHILDREN'S RIGHTS OF FREEDOM IN THE SENSE OF LIBERTIES

1 See above, pp. 24-5.
2 The most well-known of these is probably that of Sir Robert Filmer in his 'Patriarcha', against which Locke argues in the 'First Treatise of Government'. See Sir R. Filmer, 'Patriarcha and other political works', ed. P. Laslett, Oxford, Blackwell, 1949.

13 CHILDREN'S CLAIM RIGHTS OF FREEDOM

1 See, for example, M. Macdonald, Natural rights, in P. Laslett (ed.),

'Philosophy, Politics and Society', First Series, Oxford, Blackwell, 1956, pp. 39-43.
2 A. J. M. Milne, 'Freedom and Rights', London, Allen & Unwin, 1968, p. 54.
3 Ibid., pp. 94-5.
4 J. S. Mill, 'On Liberty', 'Utilitarianism, On Liberty, Representative Government', London, Dent, 1910, pp. 151-2.
5 C. Bereiter, 'Must We Educate?', Englewood Cliffs, N. J., Prentice-Hall, 1973, pp. 40-53.
6 C. A. Wringe, Pupils' rights and examinations, 'Cambridge Journal of Education', vol. 3, no. 2, Easter Term 1975, p. 199.
7 See H. L. A. Hart, Are there any natural rights? 'Philosophical Review', vol. 64, 1955, pp. 185-6.
8 R. Nozick, 'Anarchy, State and Utopia', Oxford, Blackwell, 1974, pp. 71-8.
9 See S. R. L. Clark, 'The Moral Status of Animals', Oxford University Press, 1977.
10 See J. Locke, 'Two Treatises of Government', ed. P. Laslett, Cambridge University Press, 1960, Second Treatise, para. 0, p. 313.
11 S. I. Benn and R. S. Peters, 'Social Principles and the Democratic State', London, Allen & Unwin, 1959, p. 50.
12 H. Morris, Persons and punishment, 'The Monist', vol. 52, no. 4, 1968, pp. 475-501.
13 Nozick, op. cit., p. 34.
14 National Council for Civil Liberties, 'Children in School', Discussion Paper No. 1 in the series: 'Children Have Rights', London, National Council for Civil Liberties, 1970, p. 5.

14 CHILDREN'S RIGHTS OF PARTICIPATION

1 J. Holt, 'Escape from Childhood', Harmondsworth, Penguin, 1975, pp. 131-48.
2 F. Schrag, The child's status in the democratic state, 'Political Theory', vol. 3, no. 4, November 1975, p. 454.
3 See above, pp. 88-9.
4 Schrag, loc. cit.
5 See, for example, H. Hesse, 'The Glass Bead Game', trans. R. and C. Winston, Harmondsworth, Penguin, 1972, pp. 416, 54.
6 See above, p. 72.
7 F. A. Olafson, Rights and duties in education, in J. F. Doyle (ed.), 'Educational Judgments', London, Routledge & Kegan Paul, 1973, pp. 179-83.

15 CHILDREN AND SPECIAL RIGHTS

1 See above, p. 36.
2 F. A. Olafson, Rights and duties in education, in J. F. Doyle (ed.), 'Educational Judgments', London, Routledge & Kegan Paul, 1973, p. 184.
3 See J. Feinberg, Rights, duties and claims, 'American Philosophical Quarterly', vol. 3, no. 2, April 1966, pp. 137-44.
4 D. Lasok, The rights of the unborn, in J. W. Bridge et al. (eds), 'Fundamental Rights', London, Sweet & Maxwell, 1973, pp. 18-30.
5 S. Weil, 'Selected Essays 1934-43', trans. R. Rees, Oxford University Press, 1962, p. 9.

16 CHILDREN'S WELFARE RIGHTS AND THE RIGHT TO EDUCATION

1 See G. Haydon, The 'right to education' and compulsory schooling, 'Educational Philosophy and Theory', vol. 9, no. 1, 1977, pp. 1-15.
2 H. L. A. Hart, Bentham, 'Proceedings of the British Academy', vol. 48, 1962, p. 315.
3 J. Kleinig, Mill, children and rights, 'Educational Philosophy and Theory', vol. 8, no. 1, April 1976, pp. 10-11.
4 Haydon, op. cit., p. 3.
5 The texts of the various documents mentioned in this paragraph are all to be found in I. Brownlie (ed.), 'Basic Documents on Human Rights', Oxford University Press, 1971.

6 H. K. Bevan, 'The Law Relating to Children', London, Butterworth, 1973, pp. 433–41.
7 See above, pp. 90–1.
8 I. M. M. Gregory, The right to education, 'Proceedings of the Philosophy of Education Society of Great Britain', vol. 7, no. 1, January 1973, p. 87.
9 Gregory, op. cit., pp. 93–8.
10 Ibid., p. 88.
11 Ibid., p. 91.
12 Ibid.
13 Ibid., pp. 93–8.
14 F. A. Olafson, Rights and duties in education, in J. F. Doyle (ed.), 'Educational Judgments', London, Routledge & Kegan Paul, 1973, pp. 174–5.
15 Ibid., p. 188–9.
16 A. I. Melden, Olafson on the right to education, in J. F. Doyle (ed.), op. cit., pp. 200–1.
17 Melden, op. cit., pp. 202–3.
18 See pp. 146–71.
19 M. Oakeshott, Education: the engagement and its frustration, 'Proceedings of the Philosophy of Education Society of Great Britain', vol. 5, no. 1, January 1971, pp. 43–76.
20 Ibid., pp. 45–7.
21 Ibid., p. 43.
22 Ibid., pp. 59–73.
23 Olafson, op. cit., pp. 173–4.
24 P. A. White, Education, democracy and the public interest, 'Proceedings of the Philosophy of Education Society of Great Britain', vol. 5, no. 1, January 1971.
25 P. A. White, Work-place democracy and political education, 'Journal of Philosophy of Education', vol. 13, July 1979.
26 R. S. Peters, The justification of education, in R. S. Peters (ed.), 'The Philosophy of Education', Oxford University Press, 1973.
27 Cf. Dworkin's discussion of the Defunis case in which he argues that the practice of admitting students to institutions of higher education on the basis of strict merit is a matter of public policy, and therefore not necessarily a right of the best qualified candidates. R. Dworkin, 'Taking Rights Seriously', London, Duckworth, 1977, pp. 223–6.
28 Cf. J. P. White, 'Towards a Compulsory Curriculum', London, Routledge & Kegan Paul, 1973, p. 61.
29 See Brownlie, op. cit., p. 182.

17 CHILDREN'S RIGHTS AND THE CHILDREN'S RIGHTS CONTROVERSY
1 See p. 148 above.
2 N. Berger, The child, the law and the state, in P. Adams et al., 'Children's Rights', London, Elek Books, 1971, pp. 158–9.
3 For claims to these rights see chapter 1, pp. 13–15.
4 See above, pp. 5–6.
5 See above, pp. 114–15.

Bibliography

Acton, H. B., Rights, 'Proceedings of the Aristotelian Society', Supplementary Volume 24, 1950, pp. 95-110.
Adams, P., et al., 'Children's Rights', London, Elek Books, 1971.
Adams, P., The infant, the family and society, in P. Adams et al., 'Children's Rights', London, Elek Books, 1971.
Advisory Centre for Education, A draft charter of children's rights, 'Where', no. 56, April 1971, pp. 105-8.
Austin, J., 'The Province of Jurisprudence Determined', London, Weidenfeld & Nicolson, 1954.
Bagnall, N., 'Parent Power', London, Routledge & Kegan Paul, 1974.
Barnhart, J. E., Human rights as absolute claims and reasonable expectations, 'American Philosophical Quarterly', vol. 6, no. 4, October 1969, pp. 335-9.
Barrow, R., 'Moral Philosophy for Education', London, Allen & Unwin, 1975.
Barry, B., 'Political Argument', London, Routledge & Kegan Paul, 1965.
Benn, S. I., and Peters, R. S., 'Social Principles and the Democratic State', London, Allen & Unwin, 1959.
Bentham, J., 'Works', ed. J. Bowring, Edinburgh, 1843.
Bereiter, C., 'Must We Educate?', Englewood Cliffs, N. J., Prentice-Hall, 1973.
Berg, L., Moving towards self-government, in P. Adams et al., 'Children's Rights', London, Elek Books, 1971.
Berg, L., Bust Book 'feed back', 'Children's Rights', no. 6, July-August 1972, p. 8.
Berger, N., The child, the law and the state, in P. Adams et al., 'Children's Rights', London, Elek Books, 1971.
Berger N., 'Rights', Harmondsworth, Penguin, 1974.
Bevan, H. K., 'The Law Relating to Children', London, Butterworth, 1973.
Bradford, J., 'The Spiritual Rights of the Child', London, Church of England Children's Society, 1979.
Bradley, F. H., 'Ethical Studies', Oxford University Press, 1876.
Brandt, R., 'Ethical Theory', Englewood Cliffs, N. J., Prentice-Hall, 1959.
Brophy, B., Children have rights, in M. Vaughan (ed.), 'Rights of Children', London, National Council for Civil Liberties, 1971, pp. 5-8.
Brown, S. M., Inalienable rights, 'Philosophical Review', vol. 64, 1955, pp. 192-211.
Brownlie, I. (ed.), 'Basic Documents on Human Rights', Oxford University Press, 1971.
Clark, S. R. L., 'The Moral Status of Animals', Oxford University Press, 1977.
Clarke, Sir W., The Clarke Papers, ed., C. H. Firth, vol. I, 'Camden Society Publications', New Series 49, 1891.
Cranston, M., Human rights, real and supposed, in D. D. Raphael (ed.), 'Political Theory and the Rights of Man', London, Macmillan, 1967.
Dahl, R. A., 'A Preface to Democratic Theory', Chicago University Press, 1956.
De George, R. T. (ed.), 'Ethics and Society', London, Macmillan, 1968.
Department of Education and Science and the Welsh Office, 'A New Partnership for Our Schools', Report of the Committee of Enquiry appointed jointly by the Secretary of State for Wales under the Chairmanship of Mr Tom Taylor, C.B.E., London, HMSO, 1977.
Duane, M., Freedom and the state system of education, in P. Adams et al., 'Children's Rights', London, Elek Books, 1971.
Dworkin, R., 'Taking Rights Seriously', London, Duckworth, 1977.
Edelman, P. B., Advocacy for children, 'Harvard Educational Review', vol. 43, no. 4, November 1973, pp. 639-52.

Fawcett, J. E. S., The international protection of human rights, in D. D. Raphael (ed.), 'Political Theory and the Rights of Man', London, Macmillan, 1967.

Feinberg, J., Duties, rights and claims, 'American Philosophical Quarterly', vol. 3, no. 2, April 1966, pp. 137-44.

Feinberg, J., 'Social Philosophy', Englewood Cliffs, N. J., Prentice-Hall, 1973.

Filmer, R., 'Patriarcha and Other Political Works', ed. P. Laslett, Oxford, Blackwell, 1949.

Frankena, W. K., Natural and inalienable rights, 'Philosophical Review', no. 64, 1955, pp. 212-32.

Freeman, M. D. A., 'The Rights of Children', London, Pinter, 1980.

Friedrich, C. J., Rights, liberties and freedoms; a reappraisal, 'American Political Science Review', vol. 57, no. 4, December 1963, pp. 841-54.

Gamm, H. J., 'Kritische Schule', Munich, List-Verlag, 1970.

Godfrey, G., 'Parental Rights and Duties and Custody Suits', London, Stevens, 1975.

Goldstein, J., et al. 'Beyond the Best Interests of the Child', London, Collier Macmillan, 1973.

Green, T. H., 'Political Obligation', London, Longmans, 1966.

Gregory, I. M. M., The right to education, 'Proceedings of the Philosophy of Education Society of Great Britain', vol. 7, no. 1, January 1973, pp. 85-102.

Guy, W., and Chambers, P., Public examinations and pupils' rights, 'Cambridge Journal of Education', vol. 3, no. 2., Easter 1973, pp. 83-9.

Hansen, S. and Jensen, J., 'The Little Red School Book', London, Stage I, 1971.

Hart, H. L. A., Definition in theory and jurisprudence, 'Law Quarterly Review', vol. 70, 1954.

Hart, H. L. A., Are there any natural rights?, 'Philosophical Review', vol. 64, 1955, pp. 175-91.

Hart, H. L. A., 'The Concept of Law', Oxford University Press, 1961.

Hart, H. L. A., Bentham, 'Proceedings of the British Academy', vol. 48, 1962, pp. 311-20.

Haydon, G., The 'right to education' and compulsory schooling, 'Educational Philosophy and Theory', vol. 9, no. 1, 1977, pp. 1-15.

Hesse, H., 'The Glass Bead Game', trans. C. and R. Winston, Harmondsworth, Penguin, 1972.

Hobbes, T., 'English Works', ed. Sir W. Molesworth, London, John Bohn, 1839-45.

Hobhouse, L. T., 'The Elements of Social Justice', London, Allen & Unwin, 1922.

Hoggett, B. M., 'Parents and Children', London, Sweet & Maxwell, 1977.

Hohfeld, W. N., 'Fundamental Legal Conceptions', New Haven and London, Yale University Press, 1919.

Holland, T. E., 'Jurisprudence', Oxford, Clarendon Press, 1888.

Holt, J., 'Escape from Childhood', Harmondsworth, Penguin, 1975.

Honderich, T., 'Three Essays on Political Violence', Oxford, Blackwell, 1976.

Hospers, J., 'Human Conduct', New York, Harcourt, Brace & World, 1961.

Hume, D., 'Enquiry Concerning the Principles of Morals', Indianapolis, Bobbs Merrill, 1957.

Johann, R. O., Love and justice, in R. T. De George (ed.), 'Ethics and Society', London, Macmillan, 1968.

Kant, I., 'Kant's Critique of Practical Reason and Other Works on the Theory of Ethics', trans. T. K. Abbott, London, Longmans, 1909.

Kirp, D., Student classification, public policy and the courts, 'Harvard Educational Review', vol. 64, no. 1, November 1974, pp. 7-52.

Kleinig, J., Mill, children and rights, 'Educational Philosophy and Theory', vol. 8, no. 1, April 1976, pp. 1-15.

Lamont, W. D., 'Principles of Moral Judgement', Oxford University Press, 1946.

Lamont, W. D., Rights, 'Proceedings of the Aristotelian Society', Supplementary Volume 24, 1950, pp. 83-94.

Lasok, D., The rights of the unborn, in J. W. Bridge et al. (eds.), 'Fundamental Rights', London, Sweet & Maxwell, 1973.

Locke, J., 'Two Treatises of Government', ed. P. Laslett, Cambridge University Press, 1960.

Lloyd, D., 'The Idea of Law', Harmondsworth, Penguin, 1964.
Lyons, D., Rights, claimants and beneficiaries, 'American Philosophical Quarterly', vol. 6, no. 3, July 1969, pp. 173-85.
Mabbott, J. D., 'The State and the Citizen', London, Hutchinson, 1947.
McClosky, H. J., Rights, 'Philosophical Quarterly', vol. 15, no. 59, 1965, pp. 115-27.
MacCormick, N., Children's rights: a test case for theories of right, 'Archiv für Rechts- und Sozialphilosophie', vol. 62, no. 3, 1976, pp. 305-17.
Macdonald, M., Natural rights, in P. Laslett (ed.), 'Philosophy, Politics and Society', First Series, Oxford, Blackwell, 1956.
Maritain, J., 'Man and the State', University of Chicago Press, 1951.
Mayo, B., What are human rights?, in D. D. Raphael (ed.), 'Political Theory and the Rights of Man', London, Macmillan, 1967.
Melden, A. I., 'Rights and Right Conduct', Oxford, Blackwell, 1959.
Melden, A. I., 'Rights and Persons', Oxford, Blackwell, 1973.
Melden, A. I., Olafson on the right to education, in J. F. Doyle (ed.), 'Educational Judgments', London, Routledge & Kegan Paul, 1973.
Mercer, J. R., A policy statement on assessment procedures and the rights of children, 'Harvard Educational Review', vol. 44, no. 1, November 1974, pp. 125-41.
Mill, J. S., 'Utilitarianism, On Liberty, Representative Government', London, Dent, 1910.
Miller, D., 'Social Justice', Oxford University Press, 1976.
Milne, A. J. M., 'Freedom and Rights', London, Allen & Unwin, 1968.
Moore, E. M., Human rights and home-school communications, 'Educational Review', vol. 26, no. 1, 1973, pp. 56-66.
Morris, H., Persons and punishment, 'The Monist', vol. 52, no. 4, October 1968, pp. 475-501.
Murdoch, I., 'The Sovereignty of the Good', London, Routledge & Kegan Paul, 1970.
National Council for Civil Liberties, 'Children in School', Discussion Paper No. 1, in the Series: 'Children Have Rights', London, National Council for Civil Liberties, 1970.
Nozick, R., 'Anarchy, State and Utopia', Oxford, Blackwell, 1974.
Oakeshott, M., Education: the engagement and its frustration, 'Proceedings of the Philosophy of Education Society of Great Britain', vol. 5, no. 1, January 1971, pp. 43-76.
Olafson, F. A., Rights and duties in education, in J. F. Doyle (ed.), 'Educational Judgments', London, Routledge & Kegan Paul, 1973.
Ollendorff, R., The rights of adolescents, in P. Adams et al., 'Children's Rights' London, Elek Books, 1971.
Paine, T., 'The Rights of Man', London, Dent, 1915.
Paul, J. L., Newfield, G. R. and Pelosi, J. W. (eds), 'Child Advocacy Within the System', New York, Syracuse University Press, 1977.
Peters, R. S., 'Hobbes', Harmondsworth, Penguin, 1956.
Peters, R. S., 'Ethics and Education', London, Allen & Unwin, 1966.
Peters, R. S., The justification of education, in R. S. Peters (ed.), 'The Philosophy of Education', Oxford University Press, 1973.
Plamenatz, J., 'Consent, Freedom and Political Obligation', Oxford University Press, 1938.
Plamenatz, J., Rights, 'Proceedings of the Aristotelian Society', Supplementary Volume 24, 1950, pp. 74-82.
Popper, K. R., 'The Open Society and its Enemies', London, Routledge & Kegan Paul, 1962.
Raphael, D. D. (ed.), 'Political Theory and the Rights of Man', London, Macmillan, 1967.
Raphael, D. D., Human rights, old and new, in D. D. Raphael (ed.), 'Political Theory and the Rights of Man', London, Macmillan, 1967.
Raphael, D. D., The rights of Man and the rights of the citizen, in D. D. Raphael (ed.), 'Political Theory and the Rights of Man', London, Macmillan, 1967.

Rawls, J., 'A Theory of Justice', Oxford University Press, 1972.
Ritchie, D. G., 'Natural Rights', London, Allen & Unwin, 1916.
Ross, W. D., 'The Right and the Good', Oxford University Press, 1930.
Rousseau, J.-J., 'The Social Contract', London, Dent, 1913.
Sachs, C. J. R., Children's rights, in J. W. Bridge et al. (eds), 'Fundamental Rights', London, Sweet & Maxwell, 1973.
Schrag, F., The child's status in the democratic state, 'Political Theory', vol. 3, no. 4, November 1975, pp. 441-57.
Schrag, F., The child in the moral order, 'Philosophy', vol. 52, no. 200, April 1977, pp. 167-77.
Skidelsky, R;, 'English Progressive Schools', Harmondsworth, Penguin, 1969.
Sockett, H. T., Parents' rights, in D. Bridges and P. Scrimshaw (eds), 'Values and Authority in Schools', London, Hodder & Stoughton, 1975.
Spinoza, B. de, 'Works of Spinoza', trans. R. H. M. Elwes, London, Bell, 1887.
Stone, J., and Taylor, F., 'The Parents' Schoolbook', Harmondsworth, Penguin, 1976.
Swerling, S., 'Who's Getting at our Kids?', London, The Monday Club, 1972.
Tullock, G., 'Private Wants, Public Means', New York, Basic Books, 1970.
Weil, S., 'Selected Essays 1934-43', trans. R. Rees, Oxford University Press, 1962.
White, A. R., Needs and wants, 'Proceedings of the Philosophy of Education Society of Great Britain', vol. 8, no. 2, July 1974, pp. 159-80.
White, J. P., 'Towards a Compulsory Curriculum', London, Routledge & Kegan Paul, 1973.
White, P. A., Education, democracy and the public interest, 'Proceedings of the Philosophy of Education Society of Great Britain', vol. 5, no. 1, January 1971, pp. 7.28.
White, P. A., Workplace democracy and political education, 'Journal of Philosophy of Education', vol. 13, July 1979, pp. 5-20.
Worsfold, V. L., A philosophical justification of children's rights, 'Harvard Educational Review', vol. 44, no. 1, February 1974, pp. 125-41.
Wright, Q., Relationship between different categories of human rights in UNESCO, 'Symposium on Human Rights', London, Wingate, 1947.
Wringe, C. A., Pupils' rights, 'Proceedings of the Philosophy of Education Society of Great Britain', vol. 7, no. 1, January 1973, pp. 103-15.
Wringe, C. A., Pupils' rights and examinations, 'Cambridge Journal of Education', vol. 3, no. 2, Easter Term 1975, pp. 193-202.

Index

acrimony caused by discussion of rights, 19, 160-2
Adam, paternal authority of, 47
Adams, Paul, 7, 15
administrative decisions, 158-9
adoption, parents' right to refuse, 96
adults becoming subject to welfare rights, 135-6; see also rights of adults
Advisory Centre for Education (ACE), 8, 10-15; see also 'Draft Charter of Children's Rights'
age: at which various legal rights are acquired, 91; voting, 122-3
alcohol, 154
animals, see rights of animals
appearance, see right to freedom of personal appearance
authority relations between adults and children, 92-3

Babeuf, François, 75
Barrington, Daines, 75
Bentham, Jeremy, 25, 43
Bereiter, Carl, 15
Berg, Leila, 6, 7, 10
Berger, Nan, 7, 9, 10, 11, 12, 14, 92
Berger, Viv, 7
best interests of the child, 16, 96; see also custody suits
biological tie, 100-1
'Brain Damage', 7
Brighton Borough Council, 12
Brophy, Brigid, 8

capacities as justification for rights, 75-6, 89, 147-8
'Carfax Comic', 7
censorship, see right to freedom of expression
child-centred education, 1
childhood, institutional and normative concepts of, 87-9, 118, 122-3
children: in care, 96; coercion for own good, 105-8, 138; coercion to protect rights of others, 108-10; dependence on adult power, 100; duty of obedience to parents, 100-1; in an institutional sense only, 122-3; legal

position of, 11, 97; limits of active claim rights of freedom, 110-11; limited rationality, 99-100, 120-2, 125; limited responsibility for actions, 101-2; material dependence on adults, 102-3, 118-20, 135-7; non-contribution to society, 118-19; non-contribution in school, 124-5; participation in educational decisions, 123-9, see also educational democracy; passive claim rights of freedom, 112-15; as property, 11, 94-7; punishment of, 113-17
'Children have Rights', 8
'Children in School', 17
'Cildren in Trouble', 9
Children and Young Persons Act, 1948, 9
Children and Young Persons Act, 1969, 9, 96
Children's Act, 1975, 17
'Children's Bust Book', 6, 7, 10
'Children's Rights': book, 10; magazine, 6, 9
Children's Rights Workshop, 7, 16
claims, claiming, see rights as claims, claim rights of freedom
Clegg, Sir Alex, 9
coercion: for own good, 105-8, 138; to protect rights of others, 108-10; of those rational at the level of prudence only, 109-10
common law, 42
compulsory education, 13, 16, 138
'Conference on Children's Rights', 8
conflicts: between adults and children, 107-8; see also rights in conflict
consent: as a ground of political obligation, 47; to the infringement of rights of security, see permissions
consultation, 121-2
contraceptives, right to free issue of, 15
contract, laissez-faire freedom of, 64; initial, 81-2; unequal, 72-3, 127
corporal punishment, see punishment
County Hall: pupils demands handed in to, 5, 12, 14; 'stormed', 6
'cum parente', 13

177